THE CABILDO IN PERU UNDER THE BOURBONS

JOHN PRESTON MOORE

The Cabildo in Peru
under the Bourbons

A study in the decline and resurgence
of local government in the
Audiencia of Lima
1700-1824

DUKE UNIVERSITY PRESS
Durham, North Carolina
1966

© 1966, Duke University Press

Library of Congress Catalogue Card no. 66-22590

Printed in the United States of America
by the Seeman Printery, Durham, N. C.

FOREWORD

When I published some years ago a study of local government in the Viceroyalty of Peru in the age of the Hapsburgs, I had no distinct idea of pursuing the subject further. Curiosity impelled me, however, to discover what happened to the cabildo, or town council—the only body really controlled by the important creole class—under the regime of the Bourbons. The result of the investigation, which took me to Peru for two summers and to Spain for a year in the Archives of the Indies and in other repositories, is the present volume.

In essence a continuation of the first study, it has, however, a more restricted geographical context. The vast amount of archival material available for the Viceroyalty of Peru forced me to limit research to the Audiencia of Lima, or the approximate area of the present boundaries of Peru. Founded in 1544, the administrative-judicial region counted forty-eight provinces including the district of Cercado and the city of Cuzco, since both were governed by *corregidores*.

The attempt is made to picture life and government in the Peruvian municipalities in the eighteenth and early nineteenth centuries. Prosaic as some of these local ordinances may seem, they mattered much to the colonials who saw in the cabildo the primary agency for the enforcement of law and order in the community. It was also the only instrument for relief from royal oppression.

Lastly, the role of the cabildo in the revolution is explored. It is to be hoped that this study will illuminate the genesis of nationalism in Peru. The town council became a center of resistance to Spanish authority and, simultaneously, a nucleus for the reorganization of government during the period of strife. When independence had been achieved it provided the creole with a sense of continuity with the past as well as an underpinning for the new political structure that had to be erected.

I should like to express my gratitude to many Spanish and Peruvian researchers and good friends whose advice and encouragement contributed immeasurably to the preparation of this volume. In particular, I wish to thank the following persons for their special interest and solicitude: Dr. José María de la Peña y Cámara, director of the Archivo General de Indias; Dr. Antonio Muro Orejón, professor of Colonial Law, University of Sevilla; Dr. Fernando Silva Santisteban and Dr. Raúl Rivera Serna, both of the staff of the Biblioteca Nacional, Lima; Dr. Antolin Bedoya Villacorta, Archivo histórico de los Ministerios de Hacienda y Comercio; Sr. Felipe Márquez Abanto, jefe de la sección histórica del Archivo Nacional del Perú; Sr. Enrique Azalgara Ballon, director, Biblioteca Pública Municipal of Arequipa; Dr. Jesús Covarrubias Pozo and Sr. Manuel Aparicio Vega, Archivo Histórico, University of Cuzco; Dr. Carlos Daniel Valcárcel, director of the archives, University of San Marcos; and Sr. Emilio Harth-Terre of Lima. Without the sympathetic co-operation of Dr. Luis F. Málaga, director of the Municipal Library of Lima, it would have been impossible for me to have examined thoroughly the invaluable manuscript records pertaining to the cabildo of the Ciudad De Los Reyes.

The publication of this study is due in part to institutional generosity. My thanks must go to the Louisiana State University Research Council for a grant-in-aid to finance a portion of the cost of printing. And I must acknowledge my indebtedness to the Guggenheim Foundation for appointment to a fellowship in 1960-1961, which enabled me to travel to Spain to consult the archives in Seville and Madrid.

CONTENTS

ILLUSTRATIONS

THE CABILDO IN PERU UNDER THE BOURBONS

CHAPTER I

Local Institutions in
the Peninsula in the
Eighteenth Century

"Without wishing to minimize in the least the dramatic charm of the conquest, I must insist that the important, the marvelous thing was colonization. In spite of our ignorance about it, no one can deny that it was an historic event of the first rank. To me, it is obviously the only truly great thing which Spain has done."[1] These are the words of the Spanish philosopher José Ortega y Gasset. As a corollary, he might have added that ties between the homeland and the colonies were so intimate that no understanding of the development of institutions and practices in the Spanish-American Empire is possible without a grasp of the political, economic, and social conditions in the Peninsula. This supplementary generalization, while especially true for the formative era of the sixteenth century, is nonetheless relevant for the subsequent Bourbon period.[2] In varying degrees most aspects of

1. José Ortega y Gasset, *Invertebrate Spain*, trans. Mildred Adams (London, 1937), p. 84.

2. For the Castilian origin of the colonial cabildo, or town council, see the author's *The Cabildo in Peru Under the Hapsburgs* (Durham, N. C., 1954), chap. i.

The significance of institutional background for the later evolution of this political organism should also be apparent in view of the crown's aim to assimilate the overseas possessions to the metropolis. Particularly appropriate in this connection is an assertion in 1738 by the first Bourbon ruler that from the ayuntamiento of Sevilla "were taken the rules for the establishment of my councils in the Indies." This claim is not wholly warrantable. It discloses, nevertheless, the profound importance attached by the crown to procedures and expedients already tested in the Peninsula. See Real cédula, Aranjuez, April 11, 1738, legajo 652, Indiferente general, Archivo general de Indias (hereinafter referred to as A. G. I.), quoted in Antonio Muro Orejón, "El ayuntamiento de Sevilla modelo de los municipios americanos," *Anales de la*

colonial administration and social existence reflected the attitudes of the new rulers and their advisors and the prevailing norms of Castile.

Naturally, the colonial municipalities in the Audiencia of Lima, roughly the territory of modern Peru, felt in the eighteenth century the impact of changing policies and trends in Spain.[3] In 1786 a survey ordered by the crown for the purpose of determining the state of municipal finances listed for the region twelve important cities: Lima, the capital of the viceroyalty and the seat of the audiencia, Cuzco, Yca, Trujillo, Lambayeque, Piura, Huancavelica, Guamanga, Arequipa, Huánuco, Tarma, and Jauja.[4] To these should be added Cajamarca, Pisco, Arica, and Chachapoyas. Besides, there were many towns and villages located on the plateaus, in the small valleys of the sierras, and in the irrigated sections of the coastal plain, populated by families of Spanish origin and by natives. Nearly all of the significant centers of population had been founded prior to 1700. In general, during the eighteenth century these municipalities, following the pattern of their Castilian counterparts, experienced a long era of decadence and a brief period of limited recovery. In the first quarter of the subsequent century the local regimes in America forged ahead politically to play a decisive role in the attainment of independence.

For an insight into colonial municipal history in this section of the empire under the Bourbons, an account of the personalities of the rulers and their advisors and a survey of local government in the Peninsula would appear indispensable.

In 1700 the demise of the childless Charles II, a sorry excuse for a king, led to the accession to the throne of the able Duke of Anjou, a grandson of *le grand monarque* Louis XIV of France.[5] For over two hundred years this family provided the sovereigns, both good and

Universidad Hispalense, XX (1960), 80. See also Demetrio Ramos Pérez, *Historia de la colonización española en América* (Madrid, 1947), p. 112.

3. The copiousness of materials bearing on local history in the Viceroyalty of Peru has restricted this study to the municipalities in the smaller administrative-judicial district.

4. Expediente sobre la averiguación de las rentas de propios, arbitrios, y bienes de la comunidad de las ciudades y villas del distrito, legajo 14, Archivo histórico de hacienda y comercio, Lima.

5. Perhaps the most beneficial act performed by the last of the Hapsburgs for his country was the deeding of the Spanish Kingdom and Empire to a more vigorous dynasty. Hume calls this legal donation "the most important event in the history of Europe since the Reformation." See Martin A. S. Hume, *The Spanish People: Their Origin, Growth, and Influence* (London, 1901), p. 458.

bad, for Spain. In contrast to the weak-willed, pleasure-loving Hapsburgs of the preceding century, the representatives of the new dynasty
were men of some vision, resolution, and energy. The first monarch
Philip V, though of foreign nativity, did not regard his country as a
mere satellite of her more powerful neighbor. His long reign of nearly
half a century was interrupted by a short abdication in 1724, occasioned
by the dazzling prospect of removal of his residence to the Palace
of Versailles owing to the near-fatal illness of his cousin Louis XV.
But the recovery of the French king and the sudden death of Philip's
eldest son and successor, Luis, necessitated the resumption of the
reins of government the following year.[6] Upon his death in 1746
his second son Ferdinand VI succeeded to the throne. Though a
man of average talents, with a consuming interest in the arts, he
permitted few things to interfere with the objective of rebuilding
the prestige of the monarchy. Under Charles III (1759-1788), a
half-brother of Ferdinand, Spain reached the apogee of her power.
While a person of much industry and determination, he had "the
good fortune of taking over a kingdom on the way to recovery, the
work of his father and his brother."[7] So methodical and painstaking
was he in the performance of the duties of statecraft that he regulated
his life "with the invariability of the course of the sun and the plan-
ets."[8] Not only did he rebuild Spain, both figuratively and literally,

6. Carlos Cardell, *La casa de Borbón en España* (Madrid, 1954), pp. 23-29.
He suffered severe attacks of melancholia. Once when residing in Sevilla he
sought relief by converting "night into day, altering completely the order of functions
and hours of the palace. After the sun had set, he had breakfast, ate at 1:00 A.M.; and
at 3 o'clock in the coldest part of the winter, he went out with the queen and the
court to fish in the pools of the garden of the Alcázar. At 8:00 in the morning which,
according to his errant count, was 8:00 at night, he went to bed and slept till afternoon. . . ." See Antonio Rodríguez Villa, *Patiño y Campillo: reseña histórico-biográfica
de estos dos ministros de Felipe V* (Madrid, 1882), p. 80.
7. Cardell, *La casa de Borbón*, pp. 69-70. See also Hume, *The Spanish People*, p.
488; George N. Desdevises du Dezert, *L'Espagne de l'Ancien Regime: Les Institutions*
(Paris, 1899), p. xiii, declares with no little exaggeration that "aside from Charles
III, Spain of the eighteenth century did not have a king."
8. Carlos Gutiérrez de los Rios, Conde de Fernan-Núñez, *Vida de Carlos III* (2
tomos; Madrid, 1898), I, 46.
With reference to the most controversial act of his reign, the expulsion of the
Jesuits, his *gentil-hombre de cámara* and biographer has this to say: "King Charles,
who on various occasions asserted that he was first Charles and then king, an expression worthy of his heart and humanity, had been educated by this Society . . . and
he averred at their [Jesuits] departure that Charles had regretted much what the king
had seen necessary to carry out." *Ibid.*, p. 211.

but he found time for the renovation and regeneration of colonial administration.[9]

The last two Bourbons of the colonial era have little to commend them to posterity. Unresponsive to epoch-making events in Europe and to the demand for reforms in America, Charles IV (1788-1808) was dominated for some years by his queen and her favorite, the scheming, although not unenlightened, "Prince of Peace" Manuel de Godoy. Under Charles' son Ferdinand VII (1808-1833), a dull, reactionary sovereign, Spain lost practically all of her wealth-producing colonies and sank to the level of a second-rate power.

That the political renaissance of the Spanish Empire in the eighteenth century—a fact that seems beyond dispute—was due to the personal characteristics of the Bourbon monarchs has been challenged by some historians. It is their view that the inspiration and drive for the great reforms came from ministers of outstanding ability. If this conclusion be correct, the Bourbons may at least clam credit for keen discernment in their appointments.[10]

Beyond a doubt, the Spanish crown, dating from the middle of Philip V's reign to the 1790's, enjoyed the services of a series of distinguished, even brilliant, officials. In patriotism, foresight, and zeal they were probably unmatched in the history of the country. Under Philip V the list included José Patiño, secretary of state in 1734,[11] and José del Campillo, minister of the treasury from 1739-1743.[12] In the following reign the King's chief advisor was the Marqués de la Ensenada, "of obscure extraction, but of noble mind," who aspired to

9. Alain Viellard-Baron, "L'Establissement des Intendants Aux Indes par Charles III," *Revista de Indias,* XII (1952), 521-527.

10. John Lynch, *Spanish Colonial Administration, 1782-1810: The Intendant System in the Viceroyalty of the Río de la Plata* (London, 1958), pp. 3, 4; see also Rafael Altamira, *A History of Spain from the Beginnings to the Present Day,* trans. Muna Lee (1st ed.; Toronto, New York, and London, 1949), pp. 437, 438.

The author recalls a session of the Conference of Latin Americanists of the American Historical Association in which an observation of this nature was made by Professor J. T. Lanning of Duke University.

11. Rodríguez Villa, *Patiño y Campillo,* p. 109.

He was noted for his bons mots as well as for his serious attention to issues of state. When informed on his death bed of the king's gracious bestowal upon him of the title of Grandee of Spain, First Class, he exclaimed: "Now the King gives me a hat when I no longer have a head." *Ibid.,* p. 107.

12. *Ibid.,* p. 145.

His *Nuevo sistema de gobierno económico,* though unpublished until 1789, was extremely influential with his successors. See Miguel Artola, "Campillo y las reformas de Carlos III," *Revista de Indias,* XII (1952), 690, 711, 712.

rebuild the decadent Spanish navy.[13] Charles III had at his command a seemingly unending stream of fine ministers. For the conduct of foreign relations there were the Marqués de Grimaldi, 1763-1776, and the Conde de Floridablanca, 1776-1781.[14] In the section of domestic and colonial affairs the King utilized the abilities of the Conde de Aranda, president of the Council of Castile; Pedro de Campomanes, the economist; Melchor de Jovellanos, alcalde *de corte* in Madrid; and finally as minister of the Indies, José de Gálvez. For a few years Charles IV kept Aranda and Floridablanca at his side before rejecting their advice for that of an inferior counselor, Godoy.[15]

Absolutism, centralization, and uniformity were the keynotes of the Bourbons and their ministers in the reorganization of government in the Peninsula. Of these monarchs Charles III was the most forceful exponent of regalism, which in the eighteenth century identified itself with the Enlightened Monarchy. He sincerely believed that he was being the ideal king in recognizing obligations and responsibilities to his subjects. The time-worn cliché, "all for the people, but not with the people," best summarizes his philosophy of government.[16]

Notwithstanding many obvious successes, Bourbon aims and methods at home and abroad in this period have been assailed by some students of Spanish history. They have indicted the dynasty on many counts: undue emphasis on centralization at the expense of traditional institutions, intervention in foreign wars for personal rather than national reasons, development of an oppressive bureaucracy called *Golillas*, and finally, the employment of military agents for the realization of domestic policies.[17] It has been asserted also that the new ruling family substituted the ideal of limitless progress through human exertion for the historic theory of divine guidance and revelation.[18] Manifestly, the validity of the latter criticism rests on the acceptance by secular historians of a theological interpretation

13. Conde de Fernan-Núñez, *Vida, de Carlos III*, I, 107.

14. Antonio Ballesteros y Beretta, *Historia de España y su influencia en la historia universal* (2nd. ed.; 11 vols.; Barcelona, Buenos Aires, 1929-1950), V, 168, 210.

15. Charles E. Chapman, *A History of Spain* (New York, 1927), p. 436.

16. Altamira, *A History of Spain*, p. 438.

17. In other words, according to the Bourbons' most caustic critic, "mucho despotismo y poca ilustración," or "much despotism and little enlightenment." See Manuel Giménez Fernández, "Las doctrinas populistas en la independencia de Hispano-América," *Anuario de estudios Americanos*, III (1946), 540.

18. Salvador de Madariaga, *El auge del imperio español en América* (Buenos Aires, 1955), pp. 291-293.

of national history. Despite the severity of these accusations, one cannot contest the fact that Spain gained European prestige as a result of the application of these policies.

A cursory survey of the internal political structure of Spain at the beginning of the eighteenth century must have convinced Philip V of the need for reforms. In provincial and local administration the country was far from presenting a picture of cohesion. It was, in fact, a mosaic of odd, disparate regions and institutions. Its territorial division "corresponded to the constitution of its old federative organization and had its roots in the Middle Ages."[19] The realm in 1700 comprised thirty-two provinces, unequal in size and population, twenty-four of which belonged to the crown of Castile and four to Aragon.[20] Navarre, Alava, Guipúzcoa, and Biscay completed the list. In addition, there were minuscule enclaves whose sovereignty was claimed by distant provinces. Each of the above provinces was broken up into small subdivisions, known as *partidos,* characterized by a diversity of functions and derivations.

These districts contained *ciudades* and villas of varying status and jurisdictions. Administratively, towns and cities fell into one of four classifications: *de realengo,* "royal"; *de señorío,* "seignorial"; *de abadengo,* "ecclesiastical"; and *de órdenes militares,* "under military orders." The complexity of this situation is well illustrated in the province of Asturias, where there were "one city and three royal jurisdictions, a condado [county] de realengo, five seignorial jurisdictions, five burgos [boroughs] de realengo, and one seignorial burgo; forty-five royal councils and fifteen seignorial; twelve cotos redondos [districts] de realengo, sixteen de abadengo and fifty-three seignorial."[21] It would naturally be the constant aspiration of the crown to increase the number of towns and districts under royal direction by any appropriate means.

An attack by the new regime on regional and local liberties was not long in coming. In 1707 Philip V, angry with the influential nobles and commoners in the eastern part of the Peninsula for their opposi-

19. Ballesteros, *Historia de España,* VI, 21.

20. The Castilian provinces included Asturias, Andalucía Avila, Extremadura, Galicia, Granada, Guadalajar, Burgos, Castilla la Vieja, Ciudad Real, Córdoba, Cuenca, Jaén, León, Madrid, Murcia, Palencia, Salamanca, Segovia, Soria, Toledo, Toro, Valladolid, Canarias; the Aragonese were Aragón, Cataluña, Valencia, and Mallorca. *Ibid.,* p. 22.

21. *Ibid.,* p. 23.

tion to him during the conflict for the throne, abolished the political privileges of Aragon and Valencia and replaced their *fueros* and *costumbres* with Castilian law. It was "one of the first steps toward uniformity of Law—principally of Public Law—throughout Spain."[22] While the enforcement of the decrees was modified somewhat in view of the aristocracy's subsequent profession of loyalty to the dynasty, the King found it possible to continue covertly the extension of his authority. Two new audiencias having criminal jurisdiction were set up for the region; civil suits, with minor exceptions, were to be decided as in the past according to the municipal law of Aragon.[23] Catalonia and Mallorca were likewise affected by the drive for centralization. Through ordinances issued in 1714 and 1715 the crown assumed control of the major governmental agencies in these regions, abolishing the Catalonian cortes as a separate entity but permitting its members to sit with the Castilian parliament. In 1716 it was declared that the general laws and customs of Catalonia should be modeled after those of Castile. Royal intervention took place also in municipal offices, the crown designating the twenty-four *regidores*, "councilors," of the *ayuntamiento* of Barcelona. Analogous changes occurred in Mallorca, with royal appointment of the aldermen for the chief towns of Palma and Alcudia.[24] Other instances of the reduction of regional and local rights in the Peninsula might be cited. Philip's successors on the throne, while active in other areas of administration, were unable to make further inroads on provincial fueros.[25] Despite strenuous efforts to "Castilianize" Catalonia, its language and customs survived as testimony to the vitality of separatism in the Spanish national character.

Since the primary concern in this study is the problem of municipal rights or, conversely, the extent of absolutism in the cities in the eighteenth century, it is essential to examine in considerable detail the functioning of provincial and civic administration and the character of the Bourbon reforms.

A typical regional government consisted of a captain-general aided by an audiencia. To extend royal power Philip V, by decrees of 1707 and 1716, created captaincies for Aragon, Cataluña, Valencia, Mallorca,

22. Altamira, *A History of Spain*, p. 426.
23. Ballesteros, *Historia de España*, VI, 17, 18
24. *Ibid.*, p. 20.
25. Altamira, *A History of Spain*, p. 426.

Granada, Andalucía, Canaries, Extremadura, Castilla la Vieja, and Galicia.[26] The authority exercised by the crown appointee was extensive because he had charge of the troops and was likewise presiding official for the audiencia. A few years later a significant innovation was made. No doubt impressed by the effectiveness of the intendancy in France as a device for concentrating royal power, Philip established the institution throughout Spain. The decree was soon withdrawn, however, and the office did not reappear until 1749 during the reign of Ferdinand VI. In his hands the intendant gathered judicial, financial, administrative, and military powers. In the provincial capitals he served, besides, as corregidor, with authority to oversee the work of subordinate corregidores and *alcaldes mayores*. In 1766 Charles III lessened somewhat the responsibilities of the office by depriving it of judicial attributes.[27] Revenue advantages accruing to the crown undoubtedly suggested the transfer of the intendancy to America.

In addition to their judicial duties, the *chancillerías,* "audiencias," provided counsel to the captains-general on important political and administrative issues. Sevilla, Galicia, Canarias, and Mallorca had inherited tribunals from the Austrian dynasty. In implementing their principle of uniformity the Bourbons founded audiencias where they had not previously existed and altered those already functioning to conform to a single model. In comparison with their colonial counterparts the Spanish courts had markedly less influence over governmental affairs.

The lowest unit of administration was the town. In the eighteenth century Castilian municipalities were governed by ayuntamientos, or *concejos,* comprising the corregidor, invariably a royal appointee, alcaldes, regidores, an *escribano,* "secretary," a *síndico procurador,* "attorney," and a *procurador general de las tierras,* "manager of communal properties."[28] Their organization presented an unbelievable

26. Ballesteros, *Historia de España*, VI, 23, 24.

27. *Ibid.,* p. 25.

28. Lorenzo de Santayana Bustillo's *Govierno político de los pueblos de España y el corregidor, alcalde, y juez en ellos* (Zaragoza, 1742) is an excellent description of procedure governing the functioning of town government in the first half of the eighteenth century and of the special powers wielded by the corregidor. Emphasis is placed on the expanded authority of the royal agent. According to the most reliable source on Spanish institutions of this era, Desdevises du Dezert's *L'Espagne de L'Ancien Regime*, p. xiv, his influence was less than that of the colonial corregidor who could "tyrannize populations."

diversity.[29] The number of regidores varied according to the size and importance of the municipality. Thus Burgos counted thirty-seven councilors, Valladolid thirty-three. In Andalucía, where there was greater uniformity, the quota was usually twenty-four.[30] Municipal office was regularly denied to artisans, slaves, ecclesiastics, debtors, and enemies of the crown. Alcaldes, regidores, and síndicos had to be *vecinos*, "citizens," of the town. It was permissible, however, for regidores to engage in business and trade, provided they held no contracts with the town government.[31] In some localities only individuals of noble birth could hold positions, while in others offices were divided between nobles and commoners. But in general membership was drawn from the upper classes.[32]

Conciliar posts were filled by various means, some almost incredible. By the middle of the eighteenth century the crown had extended its control over a great majority of the towns. In Castile appointments of alcaldes and regidores were made chiefly by the king and to a lesser degree by the temporal and ecclesiastical lords, but in some cases the municipalities enjoyed the right of choosing their own officials.[33] In Aragon the crown customarily designated members of the town councils. In a few cities throughout the Peninsula individuals inherited office as if it were a parcel of ground or bought a position if such were vendible. The elective power was associated generally with small towns which frequently looked to the audiencias for recommendations or suggestions. Complete democracy prevailed in Alava, the citizens holding open assemblies to choose among candidates for office and to deliberate on matters of common concern. Despite royal pressure the towns of Navarre retained their liberal fueros.

Rotation in office was a legal requirement based on the belief that honor and authority should be shared by the vecinos. An interval of three years had to elapse between an individual's terms in the same office; two years between occupation of different positions in the council. An exception was the síndico procurador who, because of the nature

29. Santayana, *Govierno político*, pp. 4, 5.
30. Ballesteros, *Historia de España*, VI, 32.
31. Santayana, *Govierno político*, pp. 6-8, 49.
32. Madrid provides a good example of an aristocratic council. See *ibid.*, pp. 10, 11.
33. *Ibid.*, pp. 12, 13.
But as late as 1787, as illustrative of the continuance of seignorial rights, nobles had a considerable measure of control over government in "17 cities, 2,358 villas, and 8,818 villages and towns." See Altamira, *A History of Spain*, p. 459.

of his duties, could serve additional terms without an intervening period.[34] In Castile *alcaldes de la hermandad* might be similarly re-elected. That this prerequisite of eligibility was always complied with is debatable.

In towns where officials were not appointed, choice was by balloting, by casting lots, or by a combination of these methods.[35] If elections were customary all of the officials, with the exception of the procurador síndico, were chosen by a majority vote in the ayuntamiento. On the other hand, the defender of the public cause was more properly named by a *concejo pleno*, "assembly of the citizens," since it was his responsibility to represent the public interests.[36]

Municipal functions required the services of a number of minor officials who fell into two classes. In the first category were those participating directly in the administration of civic affairs, including the *procuradores de Cortes*, "agents to the Cortes," *comisarios de abastos*, "commissaries," *fieles de carnicerías*, "inspectors of meat," *mayordomos de propios*, "overseers of communal holdings," *abogados*, "lawyers," *escribanos de ayuntamiento*, "council secretaries," and *contadores*, "accountants." The second group, which fulfilled services essential for the health, welfare, and security of the populace, included *médicos*, *cirujanos*, "surgeons," *maestros de gramática*, "teachers," *guardas de monte y huerta*, "guards," *vehedores*, "inspectors," and *examinadores de oficios*, "examiners of officials." In the large cities it was customary for the council to select all of the above officials, while in the smaller localities officials of the second class were chosen by *cabildos abiertos*, "open assemblies."[37] Regidores might hold minor conciliar posts, to which they could be re-elected annually.

Assemblies of the ayuntamiento were of two sorts: ordinary and open. The former was held usually biweekly, but might be dispensed with if a lack of business justified its omission. The practice of holding

34. Santayana, *Govierno político*, p. 17.
35. The localities having fueros commonly held elections. An example of a mixed procedure is to be observed in the villa of Vitoria in 1783. In the presence of officials of the ayuntamiento, the porter wrote the names of the alcaldes, procurador síndico, two deputies, and four regidores on separate ballots and placed them in an urn. A child summoned from the street drew out four of the ballots. These names were the electors, each of whom voted by ballot for the incoming alcalde. By a similar process an entirely new council was constituted. See Desdevises du Dezert, *L'Espagne de l'Ancien Regime*, p. 169.
36. Santayana, *Govierno político*, p. 19.
37. *Ibid.*, pp. 20, 21.

open assembles in the eighteenth century was restricted almost entirely to the less significant towns. Called cabildos abiertos, they were summoned for the approval of a financial levy, for the discussion of an important matter relating to the common good, and for the selection of certain public servants, such as physicians, chemists, etc. Thus, after a fashion, the assembly though frowned upon by the Hapsburgs and the Bourbons preserved certain public liberties.[38]

The chief power exercised by the Castilian ayuntamientos was that of issuing ordinances to deal with purely local questions. It was a prerogative held only by the large cities of the district. Ordinances enacted by the council concerned election to conciliar office, supplying of food and provisions, street cleaning, selection and examination of officials of the guilds, and allocation of funds from the propios.[39] Concejos in predominantly rural areas like Asturias passed many laws relating to use of land, water, and the protection of crops and vineyards.[40] Ordinances were voted upon by regidores, the corregidores having the right to vote only in the event of a tie;[41] but they would normally require the sanction of the crown before having full legality.

Cities enjoying the first position in a province sometimes had unique honors and privileges. These might take the form of immunities or exemptions. Thus the ayuntamiento could not be obliged to go in a body to receive a lord or nobleman or, in the event of the death of a corregidor who had failed to appoint a *teniente*, the ayuntamiento might name his successor ad interim.

A regidor in a Castilian town had more rights than an ordinary citizen. He was given preference in the purchase of food supplies for the town. If found guilty of violation of a law he could be sentenced to flogging or to the galleys, but if the judgment was death, he might be executed only with the consent of the king.[42] A regidor likewise had responsibilities to the city. When appointed to a municipal commission he had to render an account of his work to the ayuntamiento.[43] He had to serve a minimum of four months on the council and was obligated not to leave the city when important business was pending.[44]

38. *Ibid.*, pp. 26, 27.   39. *Ibid.*, p. 40.
40. Cesar García Fernández Castañon, "Ordenanzas municipales y de pueblos," *Revista de ciencias jurídicas y sociales*, IV (1921), 577.
41. Santayana, *Govierno político*, p. 41.
42. *Ibid.*, p. 46.   43. *Ibid.*, p. 47.
44. *Ibid.*, pp. 48, 49.

Usually, he could not be a merchant by vocation nor could he rent or lease propios of the municipality either directly or through a third party.[45] The temptation to profit at the expense of the town was apparently irresistible despite prohibitions to the contrary. Many of these rights and obligations were incorporated in the laws of the Indies and in special cédulas applicable to America.

A primary responsibility of the municipal body was to assure to the citizens a plentiful supply of food. In times of scarcity or when a threat of a monopoly existed, the corregidor or the alcalde might determine the amount of food available for the community and fix a price for each commodity. Should the need arise, the official might force merchants to sell their products rather than retain them in hope of great profit. In ordinary times, however, laws of the realm determined the maximum price of staples. In the case of minor articles of consumption regidores had much latitude in fixing the prices, inspecting the shops, and fining those who violated the price lists.[46] Prices of items other than edibles were determined by the law of supply and demand, though regidores had the right to intervene and set the sales figures if necessary.

In order to provide abundance of food, the council customarily leased the right of supplying comestibles to indvidual merchants. The leasing took place at public auction to the highest bidder. Conditions of the transaction were carefully prescribed so as to avoid fraud and to assure a sufficient quantity at a reasonable price.[47] No official of the municipality could offer a bid for a public service.[48] As a measure of precaution and insurance against famine, flood, or any unforeseen catastrophe, the town was to provide a public granary, or *pósito*, managed by an official, the *depositario*, to be elected by the regidores, or chosen by the corregidor or alcalde. Accounts of the depositario had to be examined by the corregidor and sent once every three years to the consejo of the realm for approval.[49] In Aragon the supplying of food was solved in a different fashion, the ayuntamientos having the right to make and sell bread in municipally owned bakeries.[50]

In theory every Castilian town held propios and *bienes comunes,* "communal wealth," essential for the prosperity and well-being of the

45. *Ibid.*, p. 49.
46. *Ibid.*, pp. 61, 62.
47. *Ibid.*, p. 66.
48. *Ibid.*, p. 70.
49. *Ibid.*, p. 81.
50. *Ibid.*, pp. 82, 83.

population. Propios consisted of shops, real estate, and public lands—usually inalienable without the consent of the king—which were leased to private citizens or administered directly by the town officials, if the latter practice were considered more advantageous. The income from these sources provided the revenue for the construction or repair of public works, for the salaries of the corregidor, regidores, and other officials, and for the fiestas. Bienes comunes, like the propios legally not transferable, comprised plazas, streets, roads, buildings, pastures, forests, and other areas devoted to the common use and benefit of the citizenry. To prevent the loss of propios and bienes comunes through seizure or sale, the crown ordered from time to time a survey of municipal property and the restoration of any plots of ground or buildings unlawfully occupied by private persons.[51]

The lack of propios was common to the cities of Castille and Aragon. In the eastern kingdom "they scarcely sufficed for the payment of the salaries of the alcaldes, *regidores*, and other officials of the councils, because they were so heavily mortgaged."[52] Hence recourse was made to taxes and special contributions from the citizens, but with some limitations on this power imposed by the crown.[53]

It was a function of the ayuntamiento and the corregidor to supervise the activities of merchants, traders, shopkeepers, craftsmen, and artisans in the interest of the public. Ordinances were made to insure the use of accurate weights and measures, and officials were appointed to inspect the places of business and enforce the regulations. Resale of merchandise was forbidden except under specific conditions, it being held that this practice was contrary to the interests of the consumer.[54] The municipalities outlawed monopolies. Guilds and professions came under the scrutiny of the council's appointees. The municipal justices enforced sumptuary legislation, designating types of uniforms for artisans and laborers and forbidding the wearing of extravagant dress by members of the lower classes.[55]

In the eighteenth century the crown's representative, the corregidor, was the central figure in the Castilian councils. His authority, defined by *instrucciones* of 1648 and the amendments of Charles III in 1783, was that of administrator and judge. Santayana aptly summarized his

51. *Ibid.*, pp. 84-100.
52. *Ibid.*, p. 122.
53. *Ibid.*, p. 123.
54. *Ibid.*, p. 140.
55. *Ibid.*, pp. 158-160.

role in the framework of local government: "Very extensive is the power of the corregidor; his duties are limitless so that with truth it can be said what a jurisconsult declared concerning the proconsuls and presidents of the provinces that of whatever might occur in the province that official ought to take note."[56] According to the regulations made in the reign of Philip IV, this officer had to be examined and certified for proof of his nobility and the possession of qualities requisite for a good administrator. Law stipulated the posting of a bond, an obligation not imposed upon the alcaldes and other officials of the council.[57] At the end of his term of office, the corregidor had to stand a judicial examination called a *residencia*.[58]

With respect to the municipal council, the corregidor, who was its presiding officer, had a commanding position. His major responsibilities included the conservation of food in the pósitos, examination of the accounts of the majordomos, and inspection of the municipal income.[59] Besides, he was to make a single visit to each of the ciudades and villas of his jurisdiction during his term of office, "without salary or special financial aid to himself or to any of his servants, officials, or agents."[60] While he was enjoined by law to fix the boundaries of the towns and villas in the partidos, this in practice was carried out by the alcaldes of the various pueblos.[61] No tax or levy might be collected without his authorization, "because the Prince alone can grant this right."[62] An important function of the corregidor was the preservation of the propios and bienes comunes. He was to see also to the fair assessment on the towns of royal taxes and special contributions, placing the largest burden on the rich with no exemption for regidores. In practice, the ayuntamiento drew up the estimate of quotas from the citizenry, with consideration of the personal wealth of each, after which the taxable list was turned over to the corregidor.[63]

As judge in the locality, he had wide cognizance of cases. In the

56. *Ibid.*, p. 198.   57. *Ibid.*, p. 167.
58. In seeking to improve the official conduct of the corregidor, Charles III required evidence of a candidate's knowledge, experience, and ability before signing the *título* of appointment. Tenure of office was limited to one term of six years, after which the corregidor was obliged to submit to an investigation by a judge named by the Council of Castile. See Desdevises du Dezert, *L'Espagne de l'Ancien Regime*, pp. 157, 158.
59. Santayana, *Govierno político*, p. 202.
60. *Ibid.*, pp. 203, 204.   61. *Ibid.*, p. 208.
62. *Ibid.*, p. 212.   63. *Ibid.*, pp. 252-255.

field of criminal law his authority was virtually absolute, not only in the pueblo where he resided but in the towns lying within his district. In nearby villages the alcaldes might carry out preliminary steps in the punishment of wrongdoers, such as the imprisonment of the criminal and seizure of his possessions.[64] Dating from the reign of Philip III, the corregidor claimed civil jurisdiction as well in all the places of his district, with the exception of towns that were specially exempted.[65] Alcaldes in the villages might decide civil suits involving sums up to 600 maravedis.[66] Alcaldes de la hermandad assisted the corregidor in maintaining law and order in the countryside. It was his duty finally to take the residencia of his predecessor and of the town officials, including the regidores, alcaldes de la hermandad, and "all other persons who had shared in the dispensing of justice."[67]

Thus the corregidor was the effective instrument of royal will in the local councils of Castile, the link binding the ayuntamientos to the crown. Through him the monarch enforced his decrees and stifled any resurgence of municipal rights that had been enjoyed in the Middle Ages. As an official primarily responsible for the seeming stagnation and lethargy characterizing the local councils, he was often unpopular, frequently feared, sometimes respected by the citizenry. The residencia, which may have acted as a brake on the temptation to self-profit, was removed by Charles IV in 1799, but restored a few years later when the need for it arose.[68]

It is evident that municipal government played a minor role in the affairs of the people in the middle of the eighteenth century. Independence and self-rule had largely gone. Students of Spanish administration of this era agree that local institutions were ineffective, with inadequate policing of the streets to forestall crime and an insufficiency of food and services. Civic spirit, pride, and initiative, characteristics of Castile and Aragon in the fifteenth and sixteenth centuries, were absent. There had been little or no improvement over the preceding century which saw Spain reach the nadir of inefficiency and favoritism in the central government. The aristocracy dominated the local councils, suppressing feeble aspirations for democracy by the mass of the citizenry. But that these miniature oligarchies sometimes suc-

64. *Ibid.*, p. 168.   65. *Ibid.*, p. 169.
66. *Ibid.*, p. 169.   67. *Ibid.*, p. 271.
68. Ballesteros, *Historia de España*, VI, 27.

cessfully resisted the further encroachments of the crown upon their rights is illustrated in the history of Madrid.[69]

What were the causes of these unfortunate conditions? To some contemporaries the sale of local offices was the root of all evil. The position of regidor was bought and disposed of without the sanction of the crown or was handed down from father to son as a family possession. In consequence few men of worth acquired posts, and public ends were sacrificed to private interests. In an instrucción of June 25, 1767, Charles III expressed his opposition to the traditional system of filling municipal offices, declaring with reference to the reconstitution of the civic regime of the city of Sierra Morena that "none of the offices should ever be transformed into those of hereditary tenure because they must be filled always by regular elections to avoid for these new pueblos the ills that beset the old with such acts of inalienability."[70] Ministers of the crown held similar views. Campomanes, president of the Council of Castile and one of the illustrious coterie surrounding the King, also sharply assailed the practice of selling offices: "The sale of the regimientos has been the origin of the inactivity of the ayuntamientos; the choice of individuals known for their zeal for these offices is necessary for the public weal, but the owners of the aldermancies should be compensated for their property losses."[71] Another member of this group, Jovellanos, prophesied that "one day the nation would regulate the election of deputies."[72]

The great diversity of municipal organization, ranging from oligarchical control to popular election, was also blamed for the malfunctioning of government at this level.

Among the advisors of Charles III, agreement was well-nigh unanimous on the shortcomings of local administration. As in other

69. In 1773 a *regidor perpetuo* of the villa of Madrid denounced the corregidor to the Consejo de Castilla for having interfered with the duties of the *fieles ejecutores*, "inspectors of weights and measures," more specifically for having permitted *recursos*, "appeals," from the decisions of these municipal officials. In its judgment of March 7, 1782, the council sustained the alderman's contention. See Executoria de los privilegios y facultades de los Señores Caballeros Regidores, Fieles Executores de la M. N. M. C. e imperial y coronado Villa y Corte de Madrid, June 1, 1782, Ms. 9-9-7n-1999, Biblioteca de Academia de Historia, Madrid.

70. Manuel Pérez Búa, "Las reformas de Carlos III en el régimen local de España," *Revista de ciencias jurídicas y sociales*, no. 2 (1919), p. 227.

71. Pedro Rodríguez de Campomanes, *Discurso sobre la educación popular de los artesanos y su fomento* (Madrid, 1775), p. 244.

72. Jovellanos, consulta, folio 3, quoted in Desdevises du Dezert, *L'Espagne de l'Ancien Regime*, p. 167.

areas of government and the economy, the crown sought betterment through pragmatic measures. Considering the paramount abuse the sale of offices, it regarded royal appointment and a modified form of popular selection as possible solutions. A major block in the realization of either scheme was the concept of offices as private property, which if legally changed through compensation would involve a large expenditure by the government. Conversely, to have forfeited municipal offices without indemnification and to have abolished electoral procedure in the region of the fueros would have courted serious agitation. Hence, given the considerable indebtedness of the crown, any real cure of the malady was from a practical standpoint virtually impossible.[73] But as a preliminary move toward raising standards, the King insisted on approval of all new officeholders. In Aragon, where royal power had been felt since the end of the dynastic war in 1713 municipal offices were filled for life by crown designation from a list of individuals suggested by the citizenry. Obviously, reforms were less essential in this kingdom.

Although deterred by the cost involved in carrying out what would have struck at the root of the trouble, Charles III was, nevertheless, bent on improving municipal government by other means. To instil vigor into the ayuntamientos, he advocated changes in membership. These changes would encompass the feature of popular rights. At the same time Charles III hoped that the reforms would reduce the power of the aristocracy, a potential threat to Bourbon autocracy in many parts of the Peninsula. The restoration of a vital nexus between the citizens and the council that had prevailed in the Middle Ages and the adoption of uniformity in conciliar structure were to be attained through the creation of *diputados del común,* "deputies in general," and a *síndico personero,* "special attorney." By a decree of May 5, 1766, it was enjoined that taxpayers drawn from a single parish must assemble to choose twenty-four electors. The latter elected

73. In an excess of zeal for reform Charles III tried to make over the traditional costume of the Spaniard in order to make easier the detection of criminals by the law enforcement officers. In 1766 he ordered the abolition of the long cape and the broad-brimmed hat, substituting for them features of dress more in conformity with the taste and decorum of the rest of Europe. But no rulers can very well dictate to a Spaniard what he should wear! Charles found himself faced with a popular uprising in the capital and had to give ground. Spaniards, however, fell in line when the Count of Aranda "made the long cape and the broad-brimmed hat the official uniform of the public executioner." See Altamira, *A History of Spain,* p. 444.

the new deputies and a síndico, there being four deputies for cities with a population of more than 2,000 and two for towns with a lesser number of inhabitants. The deputies served for two years and might come from any social class. A cédula of 1769 stipulated that two were to be chosen each year in the large cities and one in the minor localities in order that some continuity of policy and administration might be maintained. Thus the right of representation, albeit limited and indirect in nature, was returned to the Spanish municipality.[74]

Inevitably, the duties of the new agents conflicted with those of the regidores. Matters relating to the economy and to finance gradually came under the supervision of the deputies. A deputy was ex officio member of every committee of the ayuntamiento having to do with the food supply.[75] When suits arose over price control or contracts for provisioning, the deputies compiled the briefs and argued the cases before the audiencias. Questions of taxation and expenditures involved them also. It was the chief function of the síndico to bring to the attention of the cabildo any proposals that might benefit the citizenry as a whole. In general, close co-operation existed among the newly chosen officials.[76]

Results of the establishment of these offices were mixed. Undoubtedly there was introduced into municipal life a democratic element, a counterpoise to the reactionary aristocratic influence that had been overriding. It meant a reversal of a trend under way since the late Middle Ages and a recognition by the crown of a need to revitalize local organization. Some efficiency was promoted by the presence of persons of more ability representing the property-holders. Surely, there was more homogeneity in appearance and political make-up of the municipalities. But in some instances the councils were too cum-

74. A series of decrees supplemented the original one of May 5, 1766, which, according to Pérez Búa, "timidly represented a step toward the restoration of the Spanish municipality." Its provisions were republished in the celebrated liberal Constitution of 1812 as Articles 313 and 314. See Pérez Búa, "Las reformas de Carlos III," pp. 229-231.

It is a matter of debate as to whether the King was influenced by Louis XV's action in France in 1764 in adopting an elective system for local corporations. But Charles III maintained his reforms throughout his lifetime, while the French ruler withdrew his concessions in 1771, alleging that they fomented disorders and perturbations. See *ibid.*, p. 231.

75. Desdevises du Dezert, *L'Espagne de l'Ancien Regime*, p. 187.

76. Ballesteros, *Historia de España*, VI, 33, 34.

bersome and unwieldy to fulfil their functions, since no offices were abolished through the adoption of the reform. It was to be expected that the regidores would resent the authority of the delegates, who had a more business-like attitude toward their duties and were spokesmen for an important segment of the population. Evidence of this hostility is shown in the protest of the municipal bodies of Guipúzcoa against the royal decree requiring the holding of elections for the deputies.[77] The real merit of the innovation lay in the introduction of a new method of choosing aldermen, rather than in the assignment of additional conciliar responsibilities which were as circumscribed as before.[78]

Although the changes in the composition of the local councils in Castile may have had a wholesome effect, it is noteworthy that Charles III did not offer this reform to America. One may indulge in speculation as to the reasons for his unwillingness to apply this measure to the American colonies. If he lacked the funds to purchase offices in the Spanish ayuntamientos, it is not likely that he would seriously contemplate expenditures for this purpose in an area that was always secondary to the Peninsula in the mind of the Bourbon sovereign. Although local governments in America suffered from some of the same ills that beset their counterparts in Spain, the crown believed that efficacious devices might be evolved by the colonial intendants. It can be perceived also that colonial municipal institutions possessed a greater uniformity than was the case in the Peninsula. In the final analysis, the recurring rumors of unrest in Spanish America and the example of violent protest arising in the English colonies on the heels of changes in crown policy may have convinced Charles of the danger of making a concession to the principle of representation.

A second feature of Charles III's program of reform was related to the appointive magistrates in the ayuntamientos. During the reign of Ferdinand VI the authority of the corregidor had diminished to the advantage of the intendant, who handled matters of justice, administration, treasury, and war in the provinces.[79] By a decree of November 13, 1766, Charles III restored to the older official his former powers, differentiating them clearly from those of the intendant. A

77. Desdevises du Dezert, L'Espagne de l'Ancien Regime, pp. 187-189.
78. Pérez Búa, "Las Reformas de Carlos III," p. 231.
79. Ibid., p. 234.

royal instrucción of 1788 accorded to the corregidor a part in all phases of civic life. Henceforth he was looked upon as the chief instrument for the retention and extension of crown authority and for the remedying of the ills plaguing municipal administration.[80] The establishment by an order of October 6, 1768, of *alcaldes de barrios* in the more populous cities, officials who were to be elected in the same fashion as the deputies, brought about "even more of a reduction in the jurisdiction [competencia] of the ayuntamientos."[81]

The perilous state of municipal finances in the regions of Castile and Aragon was likewise a cause for concern on the part of the crown. Civic indebtedness due to unsound expenditures and to the peculation of officials was well known. In 1751 the Council of Castile ordered the towns under its jurisdiction to forward their accounts annually to Madrid for auditing and approval.[82] When Charles III ascended the throne, he assigned to the council general authority over the municipal *haciendas*, "treasuries"; and by a decree of July 30, 1760, he set up a *contaduría general de propios y arbitrios del reino* to deal specifically with civic expenditures. Could the municipal councils, reinvigorated by the participation of the new deputies and the special attorney, have set their own houses in order without outside interference? It is probable that difficulties of this sort had become so habitual and deeply ingrained that a helping hand was a *sine qua non*. A modern Spanish historian supports this view: "In the general debility affecting all the activities of the nation our municipalities did not have sufficient force to promote the reform by themselves."[83]

The contaduría general exercised close supervision over municipal funds. It determined how much was to be spent, when, and for what purpose, with the objective of accumulating a surplus for the redemption of the fixed obligations, or *censos*, "if they existed or if not, to relieve the town of special taxes."[84] Later decrees called for even stricter control of civic finances. Having drawn up the budget, the local junta, consisting of the corregidor and two regidores from the

80. *Ibid.*, p. 238.
81. *Ibid.*, p. 239.
    Madrid had eight alcaldes de barrios, whose powers were often confused with those of the regidores.
82. Ballesteros, *Historia de España*, VI, 34.
83. Pérez Búa, "Las Reformas de Carlos III," p. 240; see also Richard Herr, *The Eighteenth-Century Revolution in Spain* (Princeton, N. J., 1958), p. 113.
84. Pérez Búa, "Las Reformas de Carlos III," p. 243.

cabildo, was to pass it to the intendant, who in turn submitted it to the *contaduría de provincia*. After inspection at this level it was given to the Council of Castile for final approval. If the town officials proved unable to make accurate and comprehensible reports, the intendant was authorized to appoint qualified individuals for this purpose at the expense of the councils.[85]

The immediate effect of the financial reform was confusion and uncertainty. The contaduría general was overwhelmed with appeals, memorials, and suits over questions of the propios. In time, the crown issued regulations to allocate types of cases to other bodies, which eliminated a portion of the burden. Because of past squandering and petty indulgence on the part of the municipal officials, it is not surprising that there was some conniving to circumvent the restrictions.[86] As the volume of work continued to be heavy with a resultant delay in the dispatch of *expedientes*, "reports," the crown relented to permit certain exceptional expenditures by the towns.[87] The establishment of the contaduría, which was not suppressed until 1836, deprived the municipalities of their last freedom of action in the sphere of finances. But in terms of general solvency and efficiency in handling of accounts, they were better off than ever before. A Spanish economist of the nineteenth century alludes to the reign of Charles III as the "golden age" for municipal exchequers.[88] However, from the long-range point of view it may be argued that the close supervision of civic finances did not contribute to the development of a healthy sense of responsibility to the community among the municipal councils.

In still another area of the economy the crown intervened with the hope of improving conditions. The possession and use of town land by individuals and corporations came under scrutiny. The price of agricultural commodities having risen because of monetary inflation and an increase in demand by a mounting population, there was a need for the extension of areas for cultivation. In southern and central Spain the extent of pasture land, or *baldíos*, was considerable. A contemporary observer noted the amount of unused terrain: "One sees barely more land cultivated than one or two leagues around the towns. The rest is waste. One can go six or seven leagues

85. *Ibid.*, p. 244.
87. *Ibid.*, p. 240.
86. *Ibid.*, p. 245.
88. *Ibid.*, p. 247.

at a stretch without seeing a sign of human industry."[89] In a region such as Andalucía the pasturage was three times as great as in areas under cultivation. It was inevitable that any scheme for redistribution of land and assignment for the raising of crops would come into conflict with the rights and privileges enjoyed by the Mesta, the powerful guild of the owners of flocks of sheep, which rented for grazing purposes not only territory from the estates controlled by the Military Orders but also the municipal baldios.[90] In 1712, despite the influence of the Mesta at the court, the crown allowed the municipalities of Castile and Aragon to fence in a portion of the commons and sell it for farming land. Twenty years later the right was conceded to every town in the Peninsula. Many cities and villages took advantage of the concession to part with some of their inherited property on favorable terms. When it dawned upon the Mesta that its interests were being imperiled through gradual reduction of the area for grazing, it persuaded the Cortes to petition the king to stay the practice. Ferdinand VI, in deference to the wishes of the guild, not only put an end to the policy but also ordered the restoration of all lands that had been alienated from the towns in the last two decades.[91]

The occurrence of food riots throughout Spain in 1767, brought on by shortages and high prices, demanded a new appraisal by the government of the uses to which land was being put. Three years earlier the deputies in the Cortes from the towns of Extremadura had raised the question by openly criticizing the Mesta for its monopoly of certain areas. Responding to this remonstrance, the Council of Castile, on the advice of Aranda and Campomanes, commanded the cities of this province "to divide among all citizens of the towns their baldios and tierras concejiles, by the right that each has to rent them, with the preference dictated by equity in favor of laborers and farmers who lack their own lands."[92] In 1770 an order was finally issued to enclose and distribute these properties.

While well intentioned, these measures did not produce the anticipated results. Many councils refused to enforce the decrees, fearing a decline in the plentiful supply of cheap labor. In some instances

89. R. Carande (ed.), "Informe de Olavide sobre la ley agraria," *Boletín de la Real Academia de la Historia*, CXXXIX (1956), 436, quoted in Herr, *The Eighteenth Century Revolution*, p. 110.

90. *Ibid.*, p. 112.

91. *Ibid.*

92. Joaquín Costa, *Colectivismo agrario en España*, p. 120, quoted in *ibid.*, p. 114.

the land, instead of being offered for sale, was appropriated by the individual regidores and went to swell their holdings. By and large the deputies, though selected by democratic means, failed to champion the interests of popular groups, aligning themselves instead with the clergy, the members of the Military Orders, and the ayuntamientos in the exploitation of the masses. The lack of success of the program is underlined by a writer of that period: "In the few places where an attempt was made to put the baldios under cultivation, the greatest injustice in their division has been committed, so that the poor peasant has been the least cared for and the last to enjoy these benefits, because first attention was paid to the members of the ayuntamientos and the important and wealthy people of the town."[93] The allotment of communal land did, nevertheless, fulfil some of the crown's expectations in the towns of Catalonia and Asturias, regions without a strong local aristocracy, where to a greater degree than elsewhere a tendency toward social justice permeated the economic relations of all classes.

Lastly, to increase the yield in agriculture a novel experiment was given a trial. The crown proposed that German and French immigrants of the same religious faith as the Spaniards be invited to colonize a stretch of semi-arid wasteland belonging to the king and lying between Madrid and Cadiz. These progressive and energetic settlers might transform the region and set a good example to the natives throughout the kingdom. It was stipulated that no property should fall into the hands of the religious orders or the Mesta and that small holdings should be inalienable so as to forestall the amassing of big estates. As an outcome of the policy, Catholics from France and the German states founded eleven towns and forty-four villages. The fall from favor of the promoter Olavide brought the enterprise to a standstill.[94] Although it is probable that these localities had a more liberal form of government than did the Spanish towns, their foreign origin and structure had no appreciable effect on the aristocratic complexion and make-up of municipal regimes elsewhere. Through clever manipulation of laws and the secret use of communal lands the holders of aldermanic offices continued to maintain the privileged economic status that they inherited from earlier times.

93. Pedro Franco Salazar, *Restauración política económica y militar de España*, quoted in *ibid.*, p. 114.

94. *Ibid.*, p. 116.

In assessing the condition of municipal political institutions in the Peninsula one cannot forego a discussion of the Cortes. This body, essentially unaltered in form and procedure since the Middle Ages, contained procuradores, "agents," from the important towns, in addition to the representatives of the privileged classes, and therefore was a medium for the presentation of municipal petitions and memorials.

Unlike their French cousins, the Spanish Bourbons did not dispense with the Cortes. Absolutism did not proceed to the point at which the crown, relying on its prestige and the services of a numerous and loyal bureaucracy, could entirely discard the tradition of periodical assemblies of the estates of the realm. No one denies that the Spanish parliament was more a symbol than a reality of power, but it is important that it continued to meet, albeit infrequently.

With the exception of Ferdinand VI, all of the eighteenth-century Bourbons convened the Cortes at least once. In 1709, Philip V summoned the assemblies of Castile and Aragon to Madrid for the first general session of the Cortes, to depict symbolically the unity of the kingdom. When rivalries arose over precedence of the deputies in seating and voting, it was decided that pre-eminence be given to the delegates from Castile, with the Aragonese and the Valencians following. The assembly at Philip's request recognized his son as Prince of Asturias and heir to the throne. At a second convocation in 1712, the King relinquished any claims to the throne of France, which was to be vacated before long by the demise of Louis XIV. Two years later a third meeting took place to secure assent to a modification of the right of succession, which would render unconstitutional inheritance of the crown through the female line.[95] On the death of Luis I in 1724, a year after his accession, Philip returned to the throne. In order to secure the approval of this act from the influential classes, he called another session of the Cortes, destined to be the last during his reign. In 1760, the representative body, with delegates from thirty-six villas present, recognized Charles III's son as Prince of Asturias. In 1789, Charles IV issued the summons for the final convocation of the Cortes in the eighteenth century for the purpose of making invalid the Salic law adopted by his grandfather in 1714. Association of an assembly with the violent disorders and ex-

95. Ballesteros, *Historia de España*, VI, 29, 30.

cesses of the French Revolution probably precluded the calling by the King of any additional sessions.[96]

The crises of the Napoleonic era revivified the national assembly. In 1808 the seizure of the Spanish crown by Napoleon Bonaparte aroused popular resistance and a feeling of unity on a scale that could be directed only by the Cortes. During the imprisonment of Ferdinand VII and Charles IV, the body formulated for the homeland and the colonies legislation that was noteworthy for its liberal spirit. The status of the municipalities was temporarily modified in the direction of popular rights, with a repercussion on the final development of colonial local government. But, though hopeful of binding together the distant areas of the empire, the Cortes was unable to stem the rising tide of nationalism and separatism fostered by the cabildos.

In the mid-eighteenth century the Castilian ayuntamientos were in a state of decadence marked by the exercise of limited political power and unmistakable signs of maladministration. Absolutism, initiated by the Hapsburgs and furthered by the Bourbons, had not reached its logical conclusion in the destruction of all local liberties. Waste, graft, and indifference to municipal problems resulted mainly from the manner of selection of officials, the personal failings of alcaldes and regidores, and the circumscribed areas of authority left to the cabildos. Under Charles III the crown made a resolute effort to revive local administration through a variety of means. Partial democratization was introduced in order to lessen the hold of the aristocratic classes on the council and thereby to stimulate an interest in civic affairs on the part of the ordinary vecinos.

One would surmise that practices found desirable and workable in Castile would have been transplanted to Peru and to other parts of America. To what degree this is true can be discovered only by a careful examination of the policies of the sovereigns of French origin toward the colonial municipalities from the outset of the century down to the adoption of the intendency. This governmental innovation, although it came late in the reign of Charles III, nevertheless affected the evolution of colonial councils more than any other event or act and therefore deserves treatment in a separate chapter.

96. See for the subsequent development of this institution, Maximiano García Venero, *Historia del parlamentarismo español (1810-1833)* (Madrid, 1946).

CHAPTER II

Revitalization of
Old Concepts in America

If Philip V, upon his accession to the throne of Spain in 1700, had ideas of modifying colonial institutions, common sense must have imposed upon him the need for delay until political and economic conditions at home were more suitable. The exigencies of the military campaigns in Europe precluded for many years any really serious contemplation of governmental questions in America. During this extended era of international and civil conflict the Peruvian creoles, though mindful of the nature of Bourbon rule in France, expected few immediate changes beyond limited concessions to French trade in colonial ports. When the moment was opportune the King pursued policies of autocracy and centralism, the bounds and directions of which had been plainly charted by his predecessors in Madrid. However, the internal strife in the Peninsula between the followers of the Bourbon Prince and the advocates of the Austrian Hapsburg claimant may have had a serious consequence for future Spanish sovereignty overseas. According to one authority, it awakened "the creole from his political innocence. . . . [this] constitutes a factor of the greatest importance in understanding the birth and growth of a Peruvian political conscience."[1]

Thus the foundation of the Bourbon administrative system had been laid down by the Hapsburgs. The salient difference was the ardor with which the new dynasty followed the old goals. It was a regalism enforced systematically, with some knowledge of the Enlightenment, and eventually through the use of the military. To the

1. Daniel Valcárcel, "Perú borbónico y emancipación," *Revista de historia de América*, No. 50 (December, 1960), pp. 315-438.

colonial municipalities this signified a more restricted sphere of self-rule and of communal responsibility. In the early period of colonization the Spanish rulers had permitted some measure of self-government, but this right had to a great extent been canceled out by the end of the seventeenth century.[2] In contrast to the policy of "salutary neglect" followed by the English sovereigns toward their possessions in North America, in the seventeenth and first half of the eighteenth centuries the Spanish monarchs endeavored to maintain tight control of their own overseas territories. They realized early that an indispensable share of their revenues came from the rich mines of Mexico and Peru.

With autocracy and consolidation as the objectives of their policies the Bourbon rulers resorted to the strict enforcement of older governmental methods and devices. In some instances they altered devices to meet conditions that had changed since the death of the last Hapsburg. Although attention is concentrated on the application of these to the municipalities in Peru, brief reference should be made to the effects of this policy on the higher agencies of colonial government. In 1714 Philip V reduced the authority of the Council of the Indies through the appointment of a secretary or minister of Marina e Indias. The creation of the third viceroyalty, that of New Granada, out of the sprawling, cumbersome Viceroyalty of Peru was a welcome improvement in administration. Set up originally in 1717, it did not become operative until 1739. New approaches and techniques developed also in the latter part of the eighteenth century.

To grasp the relations between the crown and local officials in the Audiencia of Lima, some consideration of the major lines of policy toward America in the eighteenth century is necessary.[3] A fundamental aspect of royal government in the Indies was the distribution of powers among the numerous officials. In the fast-growing bureaucracy there was no concentration of authority in the hands of a single individual, no matter how great his reputation for loyalty and devotion to the king, nor in any body of officials. Even the town councils had rights and duties not to be impinged upon. Behind this studied allotment of powers was a profound distrust of colonial agents, a lack of con-

2. Moore, *The Cabildo in Peru Under the Hapsburgs*, pp. 265-284.
3. For a fuller treatment of this see José María Ots Capdequí, *Instituciones de gobierno del Nuevo Reino de Granada, durante el siglo XVIII* (Bogotá, 1950), pp. 17-25.

fidence engendered by the acts of rebellious conquistadors in the sixteenth century. To assure control of a region immensely wealthy and lying thousands of miles from Europe, the crown would try not to create an environment propitious for a successful movement of independence. Several serious revolts in the eighteenth century accentuated this peril.

A second phase of colonial policy was the obligation of officials to keep the Council of the Indies fully abreast of conditions in America. This responsibility, though fully understood and respected, was not specifically defined nor incorporated in a separate section of the law code.[4]

Legally and by custom, municipalities enjoyed means of access to the sovereign. Metropolitan centers, like Lima and Mexico City, might memorialize the crown directly on matters affecting their political, economic, or social interests. On the other hand, lesser towns had to obtain the permission of the viceroy or the governor to dispatch letters to the monarch or to utilize the services of royal agents. Petitions to the king had to deal with a single subject, avoiding generalizations and matters not immediately pertinent. Although special procurators might bear messages to Madrid, it was normal procedure for the capital cities to maintain agents at the court to look out for their interests in the same way in which the important towns of the Peninsula safeguarded their rights. Conversely, the crown on occasion sought *informes*, "reports," from the colonial towns in order to be enlightened on particular issues, and full replies were generally forthcoming, for the local councils missed few opportunities to be in good graces with the king. But the amount of information channeled through this medium was small in comparison with the enormous mass of reports drawn up by crown agents in the Indies for perusal in Spain.[5]

Regalism implied additionally the right of confirmation of elections in the councils and the approval of judicial acts. This royal

4. "It does not appear that there existed a precise doctrine on this particular. On occasions, in a general way or with reference to concrete cases, regulations were dictated which the authorities had to obey in fulfilment of this informative function. But the study, in connection with the documental evidence that we have had the opportunity to consult, does not permit the presentation of clear and systematic conclusions." See *ibid.*, p. 18.

5. From the author's survey of legajos in the Archivo General de Indias it would seem that the correspondence of the Peruvian cities and towns with the crown was far less in the eighteenth century than earlier.

prerogative went back to the earliest days. Obviously, in a majority of cases it was simply a routine matter with a lapse of time for the completion of the process. In other cases, the crown listened to arguments presented by judicial advisors critical of the qualifications of candidates and delayed or refused entirely petitions for confirmation.[6] Applied to the municipalities, this authority had to do mainly with conciliar elections, the sale of offices, and the enactment of local ordinances. Disputed elections for the post of *alcalde ordinario*, having their origin in factional rivalries and in the inordinate ambition of individuals, were of common occurrence. When an illegal officeholder was a person of wealth and influence and had the support of the regidores, it was difficult to oust him. The purchase or inheritance of an office invariably stipulated confirmation within a stated period, and since each act of approval entailed the payment of a fee, the crown insisted on its observance. In theory, no conciliar ordinance had full legality without royal sanction, but in practice most ordinances were enforced before confirmation had been secured. Because of the laxity of colonial administration under the Hapsburgs in the seventeenth century, many local ordinances that had never received royal approval were in force. In this connection the Bourbons demanded greater compliance with the law.[7]

A paradox of legal absolutism was the custom adopted by colonial authorities of refusing to obey directly the crown's mandate. This was summed up in the celebrated phrase *acato pero no cumplo las órdenes*, "I obey but I do not execute the orders." Some might interpret this as an anarchical symptom. It might be construed from another point of view as a device that imparted flexibility to the Laws of the Indies, an elasticity proven necessary to adjust the Castilian code to another social environment, thousands of miles from the capital of the empire and center of the law-giving process and connected with it by a relatively poor means of communication. From the viceroy down to the local cabildos the infrequent, acknowledged non-observance of a cédula was a step toward the easing of tension and the avoidance of ill feeling between the governed and the gov-

6. Ots Capdequí, *Instituciones de gobierno del Nuevo Reino de Granada*, pp. 20, 21. See also the fundamental study by Antonio de León Pinelo entitled *Tratado de confirmaciones de encomiendas, oficios i casos, en que se requieren para las Indias occidentales* (Madrid, 1630).

7. Ots Capdequí, *Instituciones de gobierno del Nuevo Reino de Granada*, p. 21.

ernment.[8] While the Bourbons resented interference with their decrees more acutely than the decadent Austrians of the preceding century, they still permitted the *de facto* existence of the practice.

Continuity in the handling of governmental business is a desirable trait of good administration. In the solution of problems involving Spaniards and natives the authorities in America sometimes lacked direction and guidance. The crown enjoined the viceroys and governors of New Granada to "preserve in their respective archives royal cedulas, expedientes, etc., including secret correspondence from the office of the Minister of the Indies, in order that it may serve as instructions for their successors," and to act as if "Reales Cédulas sent to their predecessors" had been dispatched for their compliance and execution.[9] By inference, municipalities were expected to comply by keeping records, copies of orders and decrees, and by taking a positive attitude toward their enforcement. Measures were adopted to authenticate cédulas so as to prevent forgeries and alterations that might cause damage and to insure their delivery by the dispatch of postal guards, named by the king, who would sail in the convoys carrying the mail destined for America.[10] Undoubtedly a parallel policy prevailed in Peru.

There was always the necessity of coping with officials guilty of infraction of the law or regulations. This is an important branch of administration whose praises are often unsung. No offending member of the colonial organization, whether secular or ecclesiastical, was exempt from the crown's displeasure, which might take the form of imprisonment, removal or suspension from office, heavy fines, or simply public reproof. Alcaldes and regidores were, like the higher officials, subjected to the visit and to the residencia.[11] The most com-

8. *Ibid.*, pp. 21, 22.
Juan and Ulloa believed that this contradictory practice was abused, leading to disrespect for the law, but they admitted its occasional utility: "We do not deny the fact that in many instances the viceroys have sufficient motive to suspend the enforcement of cédulas from Spain." See Jorge Juan and Antonio de Ulloa, *Noticias Secretas de América* (Buenos Aires, 1953), p. 341.
9. Ots Capdequí, *Instituciones de gobierno del Nuevo Reino de Granada*, p. 22.
10. *Ibid.*, pp. 23-24.
11. The effectiveness of the residencia in correcting abuses at the lower echelons of colonial administration is debatable. A recent authority asserts that "If we are guided by indirect testimony, the opinion of Antonio de Ulloa, the Marqués de Varinas, the protests of individuals or corporations of the period we should be inclined to regard the residencias for subordinate officials in general as fiction." But there are instances of individuals fined or removed from office, which point to the

mon misdemeanors brought to light by these institutional investigations concerned harsh treatment of the natives and embezzlement of public funds.

One aspect of administrative responsibility involved the *jueces non letrados*, "untrained, practical judges," and their *asesores*, "legal advisors." It was not until 1793 that the crown clarified their relations by affirming that governors, intendants, and other royal agents, whose duties were quasi-judicial, were not to be held accountable for *providencias*, "orders," and judgments dictated by their asesores, nor alcaldes ordinarios for decisions written by their asesores, "except in the case of collusion or fraud in their nomination."[12] Thus, liability for decisions handed down by judges lacking in formal training or education properly rested upon the shoulders of the legal secretaries. What modern bureaucrat would not want to be relieved of responsibility for the acts of his advisors and subordinates!

Another facet of Bourbon policy in the Indies derived from the insatiable need of the rulers for revenues. Peru and Mexico ranked high as sources of gold and silver. From the Hapsburgs the newcomers inherited an extensive annual income but, unfortunately, one that was heavily mortgaged because of past wars and lavish expenditures for the court. To these debts were soon added others contracted during the costly, long-drawn out War of Succession and the abortive expedition to Sicily.[13] Although Spain was at peace during most of his reign, Ferdinand VI was nevertheless preoccupied with matters of the budget. It was clear that the exchequer should not be allowed to remain empty indefinitely without a serious effort to stop up the leaks and replenish the supply of gold.

Various expedients to exorcise the demon of bankruptcy and to enlarge the flow of national revenue were therefore tried. Understandably, they affected the financial status of the municipalities and

---

fact that this was a means of maintaining the integrity of the bureaucracy, besides being a source of important information about governmental conditions. See Luis Duran Flórez, "El juicio de residencia en el Perú republicano," *Anuario de estudios Americanos*, X (1953), 384-387.

The open *visita* might well include a "general inspection of the discharge of duties" by alcaldes, regidores, lawyers, and procurators. See Guillermo Céspedes del Castillo, "La visita como institución Indiana," *Anuario de estudios Americanos*, III (1946), 997.

12. Ots Capdoquí, *Instituciones de gobierno del Nuevo Reino de Granada*, p. 25.

13. Desdevises du Dezert, *L'Espagne de l'Ancien Regime*, p. 416.

the pocketbooks of the vecinos.[14] Philip V suspended the payment of interest on the debt and took over for one year the income from virtually all types of property conceded in the immediate past by the crown to individuals and collective bodies.[15] Pursuing a similar disregard for private and corporate rights, Ferdinand VI proceeded against the towns in the Peninsula by appropriating 50 per cent of the customs duties, by decreasing the revenue from rents and offices granted by the crown, and by forcing functionaries to hand over sums of money.[16] Collection of taxes was improved by the abolition of the system of farming-out and the substitution in its place of an official bureaucracy of tax collectors. In spite of these measures and other levies, debts mounted more rapidly than the royal income.[17]

Could the revenues from the Indies be expanded? While this appeared as a distinct possibility in certain categories of taxation, there was in reality only a remote chance of increasing appreciably the sums from municipal sources. To a considerable extent the gold from this mine had been extracted. Most of the town offices had been sold in the preceding century and those yet unsold, generally in small, insignificant localities, stood then in little prospect of finding takers. It is likely also that the conflict into which Spain had been plunged at the outset of the century had encouraged laxity and connivance of tax collectors and officeholders in the assessment of funds due from the sale or inheritance of both royal and municipal posts. The secret instructions of November 18, 1725, from the Council of the Indies to the Marqués de Castelfuerte, viceroy of Peru, revealed a suspicion of fraudulence in this type of income and ordered a report to be made thereon:

> Taking account of the fact that in many offices of those kingdoms [America] awarded in past years and at the present time to various subjects the Royal Treasury suffered losses owing to the disproportion in the returns to the crown with respect to the excessive value that they [offices] had and produced for those who occupied them and bearing in mind that the crown has the right to punish any fraud that it might have suffered, I charge you to ascertain the real value of the above mentioned positions and of the income derived illegally from them by any individuals to whom they were granted

14. No attempt is made to describe the sources of the Bourbon exchequer as a whole, since it is a complicated topic and would fall outside the purview of this study.
15. Desdevises du Dezert, *L'Espagne de l'Ancien Regime*, p. 419.
16. *Ibid.*, p. 420.   17. *Ibid.*, p. 416.

and render me a report with proof of all that which is done in this.[18]

Evidently the hoped-for results did not materialize, for the council reiterated the command in the instructions to Castelfuerte's successor the Marqués de Villa García.[19] Again, in 1748 the viceroy designate, José Manso, was admonished "to take special care that the rules and regulations concerning the sale of offices be carried out."[20] The rise in revenue from this source which had occurred by 1755 may have been due to the repeated injunctions of the crown.[21]

Other levies from the municipalities to be augmented for the benefit of the treasury were the *alcabala*, "sales tax," the proceeds from the sale of *papel sellado*, "stamped paper," necessary for legal documents, and the *media anata*, which was one-half of the salary from an office for one year. The funds collected from these sources constituted a lesser portion of the total revenue from America.

In order to determine more precisely the extent of income from this provenance and its general significance in terms of crown finance, the following tables for the *caja*, "treasury," of the Audiencia of Lima have been compiled for five-year periods beginning in 1705 and running to 1755, toward the end of the reign of Ferdinand VI.

A thoroughgoing analysis of the reports from the treasury officials is made difficult by the unsatisfactory method of bookkeeping used in the colonies. For example, it is not always clear whether the sums in the strong box at the end of the year represented a collection of debts for the particular year in question or included that of past debts. Did it indicate the amount left after some funds had been deducted for dispatch to Spain? The reforms of Charles III eliminated some of the confusion and vagueness.[22]

18. Ynstruccion Reserbada de lo que el Marqués de Castelfuerte, ha de ejecutar en el Perú, luego que tome posesion de aquel Virreynato, San Ildefonso, Nov. 18, 1725, legajo 642, Audiencia de Lima, A. G. I.

19. Instruccion de lo q. ha de obserbar el Marqués de Villa Garcia electo Virrey del Perú, El Pardo, Jan. 30, 1735, *ibid.*

20. Ynstruccion que ha de obserbar el Theniente General de los Reales Exercitos Don José Manso, en el Virreynato de las Provincias de Perú, Buen Retiro, Aug. 21, 1784, legajo 643, *ibid.*

21. See table that follows.

22. There is no scholarly monograph on the subject of the eighteenth-century colonial exchequer. A *Historia general de Real Hacienda escrita por orden del Virey Conde de Revillagigedo* (6 tomos; Mexico City, 1845-1853), by Fabian de Fonseca y Carlos de Urrutia is helpful.

		pesos	reales	(from the previous year) pesos	reales	gramo.
1705	Oficios	101,658	7½			
	Stamped paper	12,628	2½			
	Alcabala	415,513	7¼	1,436	5	10
1710	Oficios	61,216	4½			
	Stamped paper	1,254	1			
	Alcabala	11,619	4½	4,608	3¼	
1715	Oficios	21,017	½			
	Stamped paper	9,541	5½			
	Alcabala	138,495	2½			

		pesos	reales
1720	Oficios	15,237	7½
	Stamped paper	3,749	5
	Alcabala	79,278	5
1725	Oficios	27,444	5¾
	Stamped paper	3,447	6
	Alcabala	13,637	1
1730	Oficios	31,248	7
	Stamped paper	5,842	5½
	Alcabala	232,819	1¼
1735	Oficios	31,135	4¾
	Stamped paper	8,292	4½
	Alcabala	269,915	½
1740	Oficios	14,366	3
	Stamped paper	6,536	3½
	Alcabala	144,455	7¾
1745	Oficios	13,902	6
	Stamped paper	15,211	4½
	Alcabala	140,315	6
1750	Oficios	13,357	6¼
	Stamped paper	6,131	6½
	Alcabala	153,982	1

		pesos	reales	pesos	reales
1755	Oficios	53,315	2½	15,198	5½
	Stamped paper	9,166	2¾		
	Alcabala	242,871	3½		

The peso, the Spanish unit of currency, had a value in this period of approximately fifty cents
The following monetary system prevailed in Spain and the colonies:
1 peso = 8 reales or tomines
1 real = 34 maravedis or 12 gramos
SOURCE. Cuentas de Real Hacienda y Caxa de Lima, legajos 1760, 1761, 1762, 1764, 1765, 1766, 1767, 1770, 1771, 1772, Contaduría general, A. G. I.

Nevertheless, one may reach certain conclusions regarding municipal taxation on the basis of the five-year sampling. The amount from *oficios*, including fees for possession of office from both royal and municipal officeholders, followed generally a downward curve from 1705, with a temporary increase from 1725 to 1735 and a more pronounced incline by 1755, because of a more determined effort to deal with evasion and the more pacific, prosperous character of the reign of Ferdinand VI. Exceeding 100,000 pesos only once, the returns must have been disappointing to the crown. The sale of stamped paper, averaging from 7,000 to 8,000 pesos, represented the smallest contribution from the citizenry in this general classification of taxes. The revenue from the alcabalas disclosed the greatest variation, with a high of over 415,000 pesos in 1705 and a low of approximately 14,000 in 1725.

Other sets of figures from the caja of Lima provide a more detailed knowledge of the returns from oficios. Since the sale of offices was closely identified with the functioning of municipal government, it would be profitable to ascertain the exact amount collected in Lima from municipal offices as distinct from that produced by sale of royal offices. For this purpose the returns for three years have been selected arbitrarily from the approximately sixty-year period under review to reveal the revenue from the two sources, with inclusion of the figures for the media anata, paid to the crown as an additional fee.[23] For further illustration, sample totals of oficios, royal and municipal, for the same years for the provinces or districts of the audiencia are given. These tables, for the years 1710, 1725, and 1755, for which there are relatively complete reports, cover in general the beginning, the middle, and the end of the reigns of the first two important Bourbons.[24]

A study of these figures indicates conclusively the meager character of the revenues for the crown from the purchase, inheritance, and transfer by individuals of colonial municipal offices. It seems clear that relatively few vendible local positions were disposed of or changed hands because of the indifference of creoles to municipal affairs or the lack of prestige attached to these positions. If the number of changes was actually greater than reported, the omission

23. In some instances it is difficult to differentiate between a purely municipal office and a royal one.

24. The length of these tables requires their relegation to an appendix. See Appendix I.

of some might be explained by the inability of the crown to make a full or partial settlement with its debtors. The sale of royal offices usually brought in sums twice as large as from municipal posts in 1710 and three times as large in 1755. The figures for 1725 appear to be an anomaly. It should be noticed that while most of the royal bureaucratic posts, both civil and military, were included, sums paid to the crown in Spain for concessions of the offices of judge of the audiencia and corregidor were omitted. The probable explanation is that the transactions customarily took place in Spain rather than in America.

Similar observations may be made regarding the proceeds of media anata. These were substantially greater from the purely crown offices, being nine times as much as those from the municipal offices in 1710 and twice as much in 1725. The possibility of increasing the income from this source would not be lost on the advisors of the next Bourbon ruler.

With the accession of Charles III in 1759, a new chapter in administration was written for the American colonies. A monarch with many years of solid experience in statecraft in Naples, counseled by a group of exceptionally alert and industrious ministers, he resolved to initiate reforms in the Peninsula and in his possessions across the Atlantic and thereby raise once more the prestige of Spain in Europe. His personal ambition to play an important role in international affairs was matched only by the sincerity of his conviction that innovations were necessary. Moreover, after the disastrous Seven Years War his plans for the future were influenced by the menacing aggrandizement of Great Britain. The conclusion of the Family Compact with France in 1761 not only strengthened his hand in Europe but also accelerated the reorganization of the colonial regime.[25] With closer ties established between the two kingdoms, the French minister Choiseul abetted the cause of reform through the recommendation of capable men for office and even through the proposal of specific remedial measures. It was inevitable, however, that primary attention would be devoted to conditions in Spain, after which measures would be initiated for the improvement of government in America and for the more thorough exploitation of its resources.

25. Céspedes del Castillo, "La visita como institución Indiana," p. 1022; see also Arthur S. Aiton, "Spanish Colonial Reorganization Under the Family Compact," *Hispanic American Historical Review*, XII (1932), 269-280.

The reforms in the colonies were well conceived and earnestly applied. It is truly said that modernization of the empire was necessary but difficult. It was to be a "mature work, realized after much time spent in preliminary surveys."[26] Economic growth and the universal observance of law were proclaimed as ideals, but they masked the monarch's desire for funds with which to achieve a brilliant court at Madrid and personal glorification through war, as well as his covert concern for the extension of absolutism.[27] Few detractors of the Bourbon sovereign would deny the social and economic advantages which his reforms produced for the influential, propertied classes. In the political sphere there was marked efficiency, but this was accompanied by a decline in local liberties and rights. The improvement in the functioning of the municipal regimes, it has been suggested, was partly responsible for the prolonged resistance offered to the crown by the cabildos in the revolutionary era.[28]

Changes occurred in the organization and structure of the governmental machinery for the colonies located in Spain. Until 1787, the king used a single minister of *Marina e Indias*; thereafter the duties of the office were divided between a minister of *Gracia y Justicia* and a minister of *Guerra, Hacienda, Comercio, y Navegación*. In the process the Council of the Indies was deprived of authority and influence. When Charles IV ascended the throne, he returned to the plan of using only one secretary adopted initially by Philip V. Although the council regained some of its power, it was temporarily extinguished by the Cortes of Cadiz in 1812. Two years later this famous institution was resuscitated by Ferdinand VII, who did not decree its demise until 1823.

In America the need for administrative efficiency and the tightening of imperial defenses was pressing. A beginning had been made in a previous reign toward the establishment of a third viceroyalty to comprise the kingdoms of Santa Fe and Quito with the capital at Bogotá. Despite its reduction in size by the creation of the new viceregal unit, the Viceroyalty of Peru still covered an area reaching from the west coast to the Atlantic and south to the Straits of Magellan. This vast territory presented complex problems of defense and economic de-

26. Miguel Artola, "Campillo y las reformas de Carlos III," p. 714.
27. Viellard-Baron, "L'Etablissement des Intendants aux Indes par Charles III," p. 527.
28. John Lynch, *Spanish Colonial Administration, 1782-1810*, pp. 288, 289.

velopment that could not be satisfactorily handled in Lima. Furthermore, the people of the La Plata region clamored for a recognition that
had been denied them in the past because of the jealousy and resentment of the merchants of Lima and Panama at the expanding commerce and wealth of the port of Buenos Aires. Seeing the need finally
for strengthening the links in the chain of defenses against England,
Charles III in 1776 consented to the appointment of a fourth viceroy,
whose domain would include the provinces of Rio de la Plata, Paraguay, and Tucumán, with the four Peruvian districts of La Paz,
Potosí, Charcas, and Santa Cruz.[29]

The creation of the new viceroyalties entailed changes in the size
and number of the audiencias. New bodies were set up and territorial
bounds were rearranged resulting in a contraction of jurisdiction for
some of the older administrative courts.[30] Prior to 1717 the Viceroyalty
of Peru contained the audiencias of Panama, Chile, Quito, and Charcas, in addition to the most significant one at Lima. The establishment
of the third and fourth viceroyalties meant the transfer of a number
of administrative courts from the control of the Peruvian viceroy.
The area of the Audiencia of Lima was reduced in 1787 by the
establishment of a separate organization for the region of Cuzco,
which had the advantage of eliminating for litigants and petitioners
the delay attendant upon the long, arduous journey from the interior
to the coast. As in the seventeenth century these juridico-administra-
tive bodies often manifested an independence toward the viceregal
representatives and the ecclesiastical hierarchy. Not uncommon were
clashes with the king's alter ego over general authority in many
administrative areas, cognizance of legal suits, and the exercise of
privileges and honors at public receptions and ceremonials. These
disagreements were an inevitable consequence of the governmental
system.[31]

Both viceroy and audiencia suffered some loss of power through
the appointment by the crown of the *regente*, "regent." By an instrucción of June 20, 1776, this official became the presiding officer for
each of the audiencias, excepting those of Santa Fe and Buenos Aires,
with responsibilities somewhat analogous to those of the corregidor
in the town councils. His function was to bridge the gap between the

29. Ramos Pérez, *Historia de la colonización española en América*, pp. 115, 116.
30. *Ibid.*, p. 114.
31. Ballesteros, *Historia de España*, VI, 667.

viceroy and the audiencia by assigning to each the proper limits of authority in disputed areas of jurisdiction.[32] As a referee his role was an unpopular one, resented by members of both institutions.

The prestige and duties of all of these officials were curtailed by the introduction of the intendancies, the greatest governmental reform in the colonial empire in the eighteenth century. Before sketching the background of this significant innovation, it is necessary to review the early policy of Charles III toward the municipalities, for the multiple and vexing problems of the local councils were a powerful reason for the appointment of the new officials.

This vigorous monarch was much concerned with the status of local government. The corruption and inertia that had characterized the ayuntamientos in 1700 still existed.[33] Unrepresentative, subject to pressure from individual interests, and using antiquated procedures, they required investigation and overhauling. Like their counterparts in the Peninsula, they were often dominated by selfish oligarchies of landowners and merchants bent on exploitation. Should serious reform be undertaken in America, the task would in one respect be simpler; the greater uniformity of organization in America, in contrast to the variety of types and practices existing in Castile, would simplify reform. But in other respects this process would be more difficult because of distance, the diversity of environment, and the frequent tendency of the citizenry to ignore royal decrees and regulations.

It was obvious that much of the trouble was rooted in the ubiquitous system of vending offices. To put an end to the nefarious practice would necessitate the crown's repurchase of offices from the legal holders or confiscation of them by the exercise of a regal prerogative. Both solutions lacked feasibility, the first because it involved the expenditure of a huge sum to be obtained by an increase in governmental indebtedness, and the second because it meant the disregard of legitimate property rights, thus provoking serious discontent among the creoles, a class regarded as loyal and faithful to the King. At the same time a minor source of royal revenue would disappear. The crown attempted neither of these two solutions in the homeland, where it had actually far more at stake. On the other hand, to plant in America the institutional reform adopted in 1766 in the Peninsula would have been comparatively easy. Yet there was no effort to democratize

32. Ramos Pérez, *Historia de la colonización española en América*, p. 115.
33. Moore, *Cabildo in Peru under the Hapsburgs*, pp. 265-269.

the ayuntamientos.[34] One might guess that the King's failure to apply this solution was the result of his fear of engendering sentiments of independence and separatism among the colonial subjects, paralleling those of the English colonies to the north. That a similar outcome would have been immediately inevitable is not, necessarily true.

The King needed to augment the revenue from the Indies to pursue his ambitious foreign policies and to maintain the court. His economic reforms eventually stimulated trade, commerce, and mining, increasing the income from royal taxes. It was hoped that greater prosperity of the region and a sounder procedure of tax collection would also increase the revenue from municipal sources.

The following table for five-year periods from 1760 to 1780, the era preceding the adoption of the intendancy, shows the receipts from the three principal municipal sources of the caja of Lima:

		(from the previous year)		Total	
		pesos	reales	pesos	reales
	Oficios	20,583	½	62,737	6½
1760	Stamped paper			35,574	6½
	Alcabala			275,132	3

		(from Lima)		(from outside)		Total	
		pesos	reales	pesos	reales	pesos	reales
	Oficios	22,937	5	12,557	1	121,101	4½
1765	Stamped paper	7,260	7	8,463	1	76,723	3
	Alcabala	283,873	6¾	107,955	1½		
	Oficios	10,471	½	11,549	6½	22,020	7
1770	Stamped paper	5,160		7,424	6¾	12,584	6¾
	Alcabala	411,670	2			468,698	2½
	Oficios	12,168	3½	11,341	5¾	28,504	¾
1775	Stamped paper	7,276		4,218	7¼	11,494	7¼
	Alcabala	115,040		102,084	1½	233,221	5½
	Oficios	9,993	6	12,529	⅞	23,621	3
1780	Stamped paper	7,035	1	5,754	5		
	Alcabala	355,213	1⅛	147,227	6⅛		

Marked discrepancies in the totals are often explained by the practice already referred to of counting sums left over in the treasury from the preceding year.

Source. Legajo B, 1772, Contaduría general, A.G.I.; legajos 1138, 1141, 1143, 1146, Audiencia de Lima, A.G.I.

34. Julio Alemparte, El cabildo en Chile colonial (Santiago, Chile, 1940), p. 367.

A consideration of the above figures discloses the futility of attempting to raise the amount of crown revenue from royal and municipal oficios. From a high of approximately 42,000 pesos in total collection in 1760, there was a downward trend to about 23,500 pesos in 1780, and a fall from approximately 22,900 pesos in collection from Lima in 1765 to roughly 9,900 in 1780. Although no differentiation is made between royal and municipal offices, it is more than likely that the ratio remained the same as in the earlier decades.[35] The proceeds from the sale of stamped paper remained at virtually the same level, with perhaps some slight decline at the end of the twenty-year period. Reflecting more favorable economic conditions, receipts from the alcabala were in general much larger than those of the previous era, attaining a high of over 500,000 pesos.[36] Against this source, oficios furnished a paltry sum indeed.[37]

Symptomatic of the malfunctioning of municipal regimes was the occurrence of disorders and riots in meetings of the cabildos. While they were the result in part of a struggle for power among certain individuals and factions and the conflict of economic interests, a major cause was the growing antagonism between creole and European. "A widespread illness," Juan and Ulloa called it in their secret report, to be witnessed in the ayuntamiento, "where the most irreconcilable enmity spreads its poison."[38] Both groups were to blame, the colonists "for their inordinate vanity and pride," and the immigrants "for their miserable and unfortunate state" on arrival, which made them excessively ambitious and greedy.[39] Basically, the creoles' dislike sprang from many factors: a jealousy of the industry of those born in Europe, their luck in contracting marriages with daughters of wealthy land-

35. There are no accounts for this period of income from the media anata. It may have been included with oficios, but this is extremely doubtful, the two types of income having been distinct in the past.

36. Augmentation of the royal revenues from the Indies may have been due in part to a better system of tax collection. In 1749 Ferdinand VI suppressed the farmers-general in Spain and replaced them with royal agents. Under Charles III the new method prevailed in the colonies. See Desdevises du Dezert, L'Espagne de l'Ancien Regime, p. 404; also Clarence H. Haring, The Spanish Empire in America (New York, 1947), p. 299.

37. Compare the above figures with those from the ramo de oficios reales y municipales from the caja of Mexico for the corresponding years: 1765-16,697 pesos; 1770-49,852 pesos; 1775-35,740 pesos; 1780-24,944 pesos. A somewhat similar downward curve is noted from 1770. See Fonseca y Urrutia, Historia general de Real Hacienda, III, 87.

38. Juan and Ulloa, Noticias Secretas, pp. 319, 320.

39. Ibid., p. 320.

owners or traders, and the favoritism shown them by the crown in public celebrations and in the appointment to high civil and religious posts.[40] In the cities and towns of the highlands, where the population was less cultured and more provincial in outlook, the greatest hostility existed.

As a remedy for this social ill, the two authors proposed restrictions on the political activities of Spanish immigrants in the colonies. It should be decreed that persons going to America "without permission of His Majesty, or who have no employment... cannot fill any position or corresponding post in any of those cities, towns or villages, and particularly those of regidores, nor be elected as alcaldes ordinarios."[41] It was a thoughtful suggestion, derived from a long sojourn in the Viceroyalty of Peru, but difficult to enforce.

Another consideration that prompted reform was the inhuman treatment and oppression of the Indians by the corregidores. The *Noticias Secretas* contains a stern indictment of the system of native labor: "The tyranny from which the Indians suffer is born from the insatiable hunger for wealth that is shown by those who govern; and as the latter have no other aim to pursue than that of oppressing the Indians by every method malice can suggest, they do not cease to practice any [device] and force from them [Indians] more work than could be obtained from their own slaves."[42]

Long known to the Council of the Indies, the suffering and debasement of the Indians went unchecked throughout the first three-quarters of the eighteenth century. Only an extensive reorganization of Indian policy and agencies could abolish the injustice.

To combat these defects and give new life to the colonial adminis-

40. *Ibid.*, pp. 319-325.
To these observers the envious attitude was well grounded, for "as soon as they [Spaniards] marry they become regidores and immediately obtain the positions of alcaldes ordinarios, in such a way that in the period of ten or eleven years they discover themselves governing a city of the former, and objects of applause and high esteem. This is the man, who before cried his goods in the streets, with a pack on his back, selling cheap merchandise and some knick-knacks that were given him to start out in business." See *ibid.*, p. 322.
The anonymous author of a "Descripción de la ciudad de Lima" (*ca.* 1774) bears witness to the "mortal aversion" of creoles for European Spaniards, which, he declares, was due to their ignorance of other lands and peoples and to a jealousy of the energetic but boastful and arrogant immigrant. See "Descripción de la ciudad de Lima," Ms. 11026, Biblioteca nacional, Madrid.
41. Juan and Ulloa, *Noticias Secretas,* pp. 325, 326.
42. *Ibid.*, p. 182.

tration, Charles III made his most decisive innovation. Having proved its worth in the Peninsula since 1749, the intendancy was applied step by step to all of the empire, to Cuba in 1764, Buenos Aires in 1782, Peru in 1784, to New Spain and the Captaincy-General of Chile in 1786, and to the remainder of the colonies in 1790.[43] The new official personified everywhere the forces of centralization and royal authority, bringing in his train unformity and efficiency. Because of the considerable importance of the office in the evolution of the municipal councils, a full treatment of the establishment of the system and its impact on the cabildos is given in later chapters.[44] Meanwhile, it is appropriate to examine the nature and practices of local regimes in Peru in the period from 1700 to 1784, the pre-intendancy era.

43. Haring, *Spanish Empire in America*, pp. 144-148; also Ramos Pérez, *Historia de la colonización española en América*, pp. 112-114.
44. See chaps. viii, ix, x.

CHAPTER III

Population and Officeholding

At the beginning of the eighteenth century the Audiencia of Lima contained a number of cities and towns. Its urban development was, however, generally less than that of New Spain. The most significant municipalities were Lima, Lambayeque, Piura, Huancavelica, Guamanga, Arequipa, Huánuco, Tarma, Jauja, Cajamarca, Pisco, Arica, and Chachapoyas. A great majority of these dated from the sixteenth century, the era of initiation of municipal life in the viceroyalty.[1]

During the course of the eighteenth century historical events and natural phenomena affected the prosperity and population of many places. The depletion of the silver mines, the exposure to raids by the English and Dutch navies and by freebooters, and the occurrence of disastrous earthquakes led to the disappearance of some towns and the reduction in size of others. Until the 1760's the audiencia suffered economic eclipse and decline. With the adoption of new commercial policies by the enterprising Charles III and the discovery of other sources of mineral wealth, the downward trend was checked, and thereafter towns evinced greater vitality and growth. New mining centers appeared and some of the older cities experienced population expansion.

As the viceregal capital, Lima, opulent and aristocratic, dominated the audiencia. Its inhabitants, according to a survey conducted by the Viceroy Monclova in 1700, numbered 22,300; a census made in 1792 disclosed that the population had more than doubled, reaching the

1. See Expediente sobre la averiguación de las rentas de propios arbitrios, y bienes de comunidad de las ciudades y villas del distrito, legajo 14, Archivo histórico de hacienda y comercio, Lima.

figure of 52,627. The creole and European-born elements of the population were less numerous than the lower classes composed of the Indians, mestizos (mixed Indian and Spanish), mulattoes, and Negroes. It is probable that the proportion of those of Spanish blood to the aborigines was, however, five to one in the middle of the eighteenth century. The group whose fortune was steadily improving was the mestizos.[2]

The merits of Lima are extolled by the author of *El Lazarillo de ciegos caminantes*. A dialogue between the Spanish *visitador* and his faithful servant and companion contrasts the capital and Cuzco:

Suppose, Señor Inca, I replied that you are enamored of Cuzco, your native city, and would wish that I should say that it was better than Lima in every way, but you are very wrong, because leaving aside the location and ejidos, you must observe that in this great capital resides a Viceroy with authority and a salary that is equivalent to the sum of income from all the mayorazgos of Cuzco. It has likewise three companies of guards maintained by the king, of cavalry with good horses and well paid; infantry and halberdiers, who serve not only for ostentation and greatness, but for the safety and repose of this great population, to which is added a full audiencia, tribunals de contaduría mayor, a royal inquisition, university, theater, public walks near the city, which Cuzco does not have nor any other city of the Kingdom.

This city has 250 coaches and more than 1,000 calashes, which alone are distinguished for having two wheels, being drawn by a mule, and having a tendency to turn over. Your city has nothing like that. In the matter of costumes one is as crazy as the other, with the difference in taste and presence of families and trade, in which Lima exceeds Cuzco greatly. In this city there are many with titles of marquis, count, and many more caballeros of the Orders of Santiago and Calatrava, who with few exceptions have sufficient income to live luxuriously.[3]

2. Rubén Vargas Ugarte, *Historia del Perú, virreinato (siglo XVIII), 1700-1790* (Lima, 1956), p. 252.

Another estimate of the population of Lima in the 1770's puts the figure at 54,000, with 16,000 to 18,000 of pure Spanish descent. See Cosme Bueno, *Geografía del Perú virreinal* (siglo XVIII), edited by Daniel Valcárcel (Lima, 1951), p. 20.

3. Calixto Bustamante Carlos Inca, alias Concolorcorvo, *El Lazarillo de ciegos caminantes desde Buenos Aires hasta Lima, 1773* (Buenos Aires, 1942), pp. 390, 391.

A comparison with Mexico City is also made, naturally to the advantage of the Peruvian capital, the author or authors stressing the more healthful qualities of a site along the coast. See *ibid.*, pp. 396, 397.

Next to Lima in prestige was the ancient seat of the Inca civilization, Cuzco. Soon after its founding the crown had endowed it with the same privileges as the Spanish city of Burgos; and because of its courageous resistance to the onslaught of the Indians led by Túpac-Amaru, the king in 1783 had bestowed upon it the additional honor of *Muy Noble, Leal y Fidelísima*. In the middle of the eighteenth century its populace was estimated at 26,000[4] and by 1793 at 32,000.[5] In 1750 Cajamarca, Trujillo, and Yca had a smaller number of inhabitants, the respective figures being roughly 12,000, 9,000, and 6,000.[6] According to a census of 1792, the population of Guamanga was 25,970; Arequipa, 23,988; Huancavelica, 5,146; and Tarma, 5,538.[7] Pisco and Arica had suffered a reduction of population and wealth through the double misfortune of piratical attack and earthquake.

Various factors determined the status of a municipality as a metropolis, a diocesan or suffragan city, or a town or village. Its selection as a center of royal government, its economic importance, its traditions, and its population gave it a position recognized by law and reflected in privileges and rights. The higher the administrative category the greater were the privileges enjoyed by the citizenry. In the eighteenth century relatively few localities succeeded in raising their classification, though some gained more civic privileges and even exemption from taxes because of gifts and acts of outstanding loyalty.[8]

4. Antonio de Alcedo, *Diccionario geográfico-histórico de las Indias occidentales* (5 tomos; Madrid [?], 1786-1789), I, 747, 748.
5. This included 16,122 creoles or Spaniards, 14,254 Indians, and the remainder mestizos, *pardos*, and Negros. See José Hipólito Unánue, *Guía política, ecclesiástica y militar del virreinato del Perú, para el año de 1793* (Lima, n. d.), p. 77.
6. According to a count made by the former corregidor, Miguel Feijoo, in 1761, Trujillo or the valley of Chimu had a total of 9,289 people, of these 3,050 were of Spanish origin, 3,650 Negroes and mulattoes (mainly slaves), 2,300 mestizos, and 289 pure Indians. See Relación descriptiva de la ciudad y provincia de Truxillo del Perú, legajo 819, Audiencia de Lima, A. G. I. But by 1793 the number had dropped to 5,790. See Unánue, *Guía política del Perú*, p. 117.
7. *Ibid.*, pp. 95, 130, 138, and 145.
8. There are several examples of elevation in status in the neighboring viceroyalty of New Granada in the eighteenth century. In 1745 the villa of Riobamba in the Audiencia of Quito petitioned the crown for the rank of "ciudad," alleging its early founding, expanding population, wealth, and loyalty of its citizens as shown by their voluntary military service and their donations. After a delay of two years the Consejo de Indias granted the boon, awarding the "title of 'ciudad' without any other privilege or distinction than that of being called 'city.'" See Expediente sobre Riobamba, legajo 139, Audiencia de Quito, A. G. I.
The *asiento* of Hambato was successful in getting the appelation of villa by real cedula of Oct. 11, 1759, because its inhabitants numbered 150 Spanish families, 4,000

As the residence of the viceroy, Lima belonged to the first category. Trujillo, Arequipa, Guamanga, and Cuzco ranked below it as centers of ecclesiastical jurisdiction.[9] To each of these municipalities were assigned two alcaldes ordinarios and anywhere from two to twelve aldermen, who together made up the cabildo. Lima and Cuzco had the maximum number of officials, that is two mayor-justices and twelve councilors.[10] A royal agent, a corregidor, a governor, or his lieutenant presided over the meetings of the councils of the more populous cities and towns with the exception of Lima. The post of alderman was often combined with other offices such as *alférez real*, "royal standard bearer," *alguacil mayor*, "constable," *alcalde provincial*, "supervisor of municipal resources," and *fiel ejecutor*, "inspector of weights and measures."[11] Although the Peruvian municipalities were expected to have the regular quota of conciliar officials, there were many towns in this period that failed to fulfil the normal requirements. Until the appointment of the intendants the crown did not insist fully on compliance with the law. Consequently, in many instances councils had only partial membership for decades. In 1745, Cuzco had only six of its twelve prescribed aldermen.[12]

---

mestizos, and 6,000 Indians, and its contribution in royal taxes exceeded 20,000 pesos annually. Its location at some fourteen leagues from Riobamba had imposed difficulties for the administration of justice by the corregidor and alcaldes of the city. It is noteworthy that the municipal council of Riobamba, in contrast to the attitude of some ayuntamientos in the seventeenth century, raised no objection to losing jurisdiction over the asiento, but wholeheartedly gave its approval to the petition. See Expediente sobre el Título de Villa para el Asiento de San Juan Bautista de Hambato en la Provincia de Quito, *ibid.*

9. Cosme Bueno, *Geografía del Perú*, p. 18.

10. Alcedo, *Diccionario geográfico-histórico*, I, 746.

11. Of the twelve regimientos in Trujillo in 1761, five were associated with the above offices and worth accordingly anywhere from five to six times more than a single aldermancy. See Relación descriptiva de la ciudad y provincia de Truxillo del Perú, legajo 819, Audiencia de Lima, A. G. I.

12. Minutes of Oct. 11, 1745, Libros de actas del cabildo de Cuzco, vol. 21, Archivo de la Universidad de Cuzco.

With only three of the possible six aldermanic positions filled and two of the occupants absent because of illness, Piura was without a legal quorum for election on Jan. 1, 1742. Thereupon the corregidor authorized the continuance in office as alcaldes ordinarios of the alférez real and the senior regidor, "in order that the administration of justice be not suspended nor the public interest suffer injury, the decision to receive, of course, the sanction of the viceroy of these Kingdoms." See the minutes of Jan. 1, 1742, *Libro del Cabildo de la ciudad de San Miguel de Piura, año 1737 a 1748* (Lima, 1939).

The paucity of regidores compelled the corregidor to repeat this procedure the following year. See minutes of Jan. 1, 1743, *ibid.*

The place of assembly for the council was the town hall or *casa de cabildo*. Most cities and towns possessed edifices, single or double-storied, of stone, adobe, or wood, built with municipal funds, but many were in a disreputable state of repair or too limited in size to accommodate the necessary functions. Earthquakes spared neither secular nor ecclesiastical structures in their devastation. Lima and its environs felt a quake of catastrophic proportions in 1746, the worst in its long memory, with an estimated loss of life from 1,000 to 6,000 in the capital alone. The casa de cabildo, along with public buildings, and nearly all private dwellings were destroyed.

The Viceroy Antonio Manso, subsequently given the title of Conde de Superunda for his heroic efforts in overcoming the effects of the tidal waves accompanying the earthquake, related in his *Memorias* the many problems and difficulties in the way of rehabilitating the capital. His first act on the morning of October 29 after the occurrence of the quake the night before was to order the cleaning of the city, the restoration of its aqueducts, and the paving of the principal streets. These measures were at first ineffective and virtually useless in view of the dimensions of the disaster. The city "without a cathedral and houses remained a place of horror, like a city that one is accustomed to see during a war, a city put to the sword and set afire, whose beautiful homes are converted into a pile of stones and earth."[13] Food was scarce, but in a few days ships with wheat appeared in the harbors and the few bakeries were able to supply enough bread to prevent starvation. In order to assist the people, the Viceroy set up temporary emergency headquarters in the main square. Bodies were exhumed from the rubble and guards appointed to prevent looting and theft.

To rebuild the city in the shortest possible time was imperative. But the Viceroy encountered many obstacles: "My wishes being all for the public good, it might be believed that they would be obeyed with pleasure and promptness. But there were many impediments that offered themselves to the speedy execution of the design. Wealth had vanished, expenditures made for uncomfortable shelters in the fields would be lost, and the costs necessary for new shops were rendered higher through lack of materials—these could not be borne

13. *Memorias de los vireyes que han gobernado el Perú durante el tiempo del coloniaje español* (6 vols.; Lima, 1895), IV, 110. See also José Eusebio de Llano Zapata, *Memorias histórico-físicas-apologéticas de la América Meridional* (Lima, 1904), pp. 436-442.

easily and it was necessary also to take precautions that the populace would not be exposed to another earthquake."[14] Because many stores were in debt and rebuilding might profit only the creditors in certain cases, some vecinos suggested that the site of the town be moved. The Viceroy rejected this advice firmly because it was "specious" and offered promises that would not materialize. A final question dealt with the method of rebuilding the houses and public edifices. It was resolved to permit no lofty structure and no first-floor wall higher than five *varas*. The Viceroy made the plaza his office for several months, until government "was being administered in a regular fashion." "Then," he continued, "I withdrew to a small lodging, next to the Sala of the Acuerdo, while work went on at the palace."[15]

Reconstruction was extended likewise to the port of Callao. Although it was within the normal jurisdiction of the capital, Superunda assumed direction of rebuilding because of the indispensability of the fort Real Felipe for the military protection of the coast and the absorption of the council of Lima in its more immediate problems.[16] To the French cosmographer and engineer, Louis Godin, he assigned the task of drawing up a plan.[17] After surveying the terrain, Godin proposed the founding of a new town to be called Bellavista at a site about seventeen varas in elevation and one-third of a league from the old town. The distance from the sea would lessen a chance of the repetition of the disaster of 1746. On February 10, 1747, the Viceroy gave his approval and ordered Godin to measure off an area of 298.859 square varas from the *chacra*, called *la Soledad*, and erect *bodegas*, "taverns," and other public buildings for Bellavista; the owner of the land was to be properly indemnified for its seizure.[18] While the planner had to make special provision for shops essential to the trade and commerce of the port, the common grid-shaped design with the central plaza was followed. There were few variations in detail from the architectural scheme for the laying out of towns introduced by Philip

14. *Ibid.*, pp. 114, 115.   15. *Ibid.*, p. 117.

16. The construction of the fort and its later history are to be found in Felipe de la Barra's *Monografía histórica del Real Felipe del Callao y guía del museo histórico-militar* (2nd. ed.; Lima 1957).

17. He was one of the French savants comprising the expedition in 1735 to Quito to measure an arc of the meridian. In the controversy between Ulloa and Juan on the one hand and La Condamine on the other he sided generally with the Spaniards. After the other members of the party had returned to Europe he remained as professor of mathematics at the University of San Marcos.

18. M. Darrío Arrús, *El Callao en la época del coloniaje* (Callao, 1904), p. 70.

II. The lots were sold to twenty-four individuals, each of whom paid according to the location of the property, "with the obligation to build on the site, without which requirement he might not alienate it, losing all ownership if he did the contrary."[19]

Despite the Viceroy's solicitude the new site did not attract merchants and tradesmen. He sadly confessed that "this town has cost me no little effort."[20] Its eventual failure was the result of its artificial location; it was too close to Lima and too far from the wharves and beaches. Contrary to the Viceroy's command, goods from the ships were unloaded on the beach, which in time was covered with *barracas*, "shelters," for the shipworkers, fishermen, and sailors. Despite this, the merchants and outfitters preferred to reside in Lima, visiting the port only when necessary. Thus ere long the old city of Callao was revived.[21]

Custom decreed that the cabildo meet twice a week, usually Tuesday and Friday, at ten o'clock.[22] In the early Bourbon era councils assembled whenever there was sufficient business to be transacted or when it suited the convenience of the members. As a result sessions were few and far between. A tabulation of the meetings recorded formally in the *libros de cabildos* of Lima discloses much diversity.[23] In no year during the period from 1700 to 1784 did the number exceed 57, or about one a week. If there is a tendency to be noted, the greater number of sessions are recorded for the first decade of the eighteenth century and for the period starting with 1778, the year in which the visitor José Areche was appointed to investigate government in the Viceroyalty of Peru. In Trujillo, the trend seems to be somewhat the same, with a correspondingly larger count of sessions for the early and later periods.[24] The Cuzco ayuntamiento met with similar infrequency. Many of the meetings were adjourned without discussion or action, since "no matter of importance was brought up, and having nothing to discuss the cabildo adjourned."[25] In any case the evidence

19. One of those getting a lot was the engineer Godin. See *ibid*.
20. *Ibid.*, p. 76.   21. *Ibid.*, p. 77.
22. The practice of semi-weekly sessions was initiated in the sixteenth century.
23. Some random counts are as follows: 1708, 36; 1711, 41; 1718, 15; 1723, 13; 1731, 11; 1735, 15; 1739, 13; 1743, 9; 1747, 10; 1749, 30; 1752, 17; 1758, 22; 1761, 26; 1766, 12; 1769, 9; 1773, 23; 1777, 15; 1779, 36; 1783, 55.
24. Some scattered selections from what appear to be typical years are these: 1702, 11; 1706, 15; 1755, 8; 1760, 15; 1765, 11; 1769, 6; 1776, 11. In the period from 1737 to 1748, the cabildo of Piura met on the average of five times a year.
25. Minutes of March 3, 1718, Libros de cabildos de Trujillo, vol. XII, B.

as to the lack of vigor of counciliar life and organization for much of the eighteen century is plain.

On the first day of January the council would meet to conduct the election of the most important officials for the coming year. In some cities, notably Cuzco, the corregidor assembled the capitulars on the last day of the preceding year in a *cabildo de propuesta* to exhort them to give careful consideration to the choice of "persons, deserving, of complete honesty, of talent, and suitable for the said offices."[26] The significant posts still subject to electoral procedure were those of the alcalde of the first and second votes and, in addition, in the larger cities that of *juez de aguas*, "judge of the water court."[27] In Cuzco during most of the eighteenth century the principal officials were known as the *alcalde de los vecinos* and the *alcalde de los soldados*, "military alcalde," the terms denoting the scope of their judicial authority. It was also the practice of the ayuntamiento to choose a juez de aguas and, because of the large number of Indians living in or near the city, a *juez de naturales*.[28] The alcaldía was never sold and seldom filled by appointment of the viceroy, the audiencia, or the corregidor. When crown officials interfered in elections, there was usually a protest from the regidor, featured by *consultas*, "remonstrances," and appeals to the higher agencies. In the event of the death or absence of the alcalde his place was regularly taken by the alférez real, with the senior regidor next in line, unless the latter held an office, such as depositario general, or alguacil mayor, considered as incompatible with that of judge.[29] If there were a number of minor offices to be filled, the following day, January 2, would be set aside for this purpose.

Procedure surrounding the elections had undergone few changes since the seventeenth century. Royal officials presided over the council and supervised the act of voting. In Lima, which had been spared the appointment of a corregidor because of its status in the kingdom and

26. Minutes of Dec. 31, 1742, Libros de actas del cabildo de Cuzco, vol. XXI, Archivo de la Universidad de Cuzco.

27. In Lima, in addition to a water commissioner, the council on the first day of the year chose the procurator-general, majordomo, and two asesores, or legal advisors, for the alcalde's court.

28. Minutes of Jan. 1, 1741, Libros de actas del cabildo de Cuzco, vol. XXI, Archivo de la Universidad de Cuzco.

29. Relación descriptiva de la ciudad de Truxillo, legajo 819, Audiencia de Lima, A. G. I.

the services rendered the crown by the vecinos, the ayuntamiento zealously guarded its right to hold elections without the presence of the viceroy or a member of the audiencia. Encroachments on this privilege were successfully resisted, evidence of the partial survival in this part of the empire of the bold, even rebellious, outlook of the sixteenth century.[30] Supervision of elections by the intendant after 1785 led to protests from the councilors as contrary to a long-standing liberty enjoyed by the Ciudad de los Reyes.[31] In the smaller cities and towns the corregidor or his teniente normally judged the elections.[32] The villages, having no royal representative, were free to make their own choice, with the proviso that confirmation must be secured from the audiencia or the viceroy.

Voting was generally by secret ballot. But this did not always mean liberty of selection, for the presence of the royal agent could lead to intimidation so that an ancient right often became a farce. The capitulars wrote the names of the candidates on slips of paper, "which were then placed in an urn, from which they were extracted" and counted. Those with the greatest number of votes were declared elected by the corregidor.[33] On the other hand, choice might be determined by a passing child, who would be summoned to the chamber and asked to draw a ballot from the urn. After the vote had been taken, the corregidor gave to the incoming officials their varas of office. In Lima, the two outgoing alcaldes, accompanied by the secretary, proceeded to the palace nearby to inform the viceroy of the

30. In 1700 the Viceroy Monclova presided over an election in Lima in violation of conciliar custom. The capitulars, though resentful, made no formal protest until Oct., 1703, when they ordered copied in the libros de cabildo certain real cédulas, notably one of Oct 29, 1693, forbidding the viceroy and the audiencia to interfere with the free elections of the cabildo of Lima or to enter the ayuntamiento at that time. Not content with recording the cédulas, the ayuntamiento on Nov. 13 resolved to dispatch the aforementioned cédula to the Viceroy and to appoint four of its members as a committee to confer with him. Two days later the committee reported that it had performed its duty. Prior to the actual voting on Jan. 1, the secretary of the cabildo read aloud to the assembly four cédulas pertaining to elections, including the one of 1693. Aware of his unpopularity, the Viceroy was not in attendance. The implied criticism of the Viceroy caused some of the more timorous regidores to leave the sala on the pretext of attending Mass, so that the choice of alcaldes had to be postponed until later in the day. Thus the cabildo was successful in preventing this interference. See minutes of Oct. 2, Nov. 13, Nov. 15, 1703, and Jan. 1, 1704, Libros de cabildos de Lima, vol. XXXIII, Biblioteca munipal, Lima.

31. See chap. ix.

32. The corregidor or his teniente was always present for the annual elections in Trujillo.

33. Minutes of Jan. 1, 1746, Libros de cabildos de Trujillo, vol. XIV.

Courtyard of the Casa de Cabildo, Cajamarca (*courtesy Municipality of Cajamarca*).

circumstances of the election and to receive approbation. When this had been accorded they returned to the casa del cabildo and presented the insignia of position to the newly chosen individuals.[34]

Candidates for the office of alcalde ordinario were sometimes disqualified by their failure to conform to law and approved usage. Submission to the residencia for former offices was a requirement in the first half of the eighteenth century.[35] Indebtedness to the royal treasury proved to be at times a bar to officeholding.[36] Of the two alcaldes for Lima, one might be from the council, but the other had to come from the populace. It is doubtful that this was strictly enforced, for the cabildo remained in control of the wealthy upper class.[37] But apparently it was not legally necessary to furnish documentary proof of nobility. On the other hand, persons of illegitimate birth, of mixed race, or of menial occupation were theoretically denied admission to the council. Marriage to a woman of obscure birth was not a disqualification.[38]

Rotation in the office of alcalde, with a lapse of two years between successive terms, was only partly observed. For example, Lima had the same alcaldes in 1726 and 1727 and again in 1728 and 1729. In fact, the practice of having the same individuals serve for two years became almost normal procedure in the 1730's and 1750's, tacitly approved by the viceroy, perhaps as a means of providing greater continuity in office.[39] In Cuzco and Trujillo rotation appears to have been common. When exceptions were made, the officials customarily obtained confirmation from the corregidor and ultimately from the viceroy.

34. Minutes of Jan. 1, 1705, Libros de cabildos de Lima, vol. XXXIII, Biblioteca municipal, Lima.

35. By the eighteenth century the oath of office for the alcalde had become more specific, including a pledge neither to accept bribes nor to permit their acceptance by members of the cabildo. See minutes of Jan. 1, 1709, *ibid.*, vol. XXXIV.

36. Special cédulas of July 15, 1620, and Dec. 17, 1679, strictly prohibited persons owing money to the crown from serving as alcaldes.

37. Minutes of Jan. 2, 3, 1704, Libros de cabildos de Lima, vol. XXXIII, Biblioteca municipal, Lima.

38. In Caracas the creoles in their rivalry with Europeans insisted on written evidence of *hidalguía* from candidates born in the Península. See Consulta del Consejo de las Indias acerca de las desazones ocurridas sobre si los españoles europeos de la ciudad de Caracas debían entrar con igualdad al goce de los empleos políticos y militares de república, Madrid, 24 de Mayo de 1776, quoted in Richard Konetzke's *Colección de Documentos para la Historia de la Formación social de Hispanoamérica 1493-1810*, Vol. III, tomo I, 1691-1779 (Madrid, 1962), 413-419.

39. There is a list of the occupants of the Lima alcaldía in Pedro Vidaurre's *Relación cronológica de los alcaldes que han presidido el ayuntamiento de Lima desde su fundación hasta nuestros días* (Lima, 1889).

If a city or town experienced a sudden crisis, the viceroy might intervene in its affairs without the approval of the Council of the Indies. Lima's tragic situation after the earthquake of 1746 induced the Conde de Superunda to authorize the cabildo to elect four alcaldes instead of the usual two to handle the heavy load of civic business. This did not become a regular practice; it was discontinued after a few years.[40] Interference by the viceroy in secondary elections was vigorously opposed by the ayuntamiento.[41]

Most councils met on January 2, to choose minor functionaries. For a metropolis like Lima the list was an extensive one, including the following officials.

2 Commissioners of Accounts
2 Commissioners of Municipal Property
2 Commissioners of Municipal Bridges
2 Commissioners of Slaughterhouse
1 Commissioner for the Election of the Alcaldes
    of Callao
2 Commissioners of the Water Supply
2 Special Commissioners
1 Corresponding Secretary
2 Commissioners of the Candles of Santa Ysabel
2 Commissioners of the Exchange (offices filled
    by the alcaldes and the alguacil mayor)
2 Surveyors (the *alarifes*)
1 Assayer of Weights and Measure
1 Procurator of Lawsuits
1 Inspector of Weights
1 Master Builder of Fountains
1 Guard for the Water Office
2 Commissioners of the Promenade (to be filled
    by the alcaldes)
1 Guard of the Promenade
1 Commissioner of Disbursements
1 Accountant[42]

40. *Ibid.*, pp. 56, 57.
41. The election of the procurator-general in Jan., 1779, led to a heated controversy with the Viceroy over qualifications for this office. See minutes of Jan. 7, Feb. 19, 1779, Jan. 7, 1780, Libros de cabildos de Lima, vol. XXXVI, Biblioteca municipal, Lima.
42. Minutes of Jan. 2, 1778, *ibid.* Cuzco chose a somewhat smaller group of func-

From the foregoing it is evident that many of these offices might be filled by alcaldes and regidores, who were thus able to supplement their normally small salaries by fees and special compensation. Confirmation of the choice of secondary functionaries by the viceroy was obligatory. Crown officials and vecinos raised few objections to their designation, execpt in the case of the procurator, who was responsible for the protection of the public interest, and that of the majordomo, whose office entailed the distribution of municipal funds.[43]

The principle of separation of church and state was rigorously maintained in the eligibility to local office. While clerics occupied lofty rank in the colonial bureaucracy, even that of viceroy on occasion, there is no record of the position of alcalde or regidor having been filled by a member of the secular or regular clergy.[44]

Elections in many localities were characterized by disturbances and occasional acts of violence. Their incidence was a matter of much concern to the viceroys. In a *carta*, "letter," of November 4, 1759, to the cabildo of Trujillo, the Conde of Superunda deplored the factionalism and petty rivalries arising over conciliar elections:

> One of the principal objects of my attention and care is the maintenance of peace and tranquility among citizens and distinguished individuals of the cities and towns, so they may pursue their business and other interests without the discord that divides and delays; believing that this originates regularly in the election of alcaldes ordinarios in which failing to carry out their obligations, the members of the cabildo only aspire to have the varas given to persons of their party and dependency, looking more to the satisfaction of their feelings rather than to the public advantage . . . I order the Cabildo, Justicia, and Regimiento of this city . . . to choose and elect as alcaldes ordinarios and the remaining conciliar officials persons of impartiality and good habits [;] in case of doubt over the interpretation of the law the Superior Government should be consulted . . . [;] likewise I order the corregidor that in no way should he indicate preference for any individual, publicly or privately, leaving the cabildo in complete liberty, under penalty of legal proceedings.[45]

tionaries. See minutes of Jan. 2, 1752, Libros de actas del cabildo de Cuzco, vol. 22, Archivo de la Universidad de Cuzco.

43. See chap. vi on the municipal exchequer.

44. Yet the ecclesiastical authorities could seriously interfere with the conduct of local business by excommunicating the corregidor or the alcaldes.

45. Minutes of Jan. 1, 1760, Libros de cabildos de Trujillo, vol. XV.

Similarly, the Viceroy Amat in his *Memoria* alludes to the inability of the capitulars to conduct their elections in an orderly, decorous fashion:

> The cabildos and ayuntamientos of the cities of the Kingdom live throughout the year in great serenity, except for the 1st of January and the days immediately following, set aside for the election of alcaldes and other conciliar offices, in which parties and dissension regularly develop (an exception being this capital where the viceroy smoothes out animosities) and they [the councils] appeal to the Superior Government, alleging vetoes, insults, and violence of the corregidores. The easiest thing is to ignore them, and meantime the alcaldes remain in office through ley 13, titulo 3, and libro 5 of the Code of the Indies, the same capitulars give up their quarrels, and the viceroy pursues a course of prudence which he considers opportune according to circumstances. Although such [elections] are free and to be determined by a plurality of votes, it behooves the viceroy to take remedial steps when he sees the possibility of grave results, hatreds, and discord.[46]

Mindful of altercations that had taken place in Cuzco in 1776, the ordinarily complacent, easygoing Viceroy Manuel Guirior forcefully enjoined the ayuntamiento of that city in a carta of December 10, 1777, "to proceed in this important matter according to law, in order to select suitable persons, who have the necessary legal qualifications as well as those of citizenship such as in the question of indebtedness to the treasury." It was expected "that conciliar offices be filled by persons of known wisdom, zeal, and love for the public good, who carry out their respective jobs with due exactitude and moderation, under penalty of failure [by the viceroy] to approve elections and of consideration to apply any serious decrees that might be necessary."[47]

The threat of coercion and punishment by the Viceroy caused the cabildo to go on record as opposing the election of "those who did not have residence in the city, those who were debtors of the Real Hacienda, and those who were under indictment for violation of the criminal code."[48] In 1779 the choice of the alcaldes was carried out with

46. Vicente Rodríguez Casado and Florentino Pérez Embid (eds.), *Memoria de gobierno de Manuel de Amat y Junient, 1761-1776* (Sevilla, 1947), pp. 178, 179.

47. Minutes of Jan. 1, 1778, Jan. 1, 1779, and Jan. 1, 1780, Libros de actas del cabildo de Cuzco, vol. 25, Archivo de la Universidad de Cuzco.

48. Minutes of Jan. 1, 1779, *ibid.*

much harmony, but the following year the council chamber reverberated with recriminations and insults on election day.

Conditions and terms of the sale of offices were a primary cause of contention between the crown and individual creoles. In the long run it was perhaps the most important explanation for the malfunctioning of the local regimes. This practice, carried out on a large scale after the sixteenth century, was universally recognized as an evil by administrators dispatched to America. Inasmuch as the crown lacked funds with which to buy up the property rights connected with the offices and obtained some income from this source, it contemplated no serious move to rectify the fault.

Nearly all of the municipal offices, with the exception of those of the alcalde, juez de aguas, majordomo, and procurator-general had been auctioned off at some time in the past by the crown's orders. The most worthwhile vendible positions were those of regidor, alguacil mayor, alférez real, alcalde provincial, and escribano de cabildo. Surprisingly, the elective principle for the aldermancy was partly preserved during this period in Mexico City and Santiago de Chile, giving to the councils in these cities a somewhat more representative character.

The office of regidor was the one most frequently sold or transferred.[49] In the eighteenth century a great majority of these positions were in the possession of private families, the title passing from father to son upon payment to the Real Hacienda of one-half of its valuation for the first transfer and one-third thereafter and of the media anata, and upon confirmation by the Council of the Indies within a specified period (at first usually three years, later six) dating from the dispatch of the documents by the governor or viceroy. If confirmation of title was not obtained within the legal period, the office was declared vacant and could be sold by the crown, with two-thirds of the amount of the purchase price to be returned to the former owner. When new settlements were formed—a comparatively unusual occurrence in Peru in the eighteenth century—and when there was forfeiture through treason, resignation, or death without

49. The oath of office for the regidor in the eighteenth century was more definite and detailed in its obligations and responsibilities. See minutes of Feb. 23, 1701, Libros de cabildos de Lima, vol. XXXIII, Biblioteca municipal, Lima.

heirs by the holder, the crown might likewise dispose of the office to the highest bidder.[50]

Procedure in a sale of office in 1750 varied little from that under the Hapsburgs. When an office was to be sold, the Real Hacienda secured affidavits from individuals of good standing in the community —usually three in number, the council secretary and two vecinos— as to its proper valuation. The final decision as to its worth was left to the treasury officials. Once this was decided upon, the crier announced the price and asked for bids. If the amount offered was below that of the predetermined price, the Real Hacienda had the right to reject it and leave the office unfilled. If the bid was approved, the buyer would then arrange the terms with the government.[51]

An examination of representative lists of the purchase prices for the office of regidor and other municipal posts in the Audiencia of Lima shows wide differences in real values. There are variations in the same municipality and among the individual cities and towns.[52] The chief factors accounting for these differences are the emoluments in the form of salaries and fees connected with the offices and the social honor and esteem that they brought the possessors. Offices in the viceregal capital naturally brought higher prices than those in the lesser cities and villas. In general, the largest sum was paid for the office of escribano mayor, followed in order by those of alguacil mayor, depositario general, alcalde provincial, alférez real, regidor, and escribano. Purchase of major municipal positions, except that of alguacil mayor, admitted the recipient to membership in the cabildo with the right to speak in discussions and debates and sometimes to vote in the elections for the alcalde. In some instances the posts of regidor and fiel ejecutor were joined for the purpose of sale. It was not uncommon for a regidor to purchase another major office for its associated fees or the additional honor accompanying its occupancy.

Another conclusion to be drawn from the figures cited is that the value of municipal positions fell in the eighteenth century, generally after 1750. For example, in Lima in 1700 an aldermancy sold for 11,000 pesos; in 1760, for 6,000 pesos; and in 1777, for 4,000 pesos. Other cases can be mentioned, bespeaking the lowered respect in

50. Haring, *Spanish Empire in America*, p. 166.
51. See Reales Cédulas, Informes sobre oficios vendibles y renunciables, sus privilegios, etc., 1595-1819, legajo 593, Audiencia de Lima, A. G. I.
52. See Appendix II.

which municipal officeholding was held. However, it was the policy of the crown to maintain prices at the highest possible level, since one-third of the proceeds normally went to the royal treasury to be paid in a year's time or perhaps over a period of three or four years. But in keeping values high, the crown ran the risk of having unsalable offices on its hands, as the honorific considerations and the slight remunerations might not compensate for the artificial prices.[53]

Complaints from potential buyers and appraisers over the excessive valuations put on offices were numerous. They became almost a general refrain in the 1730's. It was affirmed repeatedly that the offices, particularly that of regidor, no longer had the prestige and importance enjoyed in the earlier period. Because of the high prices there were many unfilled posts. In 1708 the official of the Real Hacienda declared that it was virtually impossible to dispose of the offices in the city of Arequipa because of "the great disrepute into which these posts have fallen."[54] Observations as to the futility and the lack of esteem of municipal positions were made by royal agents and vecinos in other cities. An affidavit concerning the value of the position of regidor in Lima in 1728 stated that "all of the positions in the city have suffered a decline and for this reason many posts are vacant without anyone wishing to acquire them."[55] A witness in a sworn statement before the treasury officials as to the valuation of the office of regidor fiel ejecutor in Trujillo referred to the "decadence that has befallen all the transferable offices and especially those of this nature from which their owners report no profit."[56] It was alleged that though salaries and preferments accrued to regidores in large towns, there was little opportunity for pecuniary returns in smaller places.[57] Expenses for ceremonials might also be heavy.[58] Even the office of alférez real,

53. The crown profited also from the media anata and fees connected with confirmation. The fee for offices worth not more than 3,000 pesos amounted to 10 per cent of the value of the office, plus 18 per cent of the latter for cost of conveyance to Madrid. Thus a vecino who purchased the position of regidor around 1710 for 1,500 pesos had to pay 177 pesos to the crown. See Expediente, oficios, legajo 422, Audiencia de Lima, A. G. I.
54. Informe sobre oficio de alcalde provincial de Arequipa, Confirmaciones de Oficios, legajo 451, Audiencia de Lima, A. G. I.
55. Confirmaciones de oficios, legajo 455, Audiencia de Lima, A. G. I.
56. *Ibid.*
57. All of the witnesses summoned to give an opinion of the utility of the aldermancy in Guamanga in 1731 made this point. See Confirmaciones de oficios, legajo 457, Audiencia de Lima, A. G. I.
58. *Ibid.*

normally esteemed for its social eminence, was unoccupied in some towns.[59]

Cuzco's situation was no better than that of many a lesser city. In 1752, according to the testimony submitted to the Real Hacienda, all of the aldermanic positions were vacant, and in addition, those of alguacil mayor and alférez real; "the decadence and backwardness of this city being well-known . . . the scarcity of the citizens and the lack of wealth permitted no progress and this was the explanation for there being absolutely no one who might occupy the office of reg- idor."[60] The lessened opinion of the councilor's post was reflected in the small sums paid by purchasers, the price falling from 4,000 pesos in 1706 to 1,500 pesos in 1752.

Confirmation of title was at the bottom of many quarrels and con- troversies. The endless red tape surrounding the procedure in the eighteenth century undoubtedly alienated some would-be buyers. Although a period of six years was allotted for this purpose in Peru, to many it seemed too brief a span in view of the unsatisfactory com- munications which were often disrupted by war. In addition, the dilatoriness of local treasury officials accounted for unnecessary delays. This slowness in confirmation was not occasioned, it would seem, by any protracted consideration of the qualifications of prospective office- holders.[61] Other purchasers objected to the "cushion money" that had to be paid to crown officials and to special agents in Madrid whose services were required for the approval.[62] Consequently, there were individuals who held office in the Indies for years without the formal- ity of confirmation.[63]

Faulty administration of this branch of the colonial government was in time brought to the attention of the Council of the Indies. In recommending rejection of confirmation of a title of secretary of the

59. Out of deference to the crown, one of the witnesses artfully suggested that the real reason for this was "the lack in this city of citizens of sufficient distinction to occupy the post." See Confirmaciones de oficios, legajo 458, Audiencia de Lima, A. G. I.

60. Confirmaciones de oficios, legajo 461, Audiencia de Lima, A. G. I.

Officials of the Real Hacienda were not unaware of the decline in value of municipal offices. Nevertheless, they were reluctant to accept the affirmations of wit- nesses in full, fearing collusion between the latter and the would-be purchasers who would want to make a good buy. Usually, they accepted the appraisal most favorable to the treasury.

61. With the exception of candidates for the office of escribano, rarely was a person rejected on the grounds that he lacked "ability, age, and other qualities."

62. Confirmaciones de oficios, legajo 450, Audiencia de Lima, A. G. I.

63. *Ibid.*

cabildo of Lima on the basis that the amount offered was inadequate and payment stretched out over too long a span, the fiscal of the consejo, in a *parecer*, or opinion, of December 20, 1720, went on to assail the functioning of the local treasury. It was apparent, he asserted, that many municipal offices were vacant, "causing loss of revenue to the crown, owing to poor administration in the sale of office, no doubt because of the unwillingness of those agents to fulfill the obligations of their office." He suggested that for the more efficient handling of the business a special ledger be kept with a record of "offices sold, resigned, and dates of payments, confirmations in order that those without confirmation might be resold." Viceroys and audiencias should be authorized to confer with the officials of the Real Hacienda to make certain that offices were disposed of and confirmation obtained.[64]

Until the time of Charles III, no earnest attempt was made to alter the procedure of confirmation and correct some of the abuses. In 1774 the crown dealt with a dodge that had enabled unscrupulous officeholders to evade payments to the treasury for many years. Earlier, in the absence of legislation to the contrary and with the connivance of local treasury agents, occupants of office had secured extensions of time for confirmation and before the expiration of the periods set had resigned or renounced their offices. Meanwhile they had enjoyed the preferments and compensations over a considerable time without having to pay the fees for confirmation. A royal cédula of August 22, 1774, stated that no further allotment of time for confirmation would be authorized to the second recipient of the office than had existed at the moment of resignation.[65] While this worked hardships in a few cases, it blocked a loophole in tax collection.

The burdensome costs of confirmation were eventually lightened by the crown. These had proceeded from the fees regularly levied by officials of the Real Hacienda, from charges for notarization and for conveyance of documents to Madrid, and all too frequently from fees to attorneys for clearing up disputed points. In consequence, the charge of legalizing a title often exceeded the value of the office, especially when its worth was less than 500 pesos. Accordingly, in 1777, the

64. He cited an office in Lima, for which no confirmation was secured for twenty years, yet the occupant was allowed to receive the fees and remuneration. See Confirmaciones de oficios, legajo 453, Audiencia de Lima, A. G. I.

65. Cabildos, legajo 180, Papeles de Cuba, A. G. I.

King dispatched a cédula to the viceroys of Peru, New Spain, and Santa Fe, authorizing the presidents of the audiencias in these regions to determine the value of offices, oversee the leasing, and dispatch the documents to Spain, "provided the fiscals of the audiencias solicit confirmation from the Council." This regulation was to apply to positions worth less than 1,500 pesos. For the purpose of reducing unduly high legal fees, the crown stipulated that the presidents of the audiencias should set up "a schedule of charges to be collected by the escribanos for notarizing the títulos and by the officials of the Real Hacienda for their services, with the express condition that no charges of any sort should be made for judicial writs, except those connected with the bids."[66] There were clearly advantages in the cedula for a small officeholder. No longer did he have the onerous responsibility for confirmation of his title; it was to be assumed by the officials of the government. Also, setting up an *arancel*, "list," of fees forestalled overcharging and excessive costs.

Indicative of a certain pettiness associated in this era with municipal officeholding was the constant bickering among members of the cabildo over seating arrangements and precedence in speaking and voting in the council chamber and over status at public ceremonials. Instances are countless. The officials most frequently involved were alférez real, alcalde provincial, alguacil mayor, and the procurator, whose positions were vaguely defined by law and custom. Lawsuits originating over prerogatives claimed by these officials were costly, strung out, and often settled in the last instance by appeal to the highest tribunal in Spain, the Council of the Indies. Participation of capitulars in these disputes doubtless ventilated the Spanish proclivity for legalism, but it also consumed time and energy that might have gone to the solution of municipal problems.[67]

In the basic conditions of officeholding, the Spanish government

66. The cédula of Jan. 31, 1777, El Pardo, reincorporated most of the provisions of the cédula of Feb. 21, 1776, sent by the Secretaría de Consejo de Indias. See Cédulas, legajo 593, Audiencia de Lima, A. G. I.

67. A typical case occurred in Piura in Dec., 1737, when Juan de Valdivieso presented to the cabildo a *despacho*, "communication," dated Aug. 25, 1736, signed by the viceroy and appointing him alguacil mayor. His claim to occupy the seat next to the alcalde was opposed by the alférez real. Unable to reach a decision, the cabildo appealed to the viceroy, who made no reply. Meanwhile, the alférez secured a cédula from the King, the language of which was sufficiently clear to support his claim as the most important person in the council after the alcalde ordinario. See minutes of Dec. 14, 24, 1737, and Dec. 17, 1738, *Libro de cabildos de Piura, años 1737 a 1748*.

made no significant changes during the pre-intendancy period. The traditional principle of vendibility, inherited from the Hapsburgs, was accepted. Having means and influence, the colonial aristocracy acquired the chief positions and dominated local affairs. Although conscious of the defects in the theory and practice of the sale of offices, the crown did not propose purchase from the owners or democratization to make the council more responsive to public feeling. The desire for revenue was stronger than the zeal for efficiency and improved administration. The fact that many offices were unfilled, the result partly of an economic recession in the region for many decades, caused concern primarily because it reduced income. One of the devices adopted by the treasury officials in Peru in the 1760's was the leasing of offices for a short or long time, in preference to outright sale, as a means of inducing vecinos to assume municipal posts.[68] In this way the officeholder avoided a large outlay of funds and the cost and bother of confirmation. This expedient did not materially increase the royal revenue or lead to the filling of empty positions.

Decline in the vitality of municipal institutions was the result not only of the unrepresentative character of the conciliar regimes, but also of the further curtailment of privileges and responsibilities. As will be seen, the Bourbons, to a greater degree than their predecessors, intervened in areas of conciliar jurisdiction and authority. The results were indifference and diminished respect for the municipal positions, as evidenced by a fall in the price of offices and the existence of many vacancies.

68. Thus the position of alcalde provincial of Lima was leased for two years at 300 pesos annually. See Cuentas de Lima, legajo 1772 B (año 1760), Contaduría general, A. G. I.

CHAPTER IV

Economy and General Administration

The areas of administration with the greatest freedom for the council were those of food supply and services of various sorts. By fixing the prices for commodities and the charges for services, the cabildo could exercise a powerful influence over the economy of the municipal district. The council had responsibility for the assurance of a sufficiency of food for the community at reasonable prices. Hardships through lack of rain in the highlands and through high prices imposed by unscrupulous speculators were ever-present threats which had to be met by action on the part of the local authorities, assisted by the crown. In the less significant, outlying towns the conciliar bodies obviously had greater liberty. Yet the economic problems were vastly less complicated than those in the cities, a fact that induced the crown at times to step into the latter area.

Over interregional and European trade and commerce, the crown exercised exclusive rights. Regulations defined the character of business between the colonies and the mother country, the routes of trade, and the agencies to be employed. Where there was a large shipment of food from another region, as was true for Lima after 1715 in the importation of wheat from Chile, the viceroy determined the price of the commodity. The crown had also a monopoly of the sale of certain articles, such as tobacco, playing cards, salt, pepper, stamped paper, and, in the city of Lima, of snow hauled down from the sierras for the icing of beverages. Of all of these enterprises the sale of tobacco was the most profitable. In the seventeenth century many of these articles were supplied by private individuals having special contracts with the government. Since the revenue had not panned out to expectations, the crown in the eighteenth century assumed responsibility for the purchase of the commodities from the producer and arranged the terms and conditions of disposal on the market. This procedure was not always satisfactory. As Haring says, "some of the monopolies were more an annoyance to the consumer than of profit to the exchequer."[1] Merchants who engaged in overseas trade, with the consent of the crown, belonged to the guild, or consulado.[2]

The city fathers had the responsibility of providing for the vecinos an adequate supply of the necessities of life at a moderate or just price. To accomplish this was not always easy. Although greater order and security prevailed in Peru than in the past, there were occasional crop failures in the highlands and the menace of disastrous earthquakes. Famines were on the whole of such rare occurrence in the fertile areas of the interior and in the carefully irrigated coastal plain that alhondigas, "warehouses," did not exist in the audiencia, with the exception of an ill-cared-for building at Arequipa. On the other hand, the destruction of Lima in 1746 as the result of an earthquake was a never-to-be-forgotten experience that might have befallen any other city. The danger of Indian attacks was scarcely felt until the last quarter of the eighteenth century when a descendant of the Incas launched the most serious native revolt since the first century of colonization. Along the coast the raids by the English and the Dutch caused occasional alarm. These crises sometimes led to temporary shortages of food and consequent opportunities for profit-taking by avaricious merchants and shopkeepers.

Making sure of a plentiful supply of bread, meat, and butter at a fair price for the consumers entailed other problems. To begin with, the conciliar body, composed of members of the old families of the community, frequently had little or no familiarity with problems of the vendor or the public. Despite its lack of experience, the cabildo earnestly sought to check the rise of prices by ordering the gremios, "guilds of merchants," and tradesmen to display their wares and prices.[3] Much of the council's ordinary business concerned "the

1. Haring, Spanish Empire in America, p. 294.
2. The libros de cabildos consulted by the author do not reflect an intense rivalry between the municipal and consular bodies.
3. Minutes of Nov. 26, 1732, Libros de cabildos de Lima, vol. XXXV, Biblioteca municipal, Lima.
While the cabildo sought to supervise the activities of the guilds, it gave little or

butchers, bakers, and the candlestick makers." It was the practice for the council to enter into a contract with an individual or individuals to supply essential items of the diet or other commodities at a fixed price. Litigation over the terms of the contracts was endless.

To hold down the price of bread, the main staple, was an important duty of the cabildo. Discussion of the price, which fluctuated because of the importation of wheat, occupied many sessions of the council. In December, 1700, the members of the Lima cabildo, after conferring among themselves, set 1 real as the price for a loaf of *pan de trigo*.[4] In June, 1701, the procurator-general informed the body that "wheat is selling for less than six pesos a *fanega* [one and one-half bushels] in the port of Callao," in view of which the council fixed the price for bakers at 6 pesos a fanega with a corresponding reduction in the cost of bread.[5] In June, 1703, an abundance of wheat caused the cabildo to bring the price down still further to the dismay of members of the gremio, who had bought at a higher price and did not wish to lose their profits.[6]

Difficulties in the way of arranging for a proper amount of good meat are illustrated in Lima in the first decade of the eighteenth century. On March 9, 1701, two vecinos made a successful bid to furnish *carne de Castillo* to the city and port of Callao for six years, beginning January 1, 1702, at a price of 3½ reales a *quarto*, "quarter," of beef.[7] When the contract expired in 1707, the cabildo accepted bids at the identical price for another six-year period. Complaints over the toughness of the beef having become widespread, the cabildo in July, 1709, declared that the conditions of the contract had not been fulfilled and registered a protest to the suppliers.[8] As no improvement was forthcoming in the quality of the meat, the ayuntamiento in May, 1710, again denounced the contractors, pointing out that every week a considerable number of livestock were picked out of the herds and sold to hucksters, "all of which is harmful to the well-being of the

no encouragement to the founding of industries. This would have been contrary to crown regulations. See Fernando Silva Santisteban, *Los obrajes en el virreinato del Perú* (Lima, 1964), pp. 7-11.

4. Minutes of Dec. 20, 1700, Libros de cabildos de Lima, vol. XXXIII, Biblioteca municipal, Lima.

5. Minutes of June 10, 1701, *ibid.*, vol. XXXIII.

6. Minutes of June 27, 1703, *ibid.*, vol. XXXIII.

7. Minutes of March 9, 1701, *ibid.*, vol. XXXIII.

8. Minutes of Oct. 14, 1707, July 10, 1709, *ibid.*, vol. XXXIV.

republic which lacks a proper supply." To remedy this, the council resolved to notify a landowner having 5,000 head of cattle on the heights of Pachacamac below Lima that he might become the supplier of beef.[9] The contractors appealed to the audiencia, which agreed to decide the case. Meanwhile there was constant grumbling among the vecinos over the "bad meat that is sold in the slaughterhouses."[10]

Another article of food which gave trouble to the council was lard. Disputes with suppliers were innumerable. In the early 1780's a serious controversy developed which involved at bottom the right of the cabildo to fix an arbitrary price. In December, 1782, the procurator-general of Lima, noting the scarcity of *manteca*, "fat," which was being sold contrary to municipal regulations at 2 reales a *libra*, "pound," requested from the ayuntamiento an order against the suppliers of the commodity, compelling them under penalty of 500 pesos to transport to the main square daily, beginning the next day, 100 pounds of lard to be sold at the regular price.[11] Upon the failure of the contractors to comply, the municipal official obtained approval of the council to notify "all the bakers and pastrycooks not to use lard in the bread or pastry without buying it from an approved establishment, under penalty of 200 pesos against the suppliers and fifty pesos against the cook or baker." On December 10 the contractors appealed to the viceroy for permission to sell at 2 reales a libra and, before receiving a reply, raised the price to 2½ reales. An informe of the matter was presented by the suppliers to the viceroy, who ordered all documents assembled for consideration by the fiscal. The cabildo considered the question in a number of sessions and finally decided to commission one of its members to visit the haciendas of Chancay and other farms close to the city to determine whether or not a dearth of hogs existed as claimed by the suppliers.[12] The owners of the haciendas, however, refused permission to the conciliar representative to inspect their herds. Such was the ill feeling between the *estancieros* and the cabildo that an order from the Superior Government was necessary to enable

9. Minutes of May 20, 1710, *ibid.*, vol. XXXIV.
10. The city was handicapped in the further prosecution of the suit, as the autos of the council concerning the contract were carelessly turned over to a person believed to be a clerk and lost. The escribano would have to give from memory an account of the pertinent orders and resolutions. See minutes of June 22, 1712, *ibid.*, vol. XXXIV.
11. Minutes of Dec. 4, 1782, *ibid.*, vol. XXXVII.
12. Minutes of Dec. 5, 10, 1782, Jan. 4, 14, 28, 1783, *ibid.*, vol. XXXVII.

a regidor to visit the farms.[13] Until 1786 the cabildo did not succeed
in fixing the price of lard. With the co-operation of the fiscal the
council evolved a more scientific method of reaching a price fair to
the consumers and to the raisers of pigs. Only a modest profit of 5
per cent was permitted to the sellers.[14] To the dismay of the advocates
of free enterprise of this era the procedure remained in force a number of years.

Price-fixing was deemed vital for the sale of wax and candles.
The dealings of the cabildo with the candlestick makers are illustrated
in Lima in 1751. In July of that year the council ordered all the
veladores, "suppliers of candles," to declare their recent purchases and
the prices paid. If this were not carried out in twenty-four hours, a
fine of 50 pesos would be levied by the city.[15] Upon receiving the information, the municipal authorities fixed the selling price at 9 pesos
a *quintal*, "100 pounds." Regarding this as insufficient return, the
purveyors appealed from the arancel to the audiencia.[16]

But the temptation to profit was not confined to the producers and
sellers. The capitulars themselves sometimes ignored the common
good in the adjustment of prices on foodstuffs when they saw an
opportunity for lining their own pockets. In violation of the Laws
of the Indies they often engaged in business to the impairment of the
interests of the vecinos.[17] An investigation by a judge of the residence
in Piura in 1780 disclosed the worst conditions of this sort: "Regidor

13. Minutes of March 22, April 9, July 29, 1783, *ibid.*, vol. XXXVII.
14. The system of computation used was relatively simple. Eight samples of weight
were taken and provision was then made for the cost of fattening and slaughtering
the animals.

Thus, the price or cost of a pig	16 ps.	
Expense of slaughtering	3	5½ rs.
	19	
Profit	1	
	20	5½
Value of ham, pork	—4	5½
Cost of lard (50 lbs.)	16 ps.	
Hence per lb.	2½ rs.	

See Expediente de la ciudad de Lima contra los abastedores de manteca, legajo 4
(Cabildos), Archivo nacional, Lima.
15. Minutes of July 6, 1751, Libros de cabildos de Lima, vol. XXXVI, Biblioteca
municipal, Lima.
16. If the outcome of similar suits be taken as a guide, the candlestick makers
probably succeeded in winning approval for their price from the audiencia.
17. *Recopilación de leyes de los reinos de las Indias* (2 vols. in 4 tomos; 5th ed.;
Madrid, 1841), vol. I, libro IV, título X, leyes XI, XII.

fiel ejecutor sells beef daily, the citizens agreeing to let him supply them without weighing or examining it . . . his wife being present and receiving their money; [he] selling likewise fruits and other foods and all dearly."[18] In 1734 the viceroy had to threaten the members of the cabildo of Lima with a fine of 2,000 pesos to be imposed if they did not desist from the practice of buying grain and selling it covertly and at exorbitant prices to the bakers of the city.[19]

Infrequently, the cabildo had to prohibit clerics from engaging in business in competition with the vecinos. Thus the council of Lima in 1747 enacted an ordinance forbidding any ecclesiastic from operating a bakery.[20]

In supervising the operation of the local economy, the ayuntamiento had oversight of the election of officers of the various guilds and of the general functioning of these bodies. Occasionally, the choice of officials was marred by acrimony and even resort to physical violence. A good example of a disputed election is furnished in Lima in 1778 in the selection of an alcalde and *veedor* for the gremio of shoemakers. "As is customary, according to ordinance," the masters of the guild appeared before the alcaldes ordinarios and cast their ballots in secret for two individuals. The vote resulted in the choice of one Marcelino De la Mata, a native of Old Castile, as alcalde, and the person getting the second largest number of votes as veedor. The newly elected officials were sworn in by the cabildo and, after paying the media anata, were issued their títulos of office. Certain disgruntled masters refused to accord De la Mata all of the honors associated with the office on the grounds that alcaldes in the past had been creoles. The alcalde petitioned the cabildo that "no European or chapetón [tenderfoot] as the Spanish-born are so labeled by the hostile members of the guild, should be disqualified in any way from having the right to vote in any assembly or election held by the gremio" or from enjoying any privileges in connection with the position. An *auto*, "order," of September 23, 1779, from the cabildo provided that the office of majordomo of the *cofradía* be held alternately by creoles and those hailing from Europe. As the criollos, "the American-born," still protested, De la Mata appealed to the viceroy. Supporting the council's ruling, the

18. Residencias, Piura, legajo 24, 1689-1759, Archivo nacional, Lima.
19. Minutes of June 12, 1734, Libros de cabildos de Lima, vol. XXXV, Biblioteca municipal, Lima.
20. Minutes of Jan. 5, 1747, *ibid.*, vol. XXXV.

fiscal, in an opinion of November 29, 1779, declared himself in favor of alternating the position. Thus was settled one of the many altercations between *Peninsulares* and those of American descent.[21]

Extensive litigation over fees charged by minor functionaries for services was a feature of the relations between the ayuntamientos and the guilds. A celebrated case in Lima lasted over a hundred years and involved the most lucrative position in the local government, that of escribano mayor. At stake was the right of the escribano to collect 6 pesos from each shop belonging to the city and 4 from those operated under license from the Real Hacienda. Since there were over 300 establishments and four visits of inspection annually, the secretary might realize close to 5,000 pesos from this source alone. In 1633, the office with the perquisites was valued at 45,000 pesos. Some thirty years later the gremio of the owners of food establishments, wineshops, and taverns initiated its protest against the excessive nature of the charges. The defense based its case on the sanctity of the property rights vested in the office. Meeting with no success at first, the guild reopened the suit whenever the position was assumed by a different person as the result of death or resignation. In 1743, the Real Audiencia of Lima reversed its stand and upheld the guild, declaring that the escribano had the right to collect only fees for violation of the aranceles. An appeal by the son of the officeholder resulted in a despacho, or legal decree, of May 21, 1763, from the Council of the Indies, revoking the audiencia's decision on the grounds that the court had the authority to moderate the amount of the fee but not to destroy the right itself. In 1769 the fiscal of the consejo asserted that the case must be terminated. Briefs were filed once again by both parties. The Council gave its *sentencia*, "final decision," on May 2, 1774, reducing the amount of the fee from 4 pesos to 1 peso for each visit.[22] The persistence of the guilds had its reward. While victory was not complete, the shopkeepers had materially lowered an outrageous charge for perfunctory inspection. The right of appeal from the cabildo to the audiencia and ultimately to the Council of the Indies enabled the

21. Autos sobre punto de elecciones del gremio de zapateros Españoles p. q. un año sea mre maior oficial, Europeo y otro criollo, legajo 4 (cabildos), Archivo nacional, Lima.

22. El gremio de pulperos y bodegueros de la ciudad de Lima con el escribano mayor de cavildo de dha ciudad, en nueve piezas, Consejo de Indias, legajo 20292, Archivo histórico nacional, Madrid.

guilds to find relief from unfair regulations imposed by the municipal authorities.

To insure an abundant supply of water for the city and town was essential. The construction of aqueducts and canals and the allocation of water for the cultivation of crops and for drinking came under the authority of the juez de aguas, assisted by the cabildo. The importance of the office in Lima was attested by the Viceroy Amat.[23] It was the judge's function to see that the aqueducts were cleaned at least once a year. In Trujillo the date set for the cleaning of the principal channels leading to the city was the cause of a dispute between the Indians who wished pure water for personal consumption and the *hacendados*, "the owners of the big estates," whose crops at that time of the year required much irrigation. The cabildo, siding with the proprietors, accused the Indians of malice and prejudice and instructed the procurator to draw up legal papers to protect the city in its claim that it had the right to fix the time for the cleansing and repair of the aqueducts.[24] The possibility of exchanging municipal ownership of the aqueducts for private control was of such moment that the Lima ayuntamiento, with the consent of the Viceroy, held a series of cabildos abiertos to secure the views of the prominent citizens.[25]

Supervision of the professions and crafts constituted a part of the council's duties. Aranceles were drawn up by the cabildo, and exorbitant charges by professional men and craftsmen for their services were punished by fines. The ayuntamiento authorized títulos to physicians, barbers, apothecaries, teachers, and others wishing to follow their professions or trades. It was the cabildo's business to listen to allegations against unqualified persons acting contrary to regulations.

Much of the routine activity of the council dealt with the authori-

23. "The position of juez de augas in this capital is much sought after, because it has attached a salary of 1,412 pesos 4 reales and other perquisites. This official is necessary since he determines the use of the water and thus he should be energetic and disinterested, a servant of the public good." See *Memoria de gobierno de Amat*, p. 179.

In Piura the council assigned to this official the extra duties of overseeing the slaughter of cattle and the transportation of meat to the city so that he bore the title of *juez de aguas y de fierro* (an office purchased by the cabildo from the crown in 1737 for 1,525 pesos). See Minutes of Dec. 14, 1737, *Libro del cabildos de Piura, años 1737 a 1748*.

24. Minutes of May 4, 1773, Libros de cabildos de Trujillo, vol. XV.

25. It was decided to retain the old system. See chap. vii, "Procurators, Petitions, and Popular Assemblies."

zation of the payment of debts by the majordomos. There are few, if any, references in the records to land grants by the cabildo. The right to cede public property had disappeared. Lots in the purely urban area and the commons belonging to the council constituted part of the propios and could not be alienated without the consent of the audiencia. Other tracts in the district not yet in private hands were the crown's property to be sold at auction or given to favorites.[26]

In other phases of the *policía*, "general administration," the cabildo continued to have a certain authority. The size of the municipal district had been for the most part reduced by the eighteenth century through the formation of new settlements, and even where the old boundaries persisted the power of the local officials was lessened. Lima retained some measure of control over Callao. In 1564 the cabildo was accustomed to dispatch an alcalde and a fiel ejecutor one day a week to hold court and to inspect shops. Two years later the cabildo elected an alcalde annually to serve in the port, without jurisdiction over soldiers and sailors. Objecting to a lack of voice in their own affairs, the citizens of Callao secured from the viceroy permission to have twenty of their body selected by the military commander of the port, from which number the cabildo of Lima chose one to serve as alcalde. To put an end to growing contention between the ayuntamiento and the military over the administration of the city, Philip II allotted to the council the enforcement of the civil and criminal code and the control over supplies and merchandise entering Lima by way of the port.[27]

This was the extent of authority wielded by the capital over its subordinate municipality in 1700. In that year the council defined the jurisdiction of the two alcaldes ordinarios by the issuance of a set of regulations, which were approved by the viceroy and revised from time to time. In summary, the magistrates had limited civil and criminal authority over virtually all the inhabitants of the port, with special cognizance of cases involving seizure and transportation of Indians for work on the haciendas, tippling, monopolies, property damage resulting from collisions of donkey- or mule-drawn conveyances, blasphemy, and "rigged" standards of weights and measures.

26. See chap. vi on municipal exchequer.
27. Dario Arrús, *Callao*, pp. 79-84.

Reports by the alcaldes of their activities were to be made monthly to the cabildo.[28]

Within the municipal district proper the alcaldes ordinarios were expected to enforce the law. Where corregidores existed there was undeniably some diminution in jurisdictional powers. Lima was fortunate enough to be free of their presence, except for a period in the sixteenth century. This did not mean that the crown did not subsequently consider the appointment of such an officer; the matter was vigorously debated in the seventeenth century.[29] Local interests prevailed, however, when the Marqués de Guadalcázar, viceroy from 1622 to 1629, gave his parecer on the subject to the Council of the Indies, asserting that the reinstitution of the office "would alienate the respect of the capitulars and would sow discouragement among subjects whose only reward consisted in governing their patria during a year."[30] In accepting his recommendation, the crown counseled extreme vigilance over conciliar elections.

Further threats against the exceptional autonomy of the cabildo of Lima came not long thereafter. By stretching his right to confirm conciliar elections, the Viceroy Conde de Chichón ordered the ayuntamiento in 1635 to select three alcaldes. The crown, however, forbade the adoption of any injurious innovations and the practice was dropped the following year. A danger of some gravity presented itself in the jurisdictional claims of the *alcaldes de corte*, "lawyers associated with the audiencia," who asserted sole cognizance over cases involving crown rights or powers in an area five leagues around the city conforming to law and custom in Madrid. Their authority in the eighteenth century sometimes extended to a variety of suits, even dealing with the gremios, in the event of vacillation or timidity of the magistrates.[31]

28. Minutes of Feb. 20, 1700, Libros de cabildos de Lima, vol. XXXIII, Biblioteca municipal, Lima.

29. Juan de Solórzano Pereira in his *Política indiana* [1647] (5 tomos; Madrid, 1930), tomo IV, libro V, cap. I, 26, opposed its re-establishment, since in his view the prestige of the office of alcalde ordinario exalted the civic pride of the limeños, in spite of the multiplicity of unnecessary, sometimes contradictory, orders and opinions emanating from the magistrate's court. Arguments adduced by jurists on the other side stressed the complexity of legal business in the growing metropolis, the favoritism shown by the alcaldes and their assistants to friends and relatives, and the impartiality of the corregidor who would have no civic ties or connections. See Guillermo Lohmann Villena, "El corregidor de Lima, estudio histórico-jurídico," *Revista histórica*, XX (1953), 176-179.

30. *Ibid.*, p. 179.   31. *Ibid.*, p. 175.

In the discharge of their duties as judges the alcaldes ordinarios were assisted by asesores. Their lack of a legal background made it almost imperative for the magistrates to employ men capable of giving opinions on law and drafting ordinances in appropriate language. At first the number was set at two, but later was increased to six or more. In the eighteenth century the Viceroy Amat, zealous of reforming the administration of justice in the magistrate's court, criticized the selection of such a large number on the grounds that the cabildo had perforce to pick men of inferior qualifications and lacking in sound judgment. Be this the real reason or not, the Viceroy, in January, 1762, fixed the number at two individuals, who should be in their office daily from ten to twelve o'clock. When he insisted later that the office be made proprietary to insure the retention of experienced *letrados*, "counselors," the ayuntamiento appealed to the audiencia, which declared by an *acuerdo*, "ruling," of January 13, 1776, that the office was to be filled annually by conciliar election. Meanwhile, still bent on improving the judicial system and hopeful of extending royal influence, Amat confirmed the election of a procurator-general for life. His decision was reversed by the Council of the Indies, which maintained by a cédula of March 24, 1774, that "neither cabildos nor viceroys nor governors have the power to extend the duration of the office for more than a year." In 1781 the practice of annual elections of the asesores again came under fire as causing delays in the preparation of briefs when new officials took over, "from which much ill ensued." The procurator-general recommended to the cabildo that for the common good "the present incumbents should be allowed to continue in office . . . because they are versed in the documents and have reputation as honest men." Rotation, he contended, should not apply, as the asesor was not a true conciliar figure and the council had been in the habit of choosing the same persons year after year. With the cabildo's consent the matter was referred to the audiencia, which authorized the election of legal assistants for an indefinite period since it accorded with "a custom almost immemorial." In 1787 the salaries of the two asesores were raised by the Junta Superior de Real Hacienda to 800 pesos each, "in view of the importance of these officials and the fact that the propios of this city have received an extraordinary increase since the establishment of the intendancies."[32]

Asesores were a desideratum for the local magistrates, serving in the same capacity as *fiscales* for the audiencia. Councils of all the large towns found it necessary to employ them. Although their integrity might be questioned occasionally, they were essential in the formulating of ordinances and in the preparation of briefs and appeals to higher tribunals.

In the eighteenth century magisterial jurisdiction was recognized in the fields of civil and criminal law. Despite the fact that the local alcalde had formal cognizance of all acts of a criminal nature in the first instance and of civil cases when the amount involved did not exceed a stated number of pesos, in actual practice his authority was being curtailed.[33] The alcalde stoutly maintained his immunity from a jail sentence pronounced by the *alcalde de crimen*, a royal judge, unless the sentence was passed with the express authorization of the viceroy.[34] Diminution of judicial powers came from the gradual accretion of authority on the part of the *oidor* assigned to criminal matters. To a greater degree than before, appeals from the magistrate's court were authorized by the audiencia and the *juez de provincias*. Similarly in the smaller towns there seems to have been an extension of such power by the corregidores.

The whittling down of the alcalde's juridical prerogatives was more in evidence after 1700 and did not pass unnoticed by the magistrates. It would appear that the encroachment was more because of a royalist interpretation of the law by the king's agents in America than because of the issuance of formal decrees by the Council of the Indies. As early as 1702 the procurator of Lima memorialized the

32. Expediente no. 336, Cartas y expedientes del Presidente, legajo 793, Audiencia de Lima, A. G. I.

33. The act of arresting and locking up the wrongdoer in the municipal prison was usually carried out by the alguacil mayor and his deputies. When riots occurred in the capital, the viceroy's guard, replaced toward the end of the century by a regiment of creole cavalry, came to the rescue of the hardpressed law enforcement officials. See Pablo Patrón, "Lima antigua," *Monografías históricas sobre la ciudad de Lima* (Lima, 1935), II, 202.

34. The Príncipe de Esquilache (1615-1621) upheld the alcalde's prescriptive rights on the ground that they were the "personification of the common justice, and as such should be surrounded with the most scrupulous immunities, protecting them from arbitrary sentences of the togados of the audiencia." See Lohmann Villena, "El corregidor de Lima," p. 175.

crown, pointing out that alcaldes de crimen were interfering with the execution of the law by the regular justices. Arrests were made and prisoners released contrary to custom and law. From this "results not only rivalries and discord, but the operation and enforcement of law are interrupted, with great injury to the cause of public vengeance." The fiscal's opinion, concurred in by the consejo, on March 23, 1703, was that the alcalde de crimen should obey the injunction of the Laws of the Indies in matters of the first instance.[35] The real cédula containing this command was received by the cabildo on November 28, 1703, and was referred to in a conciliar session the following year.[36]

In another petition to the consejo shortly after 1700, the procurator of Lima complained that royal justices intervened in the regulation of the food supply by the alcaldes and fieles ejecutores. Behind this unlawful procedure were the vested interests of the administrative court. The consejo, agreeing with the fiscal's parecer, ordered the audiencia not to impede the activities of the alcalde ordinario in situations of this type.[37] That this order was not carried out is apparent.[38]

Appeals from the judgments of the alcalde ordinario and the fiel ejecutor to the audiencia were a subject of contention.[39] A multiplicity of cases involving matters of the abasto, "provisioning of the

35. Cartas de cabildos, legajo 428, Audiencia de Lima, A. G. I.; see also Recopilación, libro II, título XVII, ley IV.
36. Minutes of Nov. 28, 1703, Feb. 18, 1704, Libros de cabildos de Lima, vol. XXXIV, Biblioteca municipal, Lima.
It was a grievance of the cabildo in Lima that the oidores denied permission to the alcaldes to accompany them in inspections of the jail in violation of long-standing habit, from which resulted disrespect for the alcaldes. See Cartas, legajo 428, Audiencia de Lima, A. G. I.
In Trujillo the corregidor and the alcalde of the first vote visited the jail twice a year, the names of the occupants of the cells, of the arresting officers, and the formal charges against the prisoners being written down in the libro de cabildo. See minutes of Dec. 24, 1772, Libros de cabildos de Trujillo, vol. XV.
37. Cartas, legajo 428, Audiencia de Lima, A. G. I.
38. For in 1710 the Viceroy limited the jurisdiction of the alcalde ordinario in Lima by forbidding him to have cognizance of cases relating to the abasto de la nieve. The profitable privilege of selling snow hauled down from the mountains by the Indians had been enjoyed by the crown since 1634. The cabildo defended its claim by reference to a cédula sharing jurisdiction with the alcalde de crimen. A cédula of Nov. 28, 1711, sided, however, in favor of the council. See minutes of Nov. 19, 1710, Libros de cabildo de Lima, vol. XXXIV, Biblioteca municipal, Lima.
The cabildo was obliged in 1747 to protest against the non-observance of the terms of the cédula of 1711. See Expedientes de virreyes, legajo 417, Audiencia de Lima, A. G. I.
39. The procedure of appeal often involved excessive complications. See Cartas y expedientes, legajos 421, 422, Audiencia de Lima, A. G. I.

city," were decided by the alcalde de crimen, representing the administrative court. In 1734, the Viceroy Marqués de Castelfuerte, believing that these questions belonged more properly to his sphere of authority, resolved to intervene.[40] It was evident that the future would see a clash between the two highest governmental agencies. Many years afterward the validity of the Viceroy's decree was questioned in a suit over the disposal of the municipal propios. On March 1, 1763, the audiencia agreed to listen to the appeal of one of the bidders for the purchase of certain stalls, or *toldos*, on the main plaza. He declared that his bid of 3,500 pesos as the highest should have been recognized by the cabildo. In taking the case under advisement the audiencia notified the Viceroy in a consulta that appeals from the council normally went to that body and that when the propios were sold or leased an oidor should be present. On March 10, the Viceroy responded that in the light of his predecessor's decision, appeals in the matter of abastos and, analogously, in the question of propios, belonged to the king's alter ego. In his reply the Viceroy further declared that "it is indispensable for the viceroy and governor to assume the care and supervision over everything concerning such an important matter, not so much because it is useful to the cabildo, but rather because it is necessary for the convenience of the vecinos of the city."

The final decision in the case favored the Viceroy. It was held that the toldos were, properly speaking, abastos, though regarded secondarily as propios, and a judgment had already been rendered on this point in New Spain. The consejo, by an acuerdo of October 14, 1737, ordered "to be observed in Lima what was decreed for Mexico."[41] The crown by a real cédula of 1736 affirmed that cases relating to the abasto should be handled by the alcalde ordinario and not by the alcalde de corte.[42]

It was fitting for the Viceroy to alter certain procedures associated with the right of appeal from the magistrate's court in order to correct abuses. The constant habit of legally questioning the decisions of the alcalde by the contractors for municipal victuals and necessities not only lowered the prestige of the magistrates, but also made possible

40. See *Recopilación*, libro II, título XVII, ley XXVII.
41. Cartas y expedientes del Presidente y oidores, legajo 423, Audiencia de Lima, A. G. I.; see also Expedientes de los virreyes, legajo 414, Audiencia de Lima, A. G. I.
42. See Libros de cédulas y provisiones del archivo histórico de la municipalidad de Lima, libro 1, foja 297, Biblioteca municipal, Lima.

a practice injurious to the public interest. It became the custom to suspend the enforcement of any ordinance when its legality was brought into question by the initiation of an appeal, or recurso. Hence, as a consulta from the ayuntamiento of Lima to the Viceroy Guirior indicated, the suppliers might "sell bread, candles, and other staples at less weight," or at a higher price, in defiance of conciliar measures. A prompt *decreto* of the Superior Government recognized the harm to the public weal and stated that henceforth regulations of the council would have force during the period of appeals before higher courts, unless the viceroy decreed otherwise.[43]

The judicial power of the alcalde de la hermandad in the rural area of the urban district seems to have been likewise undermined. Evidence of this is to be found in the drop in value of the office and in the sworn statements of individuals and groups. In the province of Jauja the officials of the real contaduría of Huancavelica in 1769 had to confess their inability to sell the office, which was at one time valued at 2,000 to 2,600 pesos or was leased annually for 120 to 150 pesos.[44] A witness appearing before the royal treasury in Pasco in assessing the monetary worth of the office affirmed that it had "no salary and lacks remuneration because he who seeks it will do so only for the honor it carries and for no other reason." Another witness stated that the "vara can only bring prestige to the person who buys it in view of the fact that it has neither stipend nor emoluments nor utility."[45] In Trujillo the cabildo resolved to petition the viceroy to make every effort to sell the office because "the highways are infested with thieves."[46]

That there was some justification for the repeated acts of intervention by the viceroy and the audiencia in judicial proceedings of the urban and rural magistrates is likely. A carta of October 8, 1724, from the incoming Viceroy Castelfuerte censured the negligent enforcement of law by all of the courts. There was a total "lack of justice and public correction, which the Kingdom and the city have suffered, since the

43. Minutes of June 3, June 27, 1777, Libros de cabildos de Lima, vol. XXXVI, Biblioteca municipal, Lima.

44. Autos seguidos sobre el remate de la vara de alcalde provincial de la provincia de Juaja, año 1768, legajo 3, Cabildos (1767-1778), Archivo nacional, Lima.

45. Nevertheless, the office was unexplainably sold for 4,000 pesos. See Autos seguidos por la Rl. casa de Pasco sobre el remate de la vara de alcalde provincial de Tarma, legajo 1, Cabildos (1732-1802), Archivo nacional, Lima.

46. Minutes of Jan. 7, 1775, Libros de cabildos de Trujillo, vol. XV.

use of torture to malefactors has not been permitted for the grave and heinous crimes, as used to be true, the officers freeing them at once despite the fact that it had cost the officials of the Sala del Crimen unusual risks, efforts, and expenses."[47] The same viceroy, in a carta of August 30, 1727, implied that the alcaldes ordinarios were often not equal to the execution of decrees, even for payment of debts.[48] A decreto from the Viceroy Conde de Superunda ordered the ordinary judges to prosecute cases pending in their courts.[49] In Lima the Viceroy Amat complained that the public highways were not sufficiently policed by the alcaldes provinciales. Because of the presence at a place about three leagues from the city of a band of notorious Negro cutthroats who continued their depredations and holdups despite the efforts of the alcaldes, the Viceroy ordered the Governor of Callao to send infantry and cavalry to stamp out the nuisance. This was accomplished, four outlaws being executed and four sentenced to life imprisonment in the Presidio of Callao.[50] Magistrates in the lesser towns were accused of indolence and procrastination in reporting to the audiencia the status of criminal cases pending in their courts.[51]

Jurisdictional disputes occurred likewise with the ecclesiastical authorities. A primary cause of trouble was the right of sanctuary, still claimed by the church in this period. In 1707 action taken by the alcaldes to deal with a notorious criminal was defended by the Viceroy Príncipe de Santo Buono. According to the Viceroy's version, a murderer sought by the local justices was taken forcibly from a Franciscan monastery in Lima, where he had claimed right of refuge. The provisor and vicar-general of the archbishopric drew up a protest and ordered the return of the prisoner by the alcaldes. Meanwhile, the local judge had condemned the criminal to torture, at the beginning of which the suspect had died. The wrath of the archbishop led

47. Cartas de virreyes de Perú, legajo 411, Audiencia de Lima, A. G. I.
48. Cartas de virreyes de Perú, legajo 412, Audiencia de Lima, A. G. I.
49. Minutes of May 10, 1757, Libros de cabildos de Lima, vol. XXXVI, Biblioteca municipal, Lima.
50. *Memoria de gobierno de Amat*, pp. 165, 166.
51. The regent of the Audiencia de Lima notified the Council of the Indies that in order to remedy the evil letters were sent to the alcaldes and cabildos "warning them that hereafter they must inform the crown fiscal as soon as crimes occur in their midst, giving information as to their nature and who the perpetrators, thus proving their diligence in the same case for the purposes and ends that exist in the law, with the threat, in its contravention, of the imposition of a fine of 500 pesos for the first offence." See Cartas y expedientes del Presidente y oidores, legajo 792, Audiencia de Lima, A. G. I.

to the publication of an anathema, carried out with "ceremonies of a Roman origin, never seen nor used in this city," and to excommunication of the alcaldes ordinarios, "with utmost confusion and disorder of the entire community, and with full risk of a complete breakdown of law and order." At the Viceroy's suggestion the audiencia presented a petition to the archbishop for clemency. In the end the censure by the church was withdrawn. One aspect of the episode, the manner in which the bans were published, alarmed the Viceroy, who in his report to the Council of the Indies regarded it as a possible threat to the Real Patronato. In Spain the fiscal of the consejo upheld the Viceroy's interpretation of the justifiability of the action taken by the alcaldes on the basis that the right of sanctuary could not exist if the criminal were dangerous and constituted a menace to the lives of the citizens.[52]

The cabildo was often displeased with petty acts of the lesser clergy. In July, 1737, Piura remonstrated to the crown against the closing up of an oratory, "which has been used since time immemorial for services of the Mass for prisoners in the jail cells and for the justices and the cabildo." The pretext given by the commissary of the bishop was that chapels of this type had to have a license from the church before being made available for public use. Inserted in the petition of the regidores was an indictment of a certain slothful priest who had been appointed as curate of an Indian village but had not visited there in ten years. The fiscal of the consejo in his parecer censured the lazy pastor and recommended that the chapel be reopened.[53]

Construction and maintenance of public works were also functions of the local authorities. In general, little was done in the way of new buildings in the pre-intendancy era because of the slackness and indifference of municipal officials and the deplorable state of civic finances. The erection of palaces, courts of justice, and fortifications was the result of crown initiative; the spread of churches, chapels, and monasteries, of the wealth of the church, aided by popular donations.

52. Cartas y expedientes, legajo 410, Audiencia de Lima, A. G. I.

Another less serious incident occurred in Guamanga in 1734, when the bishop of the city accused the alcaldes ordinarios of threatening him with popular demonstrations because of his stand on a local issue. The Viceroy investigated the complaint and cleared the justices of malicious intent. See Informe con testimonio de los autos practicados en la ciudad de Guamanga, Cartas y expedientes, legajo 416, Audiencia de Lima, A. G. I.

53. Cartas de cabildos, Piura, legajo 428, Audiencia de Lima, A. G. I.

Repairs of buildings, bridges, streets, and aqueducts were a constant preoccupation of the cabildo.[54] Earthquakes accentuated the difficulties of the councils. The rehabilitation of Lima after the holocaust of 1746 was beyond the capability and resources of the ayuntamiento, and only the efforts of the Viceroy saved the capital from still further heavy loss of life. Illustrative of the interest of the cabildo in facilities of communication and transportation is the preservation of the bridge over the Rimac. In 1709, the Lima council accepted a bid for 2,990 pesos for the repair of the arches of the structure.[55] Again, in 1713, some restoration being necessary, the ayuntamiento ordered the crier to announce the submission of bids by interested contractors and carpenters. When no bids were forthcoming, it ordered the majordomo to have the work done.[56] Four years later, in October, 1717, the council ordered a commission comprising the alcalde, the juez de aguas, and the two alarifes to inspect the bridge and, if necessary, to rebuild certain sections, with bills being paid by the majordomo.[57]

The general appearance of the city, its neatness and sanitation, was a responsibility of the council. Needless to say, it was one frequently shirked and overlooked. A contemporary *limeño* depicts the heavy traffic moving through the streets of the capital, with the attendant discomforts and perils for the unlucky pedestrian:

54. It had the right to approve or disapprove plans for the construction of private dwellings, or any modifications or additions. In 1782, the proud creole aristocracy of Lima thought it saw an opportunity to take revenge on its erstwhile enemy the Viceroy's mistress and favorite, the actress Doña Micaela Villegas, familiarly known in history as "La Perricholi." The beautiful but designing heroine of Hoffman's operetta had caricatured Lima society and in turn was the object of ridicule and haughty contempt. Even the Viceroy did not escape the derision of the upper class because of his age, obesity, and a Catalan accent, rendered more difficult by an impediment of speech. In that year she had built for her residence in the city an exterior wooden balcony, then much the vogue in Lima. Upon learning of this, the procurator of the cabildo visited the spot and condemned the projection as blocking the traffic and obstructing the view along the street. To the discomfiture of the council Doña Micaela won her case by proving that the balcony was built over a *camino* not a *paseo*, with the normal dimensions permitted for such dwellings. The celebrated courtesan had gained another victory over high society! See Expediente promobido pr. el Sr. Procr. Gral. de la ciud. contra Da. Micaela Villegas, sobre la fabrica de una piesa alta, y baja, en el Molino de la Almeda, año de 1782, legajo 8, archivo nacional, Lima; see also Emilio Harth-Terre, "Un balcón para Micaela Villegas," *El Comercio* (Lima), July 13, 1959.
55. Minutes of Aug. 3, Nov. 12, 1709, Libros de cabildos de Lima, vol. XXXIV, Biblioteca municipal, Lima.
56. Minutes of June 27, Aug. 3, 11, 1713, *ibid.*
57. Minutes of Oct. 9, 1717, *ibid.*

In carriages, sedan-chairs, or on saddle mules the people of the city passed by; since there were no paved sidewalks and although the cabildo had slaves and carts for cleaning up refuse, much is to be desired; it was annoying to walk on foot, elbowing one's way at each step with burros loaded with hay, lime, and bricks, and breathing the dust and ordure raised by the animals. Such a number of beasts, as those engaged in transportation, meant a heavy expenditure for grass, and to provide supplies, all the farms of the country around about were sown with alfalfa, whose cultivation replaced that of wheat, which grew well here at one time.[58]

The repulsive condition of the streets with their accustomed dirt and filth and the threat to life and limb of the citizenry posed by cutthroats and pickpockets reached such a height in 1761 that corrective action by the crown was almost imperative. The Viceroy Amat, with his usual energy, appointed alcaldes de barrios, having full economic and judicial authority and responsible only to him, to assist the regular alcaldes.[59] Each new official, in addition, drew up a register of the vecinos of his district, enabling the government to ascertain the number of citizens and the residence of each. For the protection of the urban population from assaults at night by robbers and thieves, the Viceroy put into operation the first system of street lighting in Peru. A regulation stipulated that every citizen, with a house or shop on the corner of a square, must keep a lighted lantern near his front door throughout the night.[60] Lima benefited also by the strengthening of the principal bridge over the Rimac, long a concern of the city fathers, and the enlargement and beautification of the alameda.[61]

Measures for the defense of the kingdom often required the cooperation and support of the municipal authorities. The cabildo made donations to the crown in time of war or when the city was threatened by pirates or attacks of Indians. The funds sometimes went to the construction of the walls of the city, constantly in need of repairs. As a

---

58. Patrón, "Lima antigua," Monografías, p. 218.
59. Memoria de gobierno de Amat, p. 168.
60. Vargas Ugarte, Historia del Perú, virreinato, siglo XVIII, p. 320.
61. Memoria de gobierno de Amat, pp. 169, 170.
Amat wrote discouragingly of the gap between his aspirations for the city and his achievements: "Although my efforts have been great for the perfection of the capital of Peru, I have not been able to accomplish as much as its importance deserves, owing to the negligence of its citizens or their little zeal, injurious to its own glory and, what is more, even to its preservation." See ibid., pp. 168, 169.

major, if not the most important, link in the chain of defense for the Spanish possessions on the west coast of South America, the presidio at Callao demanded expenditures for repair and enlargement, to be met in part by contributions of the vecinos of Lima and those of the coastal cities.

To a lesser extent, the cabildos of Peru participated in actual preparations for the use of the armed forces. For the first time regiments of colonial militia were organized at the crown's command during the regime of the Viceroy Amat. The increasing peril of British aggression in the Pacific led him to enlist colonials into the army for the protection of the region. Beginning in the City of the Kings, he ordered a general census of available men in all classes, from whom urban regiments would be formed, with discipline and training to be furnished by Spanish officers. In all there were twenty-seven companies, maintained chiefly at the cost of the individual soldier and the local treasury, and comprising 5,000 infantry and 2,000 cavalry.[62] The example of the capital was followed by other cities and towns and gradually a military organization came into being. While these new troops were drawn from all ranks and stations of life, they proved amenable to orders from Spanish officials until the later phase of the revolutionary movement.

In the eighteenth century the most serious military crisis was the rebellion of the Indians under the leadership of Túpac-Amaru. There had been no movement comparable to this in duration and potentiality for destruction since the sixteenth century. Of the cities in the Audiencia of Lima the chief one affected by the uprising was Cuzco, which had a large native population and was surrounded by many Indian settlements. In this emergency, support given by the cabildo of the city to the Spanish forces was fundamental to the defense of the region. On December 28, 1780, the Inca chieftain began his advance upon the city. Hoping to win the creoles over to independence, he sent, on January 3, two messengers to the cabildo to explain his reasons for revolt. Upon the rejection of his demands, the Indians proceeded

62. *Ibid.*, p. li.
Titles and uniforms appealed to the vanity of the creoles: "Knowing how much the ordinary people are moved by the example of the nobility, he [Amat] persuaded the distinguished men of the city to form a regiment among themselves . . . with a personage at its head bearing the title of Colonel, which was revered as if it were that of Captain-General of the whole Kingdom." See *ibid.*

to make an assault upon the walls. Although strong reinforcements had arrived in Cuzco from Lima and from a neighboring *corregimiento*, companies of local militia and even women and children took an active part in the defense. An account of the action by the secretary of the cabildo tells of the efforts of "the company of merchants and tradesmen counting 130 fusiliers with their captain D. Simon Gutiérrez, which was ordered to scale the hill with its colonel D. Isidoro Guisasola and D. Francisco Morales, who had trained it. This company was ready to march with valor and spirit, of which it gave evidence, since the greater part of it was composed of men of honor, commercial folk of all classes and other members of the guild, all people of Spanish blood."[63] Similar action by other cabildos in the *cordilleras* was decisive in the failure of the great Indian uprising.

The role of the local council in the areas of education and charity was relatively slight. Elementary and secondary training was the work of the secular clergy and the orders, in particular the Society of Jesus. Occasionally, the cabildo might license a schoolmaster to instruct the less fortunate children of the city. For example, in 1748, the procurator of Lima presented to the ayuntamiento a petition, in which it was stated that "there was no master of reading and writing, from which lack and the little care with which children are taught ensued barbarism and deficiency of culture, so that sons of this land spoke and wrote in a manner unworthy of a city which is the center of the entire Kingdom; and that D. José Manuel de Vitoria was an excellent penman, as it appeared from the sample presented in his handwriting and also a good speller." It was resolved to grant the said applicant a título, if approved by the viceroy.[64]

The Catholic church fulfilled its traditional function as the chief dispenser of charity and healing services. The larger cities possessed hospitals and almshouses. As the capital, Lima had the greatest number of hospitals, twelve in all, including that of San Andrés, with "250 beds for Spaniards, patio for the insane, chapel with tower and clock, a good apothecary's shop, and a beautiful garden," and that of Santa Ana "for 300 Indians of both sexes, well run, with chapel, an upper floor with elegant columns and garden." Endowment for

63. Quoted from Lewin Boleslao's *La rebelión de Túpac Amaru y los orígenes de la emancipación Americana* (Buenos Aires, n. d.), p. 466.

64. Minutes of July 11, 1748, Libros de cabildo de Lima, vol. XXXIV, Biblioteca municipal, Lima.

these was provided by the church and the crown. Brotherhoods, organized under the auspices of the church, managed the hospitals, paying the salaries or fees of physicians and surgeons and seeking additional funds for their maintenance.[65] With limited financial resources the cabildo made only a small contribution to the feeding of the hungry and the upkeep of houses for the needy and the ill. In Cuzco, however, of four hospitals in operation, that of Espiritu Santo for male and female Indians was administered by a junta of thirty-three persons, presided over by the first alcalde.[66] Contrary to the trend in America, the Spanish ayuntamientos expanded their charitable activities.

In the eighteenth century many aspects of the local economy and the policía felt the authority of the cabildo and its elected agents. Protection of the consumer against high prices caused by real or synthetic shortages was obligatory. Strict control was precluded by the intervention of the crown and the increasing play of the forces of supply and demand that often recognized no national or colonial frontiers. As a dispenser of justice, the municipal magistrate cut a less important figure. Through the issuance of orders and the clever exploitation of the right of appeal from the lesser courts, the crown officials in America gradually augmented their power in this field, even though it was contrary at times to the announced policy of the Council of the Indies. Construction of public works was neglected. For greater internal and external security the cabildo threw its support behind the organization of a colonial militia and donated funds for the maintenance of city walls and fortifications. It accomplished little for the realization of educational and eleemosynary goals. But, as will be observed, in the celebration of public acts and in social functions the prestige of the members of the cabildo was relatively undimmed.

65. Patrón, "Lima antigua," *Monografías*, p. 194.
66. Alcedo, *Diccionario geográfico-histórico*, I, 744.

CHAPTER V

Ceremonies and Fiestas

The Bourbon epoch witnessed a proliferation of public celebrations and festivities. A great majority of these had been inaugurated in the past, but the advent of the new dynasty reflected the prestige of the descendants of the Sun King and the glitter of Versailles. The spirit of the pagentry and the ceremonies was more secular, less religious. New celebrations arose to express the changed outlook of the times. Undoubtedly, the older ones were modified over the passage of time as a result of the acquisition of different tastes, perhaps a finer sense of decorum, and the costs of the entertainments.

Sociological and psychological factors perhaps explain the greater stress in the American colonies on ceremony and social life. For the upper class wealth was a means of gratification of a profound desire for ostentatious display. To compensate for their lack of self-rule, the creoles, dominating the local regimes, expended money, time, and energy on the more frivolous and decorative side of municipal existence. As long as the celebrations disclosed no disrespect for royalty and did not bankrupt the local treasury, there was little interference from above. From the first, the church lent encouragement as a way of strengthening its hold on the Indians and appealing to the social conscience of those of Spanish ancestry. In the splendid tableaux and the exciting parades the official representative of the municipality was the alférez real, and his rank was eagerly sought after by those aspiring to social prominence in the community.[1] The worth of the office of regidor

1. A título of alférez real of Cuzco was sold in 1702 for 8,000 pesos, giving the possessor the rights enjoyed by "the other alfereces reales of other cities, villas, and places of this kingdom with seat and vote in the cabildo of the said city and in other public acts with active and passive vote and [you] may be chosen in the election for alcaldes ordinarios and in the absence, death, or disqualification of anyone of the said alcaldes ordinarios you may occupy the office as senior regidor and wear

was often measured in terms of opportunities for public display and participation in municipal acts.[2]

In Lima, the greatest social occasion was the *recibimiento*, the "reception," accorded the king's alter ego by the royal officials, the church dignitaries, and the cabildo. Those sharp observers of the colonial scene, Juan and Ulloa, did not fail to recognize its signal importance for the creole aristocracy:

> In all those of the Indies [Lima and Mexico City] it is one of the most notable acts, in which is revealed the wealth of the city on the instance of the entry of he who governs. This opulence characterizes Lima more than any other, since by riding in their carriages and coaches throughout the city and wearing their court-dress, the nobility exhibit a deportment that leads them to adopt a livery of the richest and costliest cloth for their servants in order to show off in this way the power of their masters, who not finding in their own persons full expression of their generosity try to call attention to it in the adornment of their retainers.[3]

The momentous event of the arrival of a new viceroy took place every three to ten years. The length of his term would depend on many things: his success as an administrator, the circumstances of his personal standing with the ruler and at the court, and finally, his physical health. Prolongation of his stay might also result from popularity with the vecinos of the viceregal capital. In the last quarter of the eighteenth century the average length of a viceregal term was five years, whereas in the earlier period only five individuals held office for five years or more.

It would even appear that the reception of the viceroy overshadowed the celebration of happenings affecting the royal family itself. To the

the sword and dagger in the said cabildo and every time the vacancy occurs you may pick up the vara without other formalities than knowing of the vacancy . . . you are to be preferred in seating and voting in public acts to the alguacil mayor, unless there is custom to the contrary as in the city of La Plata and other parts where the alguaciles mayores take precedence . . . and you may raise the royal standard in the fiestas occurring in the said city of Cuzco in tribute to Our Most Royal Person." See Confirmaciones de oficios, legajo 450, Audiencia de Lima, A. G. I.

2. Time and again witnesses summoned before the officials of the Real Caja in connection with the appraisal of local offices use the term "honor" as the main, if not the sole, justification. It should be kept in mind, of course, that some were biased and hoped to see a reduction in the cost of the office. See Confirmaciones de oficios, legajo 456, Audiencia de Lima, A. G. I.

3. Quoted in Juan Bromley's "Recibimiento de virreyes en Lima," *Revista histórica*, XX (1952), 5.

ordinary vecino in a Peruvian town the king was a vague, insubstantial figure, never seen in the flesh, for the obvious reason that, like other monarchs of his day, he regarded it beneath his dignity to inspect his American dominions. Nevertheless, homage had to be paid on the accession of a new sovereign to the throne and fitting ceremonies were to attend the announcement of a royal nuptial, the birth of a Prince of the Asturias, and the demise of the king or queen.

However, the viceroy was a living symbol of the Spanish crown. He was visible to the populace in the public acts and, in the popular mind, accessible to all in the palace. Born in the Peninsula, usually of a noble family, with the background of a capable administrator or at the time of the later Bourbons of a respected general, he was the embodiment of royal authority. Few viceroys ever forgot the fact that they enjoyed the greatest share of power in America, to be wielded in theory under the Council of the Indies, but in reality with much leeway for independent action and judgment. In such a position it is not surprising that a viceroy was a victim of flattery or, in its worst form, of sycophancy. That there were intangible influences which might determine his attitude and decisions was not lost upon the citizens of the capital. Like a host of others, the members of the cabildo curried favor with this powerful personage. To get off on a good footing with him was considered well worthwhile.

Lima outdid itself in its efforts to impress each successive royal executive with its show of warmth.[4] References in the libros de cabildos to this ceremony are more frequent than to any other. Preparations had to be made well in advance, for they involved much planning and a considerable outlay of funds. To halt extravagance and wastefulness on the part of the council, the crown stipulated a limit to expenditures for this purpose.[5] But this did not forestall short-term loans, often winked at by a viceroy who secretly wanted to surpass his predecessor in magnificence of entry and display of pomp.

No more appropriate setting for the brilliant tableaux and gay processions could have been found in America than Lima. A minor governmental official, employed by the Viceroy Amat, has left a fairly

4. Actually, the height of extravagance was reached in the seventeenth century when the municipality on one occasion literally paved sections of the main street with silver.

5. See chap. vi on municipal exchequer.

accurate description of the city as he saw it during his period of residence:

From the section of San Lázaro one makes his way into the city by a majestic bridge, whose length is 130 castellanos varas, and twelve and one-half in width, without including six half circles and six triangles that make its construction steadier and more secure. Seven of the strongest arches, eight varas in height, support it. The Viceroy Monteslaros built it in 1610...

The main square measures 150 varas on each side, and in all 600, which reveals its excellent design, and [it] has a beautiful bronze fountain, which in its center is adorned with various lions and receivers of the same metal with an unique statute of regular size on top.

To the south and east are seen eighty stone columns, which, well constructed, constitute elevated arches, and on the northern and western sides the Viceroy's palace, the riverside stalls, and the cathedral....

Situated to supply the needs of the square are 600 stalls, loaded with everything that nature produces for the enjoyment and delight of man, in such abundance that in agreeable harmony the appearance, fragrance, and diversity of food compete with the most celebrated in Europe.

The Duke de la Plata built the walls in 1685, crowned with thirty-five bastions, which, although of adobe, and without embrasures for the artillery secure the interior...

The entire city is undermined by canals or conduits for the cleaning and washing of the houses only and then for drinking water there are separate reservoirs beyond the walls, from which it is drawn by special channels to the fountains and troughs.

The principal section of the city has 360 streets, some from the northeast to southeast, others at right angles, and some from east to west; it has a circumference of two and one-half leagues, without including the barrio of San Lázaro, and its area totals 2,515 castellanos varas . . .

For common drinking there are twenty-five fountains, not counting those in the monasteries, convents, palace of the viceroy, episcopal palace, residence of the Inquisition, schools, and homes for pious women.

Commerce in various merchandise is conducted in 342 shops and storehouses; eighty silversmithes, in which art and skill acquired by practice transform the many precious metals that are furnished by the mines abounding in the highlands.

Churches and sumptuous buildings number eighty, and, in addition, [there are] five parish churches, twenty-six monasteries, fourteen convents, four homes for religious women, ten chapels, structures for the Inquisition, University, mint, cockfights, the Coliseum, and the bullring.

The regular clergy residing behind the walls of their edifices total 914; the teachers in the *colegios,* 252; the secular clergy, 350, in the city, and 560 in the entire archbishopric; doctors of the University, 600, professors, twelve. The population is approximately 100,000 persons, not counting youth and children. . . .[6]

Since the inauguration of the ceremony of the recibimiento in the sixteenth century, general procedure had changed in some details. The principal difference was the length of the *paseo,* "parade," through the streets of the capital. Preparations varied, however, depending on the residence of the administrator at the moment of his nomination and the route chosen to reach the city. Appointees living in Spain usually set out for the Indies in the *flota,* "fleet," a mode of transportation that delayed departure indefinitely, so that six months often elapsed between the date of selection and that of arrival in Lima. In the eighteenth century a number of viceroys already held administrative posts in New Spain or Buenos Aires or Chile and were simply shifted to Peru, thus cutting down the time involved in travel.

Upon the arrival of the fleet from Spain at Cartagena, it was customary for the appointee to dispatch news of his coming to Panama and hence to Lima. On receiving intelligence of this event, the cabildo of the capital forwarded a message of welcome, with a reply expected from the viceroy. From Panama the customary route was by sea to Payta, whence it was possible to proceed either by ship to Callao or by land down the coastal plain to Lima. In the eighteenth century a viceroy would ordinarily sail from Payta to Callao at the request of the crown, hopeful of preventing the inland cities from making exorbitant expenditures from their limited propios to honor the functionary during his passage through their districts. If he were a resident of Chile at the time of his appointment, the viceroy would reach the capital by a voyage up the coast to Callao and there would be welcomed by a group comprising the retiring official, members of the audiencia, and a delegate from the town council. Should he decide to travel overland from Payta—a temptation not easily dismissed considering the tedium and physical discomfort of the long voyage down

6. Gregorio de Cangas, "Descripción de la ciudad de Lima," *Revista histórica,* XIV (1941), 327-329.

the coast—a committee of the ayuntamiento would greet him at Huarmey, a town near the boundary separating the jurisdictions of Trujillo and Lima, or occasionally at Chancay, Bocanegra, or Carabayllo.[7]

Long before the appearance of the new governor in the streets of the capital the ayuntamiento had begun its preparations for the reception. The news of the nomination was itself the excuse for an immediate celebration, marked in the evening by special lighting of the casa de cabildo and of the dwellings of important citizens and by a parade of prominent vecinos on horseback, carrying four long wick tapers around the *plaza mayor*. Sessions of the council were given over to the raising of funds for the purchase of cloth for the canopy, wood for the triumphal arch, a horse and chair for the viceroy, and fine material for the resplendent costumes of the capitulars. To heighten the excitement of the event and from a practical standpoint to co-ordinate the activities of the welcoming bodies, the viceroy dispatched an envoy to the city, who gave the approximate time of his coming. Met on the outskirts by an alcalde and a regidor, the ambassador rode first to the palace to inform his master's predecessor and the audiencia, and thence to the town hall for a similar announcement. Criers proclaimed the news at the four corners of the main plaza; and, occasionally, bull fights and *cañas*, "sham battles," between riders armed with long reeds, added to the rejoicing of the populace.

The curtain rose on the main show when the viceroy's ship hove into view at Callao. Salvos from the artillery at the fortress of Real Felipe boomed out over the water. Ensigns and pennants of the units of cavalry and infantry assembled at the beach were lowered and raised again in homage to the highest authority in the Indies. The first night, however, he spent on shipboard. Disembarking the next morning, he greeted the man whom he would succeed, the audiencia, the representatives of the ecclesiastical and secular cabildos, and then proceeded to the mother church of the port for a *Te Deum Laudamus*. For some days he remained in Callao, inspecting the garrison and guns of the presidio and, incidentally, giving the cabildo time to complete its preparations.[8]

7. Bromley, "Recibimiento de virreyes," pp. 9, 10.
8. *Ibid*., pp. 11, 12.

In due time the viceroy set out for the capital in a commodious coach. Although the distance to the Plaza de Armas was less than eight miles, he passed a night at a manor house along the way. The following day he halted at the triumphal arch to be welcomed by the municipality. The arch stood at the end of the road to the port or in the last street on the west side of the city and was "made of wooden lathes, covered with linen cloth, painted white to resemble marble, and capable of being taken down and reassembled. . . . On it were woven the royal coat of arms and those of the city."[9] If the viceroy came by the land route from the north, the arch was erected at the approach of the bridge over the Rimac.[10]

Stepping out of the conveyance at the foot of the wooden structure, the viceroy entered a small theater, the entrance to which was covered with hangings, to take the oath to preserve the *fueros y honras*, the "rights and honors," of the city. On his knees in the presence of the ayuntamiento, he pledged his word not to infringe upon or violate the charter. Thereupon the alférez real or the alcalde mayor handed him the keys of the city and the *bastón*, a small mace with a gold handle studded with diamonds. To the council it was an act of trans-cendental importance, a solemn promise of the preservation of basic liberties.

Next, according to protocol, was the paseo. Leaving the theater, the viceroy mounted a mettlesome charger, which with gold and silver trappings and a velvet cover extending to the stirrups, was the gift of the municipality.[11] Then the procession formed to make its way to the plaza mayor. At the head of the column were the infantry companies, both Spanish and Indian, followed by the archers, a squad of cavalry, representatives from the *colegios*, the consulado, the university, the exchequer, and the audiencia. Astride his brightly be-decked horse, the viceroy rode slightly in front or behind the canopy, or *palio*, which was eighteen feet in length and fourteen in width. The canopy, stretched to four twelve-foot poles gilded or silver plated and carried by four regidores, was the symbol of royalty and its use a bone of contention between the king's representative and the local councils. To the creoles it was an act of unbecoming and extreme

9. *Ibid.*, p. 20.   10. *Ibid.*, p. 21.
11. The horse and saddle for the Viceroy Agustín de Jáuregui cost the cabildo over 2,000 pesos. See *ibid.*, p. 23.

Plaza de Armas and Casa de Cabildo, Lima, in 1874 (*courtesy Biblioteca Municipal, Lima*).

deference to a person of non-royal blood.[12] The two alcaldes ordinarios walked on either side of the viceroy, grasping silken cords tied to the steed's reins. Accompanying this important personage were the president of the audiencia and the ex-viceroy, who were then followed by the new official's entourage, palace guards, nobles with pages, and the royal and municipal mace bearers. Few of the onlookers could help but be stirred by the sight of this glittering display. As the gay cavalcade moved through the narrow cobblestone streets to the Plaza de Armas, the people waved from their balconies, shouted greetings, and tossed flowers upon the heads of the marching band. In front of the cathedral, where the clergy had gathered, the procession came to a halt. Dismounting, the viceroy knelt for a few minutes before the cross set up at the portico, and then entered the interior where he prayed and listened to the *Te Deum*. The last lap of the paseo brought him to the palace. At nightfall a brilliant exhibition of pyrotechnics illuminated the Plaza de Armas and its environs.

There is to be found in the Libros de cabildos de Lima a simple, matter-of-fact account of the reception of the ingratiating Viceroy Manuel de Guirior on December 3, 1776. The simple language probably reflects the non-literary style of the conciliar secretary:

In the very Noble and Loyal City of the Kings of Peru, on the 3rd day of December, 1776, was celebrated the public entry of the His Excellency Sr. Manuel de Guirior, Caballero of the Order of St. John and Lieutenant-General of the Real Armada of His Majesty, as Viceroy, Governor and Captain-General of these Kingdoms, on which occasion were present at slightly before four o'clock in the afternoon, the Real Audiencia, the Tribunal of Accounts, royal officials, Tribunal of the Consulado, the University, and the teach-

12. In the eighteenth century the viceroys customarily made their entrance into the city in this fashion. A cédula of Aug. 20, 1749, recognized the practice, though the crown secretly disapproved of it because it had the effect of swelling the vanity of the functionary and of encouraging a spirit of independence on his part. The cabildo had a temporary triumph when this obnoxious part of the ceremony was dropped in the entrance into Lima of the Viceroy Gil de Taboada y Lemus in 1790. But on July 1, 1796, Viceroy Ambrosio O'Higgins informed the cabildo that he intended to re-establish the custom. In obedience to a royal order of March 3, 1806, the thirty-ninth viceroy, Joaquín de la Pezuela, in 1815 permanently abandoned the formality. See *ibid.*, pp. 12, 24-26, 103-107; see also Rodríguez y Pérez, *Memoria de gobierno de Amat*, pp. 157, 158.
The material used in the palio was expensive, that for the reception of Jáuregui in 1780 costing over 1,200 pesos. See Bromley, "Recibimiento de virreyes," p. 26.

ing brothers on horseback, at the gate, which is at the entrance
of the street Montserrate, His Excellency having gone in his coach
by out of the way lanes to that place [.] There on a little table
serving as an altar with a figure of Christ and four candles, and
the Holy Apostles, he took the customary oath to be loyal to Our
Sovereign and to the fueros and privileges of this city before the
secular cabildo, which awaited him there, with the secretary of the
cabildo Andrés de Sandoval y Davalos giving the oath. Accompanied
by the two alcaldes ordinarios Joseph de Velarde y Tagle and Dr.
Juan Estevan de la Puente, the alguacil mayor of this city Don
Agustín Joseph de Ugarte, to whom belongs this right, handed
him the keys [of Lima]. This ceremony completed, His Excellency,
followed by the secular cabildo, proceeded to the Church of Our
Señora de Monserrate, where the ecclesiastical cabildo with the
prior was waiting for him, to hear the benediction and listen to
the Te Deum; afterwards His Excellency mounted his horse and
began the public paseo, the secular cabildo behind him, with the
canopy and the two alcaldes ordinarios holding cords attached to the
reins of His Excellency's horse and the majordomo of the city in the
rear with the council secretary; he came by the customary streets to
the Cathedral, at the main door of which stood the archbishop with
the ecclesiastical cabildo and nearby an altar for the utterance of a
prayer[.] This done all the participants resumed the paseo and got
on their horses to accompany His Excellency to the palace[.] And
thus concluded the function of the day.[13]

On the ensuing days receptions and entertainments augmented
the gala mood of the populace. The viceroy shared the hospitality of
the cabildo at a banquet in the casa de ayuntamiento. For this occasion
the capitulars and their ladies exhibited their finest apparel, imitating
the latest style and fashion of the court at Madrid. The conciliar uniforms were of crimson velvet or of damask lined with satin, bedecked
with jewelry. For the reception of Velasco in 1596 the costumes were
"of crimson velvet, lined with mulberry-colored satin, velvet caps,
and with bands of taffeta of the same color around the crowns, with-

13. Minutes of Dec. 3, 1776, Libros de cabildos de Lima, vol. XXXVI, Biblioteca
municipal, Lima.

It is curious to note that the only record in the libros de cabildos of a communication from the city of Buenos Aires prior to 1800 has to do with this ceremony. The
La Plata council, remembering Lima's abundant experience in this connection, solicited
in 1790 an account of the "ceremonial that was observed in the public acts and
fiestas in honor of the viceroy and the real audiencia." See minutes of Feb. 19, 1790,
ibid., vol. XXXVIII.

out gold or plumes, or other finery, except for gold chains about their necks."[14] Even their servants wore a special livery for the occasion.[15]

Typical costumes for limeño aristocrats for *fiestas de gala* are described in this way:

[They were] clothed according to Spanish style, in black hose of costly workmanship, short mantle or cloak with gold clasps or crystal buttons planted in gold [castings], caps with bands set with diamonds, with crests and graceful plumes, valuable jewels on top of the fold of the cap with richest pieces of gold with most curious enamels and enchased in them diamonds, rubies and topazes of great value.

They were accustomed to go richly adorned with flesh-colored or deep-red cloth and cloaks of velillo silver and gold, of the color of mother-of-pearl, a lo gascon . . . [in] garments of color, the finest fabric of gold and scarlet and velvet with gold borders, mantles of flesh-colored velillo, plumed hats with bands set with precious stones. . . . He [a limeño] was wearing on the lower part of his body a crimson hose richly embroidered with spangles and caught with silver, white boots, and gilded spurs, and from the waist upwards, a coat of mail, breast plate and shoulder piece gilded with seven [bands of cloth] and fashioned with parts of gold, sleeve of crimson and over it half bracelets and the edges of the armour of rich crimson material and of silver, a black court hat, with two angles, red and white, with crests and a jewel and band of diamonds, a red sash a lo español, decorated with silver, a sword, and gold dagger.[16]

Invariably, bullfighting was a feature of the public spectacle promoted by the cabildo to celebrate the event. It was a delight for the masses and the upper class. As a general rule, there were five *corridas de toros*, two in honor of the viceroy's emissary and three for the Spanish dignitary. The site for the Iberian equivalent of the Roman circus was the Plaza de Armas, enclosed for the event and sometimes provided with a wooden floor. At three o'clock in the afternoon, the municipal alcalde, who held the keys of the plaza, entered the ring astride a horse and rode around it to make sure that preparations had been completed. From seats on a platform under the arches of the portals of the casa de cabildo, the viceroy, his wife, members of the audiencia, and the captain of the guard viewed the mortal combat

14. Bromley, "Recibimiento de virreyes," p. 27.
15. The cost of the outfits used by the eleven regidores of Lima for Jáuregui's reception was over 1,900 pesos, the livery for the servants amounting to over 1,200 pesos. See *ibid.*, pp. 27, 28.
16. *Ibid.*, p. 27.

of man against beast. In each corrida twenty to twenty-five bulls were killed by paid matadors or sometimes by *caballeros* out of mere sport.[17] *Juegos de cañas*, in which squads of horsemen pretended to engage in ardent warfare, aroused the excitement of the crowds. Having wide appeal also were *juegos de sortiza*, which required dexterity on the part of riders in piercing a small iron ring with a lance at full gallop. After each taurine exhibition the cabildo served a collation to the Spanish guests, refreshments consisting of sweetcakes, lemon peels preserved in sugar, and quinces, together with beverages. The expense for the council was often not inconsiderable.[18]

In the last quarter of the eighteenth century Charles III introduced modifications in the ceremony of the recibimiento. His thought was to de-emphasize still further the role of the cabildo in colonial administration. The changes symbolized his policy of subordination of localism to centralism, of creole to crown. An additional reason was to alleviate the sorry state of municipal finances, induced in part by expenditures for viceregal entertainment. At his request the audiencia altered traditional rites in various ways. The retiring viceroy was authorized to meet his successor in Callao and deliver to him the bastón and on the following day the incumbent would enter the palace and there receive the oath of office from the *escribano de cámara*, a royal official, in the presence of the audiencia. Obviously, the cabildo played a minor part in the drama.[19]

A careful inspection of the protocol of the ceremony by the Visitador-General Jorge de Escobedo led to the issuance in 1787 of a set of regulations to be followed by incoming viceroys. A stickler for solemnity and dignity in every stage of the reception, Escobedo pre-

17. The conciliar bill for five corridas for Jáuregui was 16,673 pesos 4 reales. See *ibid.*, p. 32.
18. The account for five conciliar collations for Jáuregui and his entourage was rendered thus:

31 flasks of *helado* ("iced drinks") 9 ps. ea.	1,395 ps.	
23 platters of sweetmeats each day at 10 ps. each.	1,150	
Conveyance and serving the above	33	6 rs.
10 dozen glasses for the drinks	30	
3 dozen Chilean pitchers for the iced water	4	4
5 *arrobas* of snow	15	5
Total	2,628 ps.	7 rs.

See *ibid.*, p. 33.
19. Teodoro de Croix, whose induction did not occur until Aug. 25, 1784, some four months after his arrival in the city, was the last viceroy to take the oath before the cabildo according to tradition. See *ibid.*, pp. 102, 103.

scribed in detail, with few omissions, almost every movement of the new functionary from the moment of his arrival at the port until he occupied his quarters in the palace. Not only was the hour of disembarking at Callao prescribed, but even the seating arrangements in the coach that was to carry the high officials of the government to the capital. His meticulousness in this respect approaches the point of the ludicrous.

Before Escobedo's rules for the reception were approved by the crown in 1788, they were amended by the audiencia. The chief modification related to the status of the cabildo:

> As to the acceptance of the oath, let the fueros and lawful privileges of the cabildo be kept, or let it be understood that this is included in the obligation that His Excellency takes in the Real Acuerdo to maintain justice, or let the cabildo have recourse to His Excellency by convenient declaration once the solemnity of the public entry is abolished, at the beginning of which the oath was formerly taken.[20]

The revised protocol relegated the cabildo to the background in the ceremony in line with general crown policy. The intentional neglect by Escobedo of the oath to maintain intact the municipal fuero was pointed out by the audiencia and at its insistence was apparently reinserted. In the new procedure members of the ayuntamiento met the incoming viceroy near the capital and escorted him to the palace. The swearing-in of the royal representative took place in the *sala de acuerdo* in the presence of the oidores of the audiencia. As in the past, the alcaldes and regidores provided the banquet and sponsored the public entertainment. A distinct gain for the cabildo was the ending of the unpopular practice of the palio, which was in disuse until restored by O'Higgins in his *entrada* in 1796 by virtue of a royal order of May 7, 1794. There is little doubt that Escobedo believed that the effect of his order would be to avoid undue expenses by the capitulars for uniforms and other paraphernalia essential for a paseo. In this respect it had a temporary success. However, a rising price level in the 1790's compelled the cabildo to petition the audiencia for authority to spend more than the regular quota, a request that was generally granted.[21]

20. *Ibid.*, pp. 16-18.
21. Escobedo's *reglamento*, "regulations," were in part disregarded after 1794, but

The arrival or the departure of a viceroy elicited letters from the municipal councils. For the new official there were expressions of good wishes for his success and offers of co-operation in the solution of problems. When a viceroy relinquished office, commendatory notes from the cabildos or the lack thereof might be a clue to the extent of his accomplishments or to his popularity. Such communications were sometimes of value in the outcome of the residencia. The meritorious achievements of the Conde de Superunda in the salvation of Lima after the great disaster of 1746 and in the general implementation of good works drew praise from the capital, Oruro, Guamanga, Piura, Trujillo, Arequipa, La Paz, Potosí, and Cuzco. In reply to a carta of May 20, 1761, from the Viceroy, announcing his impending retirement, the cabildo of Lima had difficulty finding words to indicate the depth of its gratitude for his efforts in behalf of the city:

> The satisfaction that this city and all the Kingdom has had from the Glorious Policy with which Your Excellency has governed, happily over a long period of sixteen years—as much in the rebuilding of this capital, after its total ruin in the earthquake of 28 October, 1746, and particularly in the splendid works of the fortress at Callao, of the cathedral, of the royal palace, of the mint . . . as in the subjection of the Indians, who for many years threatened the peace of the mountains beyond Tarma—[all of this] brings home to this city the departure of the most important figure of Your Excellency. . . . But our acceptance of the royal decision is necessary and when Your Excellency leaves he has the consolation of knowing that this capital and the entire kingdom will manifest forever in its eulogies a well-deserved gratitude.[22]

Formal notice of the resignation on August 8, 1796, of Gil de Taboada y Lemus, viceroy during the critical period of conflict with the

were reintroduced *in toto* by real cédula of March 3, 1806. The last viceroy, de la Serna, chosen by a junta of the military officers in 1821 during the final stage of the revolution, had no recibimiento. See *ibid.*, pp. 106-108.

22. Representaciones de cabildos, legajo 787, Audiencia de Lima, A. G. I.

Another viceroy possessing the esteem of the limeños was Manuel de Guirior (1776-1780). Upon his recovery from a serious illness, shortly before his departure from the city, the council instructed the majordomo to provide funds for a solemn mass in the cathedral "to give thanks to God for the speedy convalescence of the Most Excellent Viceroy." See minutes of July 17, 1780, Libros de cabildos de Lima, vol. XXXVI, Biblioteca municipal, Lima. The act taking place on the anniversary of his reception became a target during the residencia for his enemies, who sarcastically referred to it as the "coronation." See Vargas Ugarte, *Historia del Perú, virreinato (siglo XVIII) 1700-1790*, p. 389.

revolutionary government of France, brought commendation from many councils. The resolution adopted by the ayuntamiento of Trujillo expressed admiration for his exercise of impartial justice to all subjects of the realm and for his bold measures of defense in the late war.[23]

Important events affecting members of the royal family were noted in the colonial municipalities by acts of jubilation or mourning. The cabildo of Arequipa informed Ferdinand VI in a carta of May 28, 1748, of the celebration of the good tidings of his accession to the throne. Even comedies were staged as a special feature in the main square, there being no theater to accommodate the actors and audience.[24]

Lima honored the birth of the Prince of Astrias Luis, son of Philip V and Isabel of Savoy, with two days of bullfighting and acts of largesse by the council at a cost of 4,000 pesos.[25]

By the eighteenth century some cities and towns had developed celebrations and fiestas peculiarly their own. Their uniqueness is evidence of a survival of local pride and self-reliance. Needing something to take the place of the brilliant occasion of the reception of the viceroy in Lima, the lesser places commemorated annually incidents in their past or customs associated with civic institutions. Naturally, Cuzco, as the second city in the audiencia in renown and wealth with the visible remains of the Inca civilization in its temples and thick walls, disclosed originality in its fiestas and social life. The election of the members of the ayuntamiento was the pretext for a splendid fiesta, which, according to travelers, surpassed in magnificence and duration the festivities honoring royal officials and even the festivities honoring the day on which the city was founded by the conquistador Francisco Pizarro. A holiday mood pervaded the entire city and eased the strain and tension of racial and class distinctions. To the *corridas de toros*, "bullfights," the populace looked for its major source of entertainment.[26]

23. Residencia del virrey Gil de Taboada y Lemus, legajo 21293, numero 220, Consejo de Indias, Archivo histórico nacional, Madrid.
    There are also letters in this legajo from Arequipa, Huánuco, Moquegua, Yca, and Tarma.
24. Correspondencia de los virreyes, legajo 417, Audiencia de Lima, A. G. I.
25. Minutes of March 9, June 2, 1708, Libros de cabildos de Lima, vol. XXXIII, Biblioteca municipal, Lima.
26. Bustamante Carlos Inca, *El Lazarillo*, pp. 353, 354.

Throughout the colonial period the municipalities called special attention to the anniversary of the day of founding. There were parades, headed by the alcaldes and the regidores, acts of homage to the king, and the final ceremonies taking place in the cathedral. But in the last century of royal rule references in the libros de cabildos to the annual act of raising the sovereign's standard are scattered and perfunctory. Apparently, it had less significance than in earlier times when the municipal councils exercised greater authority.[27] The indifference of the ayuntamiento of Lima in 1793 toward the *paseo del estandarte* prompted an oficio from the viceroy, requiring all regidores to take part in the ceremony. In 1797, the viceroy's successor O'Higgins was forced to impress upon the councilors the gravity of the occasion.[28]

In the lives of the people of all classes it goes without saying that religious fiestas played no less important a role than in the past. The number of these had increased rather than decreased with the passage of time. The affluence of the church and the orders and the almost innumerable secular and regular clergy made the age-old, slow-moving processions awesome and the crowded but dignified services in the cathedral or temple impressive.[29] While the creoles offered proper obeisance to the representation of the Virgin as she was borne through the streets on the shoulders of the believers, Indians knelt in the crowd, overcome at the sight of their patron and benefactor. With the passing of the mood of religious exaltation, the natives gave vent to their pleasure by imbibing excessive quantities of *chicha*, a favorite fermented drink, or by experiencing the stupefying effects of narcotics. For this failing, custom, and the dread of cold, hunger, and hard work were to blame.

In the opinion of the visitador and his devoted companion Concolorcorvo, Cuzco celebrated Corpus Christi with more earnestness than it did any other feast of a religious character. Although deeply spiritual, to the Spanish observers it had a humorous side. The gro-

---

27. Minutes of Dec. 11, 1771, Dec. 10, 1772, Libros de cabildos de Lima, vol. XXXVI, Biblioteca municipal, Lima.

28. Libros de cédulas y provisiones del archivo histórico de la municipalidad de Lima, libro XXX, fojas 349, 415; libro XXXI, foja 1, Biblioteca municipal, Lima.

29. But some aspects of the church's financial policy were less appealing toward the end of the eighteenth century. Limeños were reluctant to contribute to the Santa Cruzada, or special levy, so that the crown had to issue cédulas to compel acceptance in 1783, 1785, 1787, 1791. See *ibid.*, libro XXX, fojas 67, 73, 76, 113, 126, 186.

tesque costumes and movements of the Indians seemed hardly in keeping with the profound gravity of their mien:

> The second part of the procession is truly ludicrous, but it appears to me that it goes back to great antiquity because it is not possible to judge it from the standpoint of obsequiousness, much less from that of superstition. The dances of the Indians, who come from all the parishes and provinces roundabout, are very serious in their execution, because the nation is so by nature. The chiefs are adorned with solid silver pieces, rented from mestizos in this business, and likewise with linens, mirrors, plates with pictures engraven thereon, and candlesticks.[30]

Lima added to its roster of patrons in the eighteenth century Our Lady of the Mercedes, *Patrona de los Campos*. It was claimed that intercession by the Virgin of the Mercedes had brought an end to a long, drawn-out drought affecting ranches in the neighborhood of the city. Thereupon the council stipulated an annual fiesta in her honor.[31]

Over points of etiquette during the fiestas and ceremonials the cabildo found itself frequently at loggerheads with ecclesiastics and royal officials. For the most part these disputes originated in the seating arrangements in the church or palace and in the matter of rank in the multitudinous processions characterizing colonial public life. The ayuntamiento struggled tenaciously to preserve its position and self-respect. Some of these quarrels could not be easily patched up and eventually went to Spain for arbitration. While the Council of the Indies undoubtedly disliked such trivia, it recognized the fact that they were a by-product of a system that permitted appeals from virtually all governmental bodies to the highest authority.

---

30. Bustamante Carlos Inca, *El Lazarillo*, pp. 352, 353.

31. Minutes of Feb. 20, 1730, Libros de cabildos de Lima, vol. XXXIV, Biblioteca municipal, Lima.

The Order of the Merced had one of the churches in Lima worthy of mention in this period. It was especially noted for its "high altar, an admirable work of art, the arrangement of its stalls of the sacristy, each costing 9,000 pesos, and for its magnificent jewelry, such as a lamp of more than a thousand silver marks, a Christ child, whose cradle had gold and pearl nails, a silver carriage, and in it a sphere of gold with a piece of cloth adorned with pearls and another with emeralds of prodigious value." See Patrón, "Lima antigua," in *Monografías históricas*, p. 192.

It was one of the orders whose financial activities were regarded with suspicion by the Viceroy Castelfuerte, because its vicar, dying unexpectedly in Portobello, was found to be carrying to Spain on his person the sum of 180,000 pesos in silver and doubloons. See Vargas Ugarte, *Historia del Perú, virreinato (siglo XVIII), 1700-1790*, p. 167.

The history of Lima provides a typical instance of contention between the secular and the ecclesiastical bodies over precedence in public functions. On one occasion the Tribunal of the Inquisition declared that the ayuntamiento should march as a body behind its members during the ceremony of the promulgation of the Edicts of Faith in accord with a real cédula of May 23, 1649. At the instigation of the cabildo, who regarded this as contrary to immemorial custom, the Viceroy Marqués de Villagarcía permitted the aldermen to mingle as individuals with the Inquisitors. The controversy was renewed again in February, 1746, when the tribunal endeavored to enforce its former directive. In a carta of July 31, 1746, the Viceroy Superunda referred the question to the Consejo de Indias, which finally rendered a decision in favor of the Inquisition.[32]

The Lima ayuntamiento resented the disdainful and condescending attitude shown by the audiencia at receptions attended by the viceroy. The members of the administrative court preferred to stand apart and have little to do or say with the capitulars. In November, 1761, the cabildo took steps to assure its proper status and rank at the reception and ball to be given by the Viceroy Amat. It was resolved to prepare a consulta to the retiring Viceroy Superunda, pointing out the fact that the cabildo and the audiencia should be "a single body as His Majesty desires it at the repasts that are offered in the viceroy's palace."[33] There being no immediate response, the cabildo discussed the matter again a month later.[34] Since the question disappears from the conciliar records, it is probable that the council won its point.

Insistence by the council on its social prerogatives sometimes involved it with notorious personalities of the day.[35]

32. Informe con testimonio de los autos formados en punto de la asistencia del cavildo secular de Lima con los ministros del Sto. Oficio, Cartas de virreyes, legajo 417, Audiencia de Lima, A. G. I.

33. Minutes of Nov. 18, 1761, Libros de cabildos de Lima, vol. XXXVI, Biblioteca municipal, Lima.

Complaints against the overbearing attitude of the oidores were common. See Cartas de cabildos, legajo 428, Audiencia de Lima, A. G. I.

34. Minutes of Dec. 19, 1761, Libros de cabildos de Lima, vol. XXXVI, Biblioteca municipal, Lima.

35. The ayuntamiento of Lima asserted exclusive right to certain boxes in the local theater, the only one of its kind in the audiencia. The claim involved the cabildo in a dispute once more with the famous comedienne La Perricholi, the Viceroy Amat's mistress. According to the local scribe, the actress had converted one of the three rooms assigned to the cabildo into a dressing room, with space for her friends and relatives. So outraged were the regidores that it was resolved to dispatch the alférez, alguacil mayor, and the procurator to clear the room. Apparently,

The evidence clearly indicates that the capitulars gave excessive attention and thought to the public social functions and ceremonials. Conciliar time and money could well have been put to better ends![36] Yet the need for the creole to compensate for the denial of real self-government and a natural inclination of both Spaniard and Indian for leisure and rejoicing made them inevitable. The most important celebration in Lima was the recibimiento of the viceroy, always attended by pomp and ceremony. In a more modest way lesser cities honored the arrival of a new governor or corregidor, or centered their efforts on the commemoration of an event connected with their past. Still respected, though to a lesser degree, was the day of founding of the municipality. Religious holidays bulked large in the minds of a people who cherished orthodoxy to the point of fanaticism.

The crown's curtailment of the traditional role of the cabildo in the reception of the viceroy was looked upon as an unwarranted interference with its rights. The unique popular concession was the temporary abolition of the distasteful feature of the palio.[37] The disappearance of certain of the outward trappings of local authority deepened the distrust of the creoles. On the other hand, the deplorable state of municipal treasuries, unimproved materially by limitation on expenses for social functions, demanded scrutiny and overhauling by the crown.

---

this time the tables were turned and the cabildo emerged victorious. See minutes of Feb. 17, 1775, April 29, 1778, Libros de cabildos de Lima, vol. XXXVI, Biblioteca municipal, Lima; minutes of Dec. 11, 1783, *ibid.*, vol. XXXVII; see also note 54, chap. iv.

36. In 1702 the procurator of Lima petitioned the viceroy to the effect that alcaldes and regidores wasted a large part of their time attending baptisms, betrothals, and receptions of persons newly arriving, thus neglecting their duties. In response a vice-regal provision of 1702 forbade the council to assemble for the above-named purposes unless the person honored was the viceroy or a member of the audiencia, under penalty of a fine of 50 pesos for each individual, double the amount for the second offense, and for the third, suspension from office. Subsequent publication of the same order points to its non-observance. See Cartas de virreyes, legajo 428, Audiencia de Lima, A. G. I.

37. See chap. x, "Limited Resurgence of Municipal Rights."

CHAPTER VI

Civic Finances

From the early days of the Conquest finances posed a serious problem for the municipalities of Peru.[1] This perennial problem became progressively acute in the eighteenth century for a number of reasons that are associated with the gradual decline of the civic regimes. The loss of established income through sale or seizure by private individuals of municipal property, an increase in expenditures and costs of government operation, inflationary prices, and finally faulty administration by the local councils tell the unhappy story. These factors are best seen in the history of Lima, for which the records are fullest. The difficulties and embarrassments that at times beset the viceregal capital confronted the lesser places in a similar fashion. Illustrations from the experience of Trujillo, Piura, and other towns bear this out. It should be noted that while there is a strong connection between the economic prosperity of the community and the state of the local treasury, this is not always the case. Nor did municipal income necessarily parallel receipts of crown taxes.

Was the crown unaware of the wretched condition of the municipal treasuries in the pre-intendancy period? Did it fail completely to recognize the need for improved administration of this branch of local government? That the Council of the Indies had ample opportunity to learn of the financial distress of the municipalities in the Audiencia of Lima is evident from the memorias of two prominent viceroys of the mid-century era. These reports stress the plight of the localities, though attributing it primarily to conciliar neglect in the handling of funds. The Conde de Superunda deplored the state of Lima's finances: "The propios and rents that this cabildo

1. See Moore, *Cabildo in Peru*, pp. 157-167.

has would be sufficient if those who should look after them would use the same vigilance that they do with their own affairs; but they do not attend to such important business, and when it is necessary to implement some public work, the money is lacking and cannot be collected from arbitrios."[2] His successor, the Viceroy Amat, continued in the same vein with reference to the cities of the region in general: "The propios and rents of the cities are of limited extent and those of this one [Lima] amount to 25,000 to 28,000 pesos each year; they could be greater if there was the attention and care that these privileged funds should have and they [would be] of advantage for so many public works."[3]

It would seem that the long existence of this condition was because of the apathetic, neglectful attitude of the early Bourbons toward over-all colonial reform and an optimistic but naïve assumption by the crown that a sufficient number of laws were on the statute books to curb the improvidence of the local councils if duly enforced. If it occurred to these rulers that more drastic measures might be required than mere enforcement of existing legislation, they lacked the will to act.

To safeguard municipal finances, numerous regulations had been issued in the past by the Hapsburgs. They aimed at the avoidance of unwise expenditures by the cabildos and at the protection of local treasuries from unscrupulous and dishonest bursars. The Laws of the Indies declared that the council of Lima might not spend more than 12,000 pesos for fiestas and ceremonies attending the installation of a viceroy. If the amount was greater than that stipulated, the crown might collect the difference from the person authorizing the payment.[4] By a decree of 1564, reissued by Charles II, municipalities were required to observe to the letter the ordinances enacted by the crown governing financial procedures. No extraordinary expense beyond 3,000 maravedis could be incurred without royal permission; nor could salaries be assigned to any person without royal approval having first been secured, under penalty of recovering the amount or amounts from those responsible for the payment. No regidor was to assume duties as commissioner in the pay of the municipality. Municipal

2. *Memorias de los virreyes que han gobernado el Perú*, IV, 107, 108.
3. Rodríguez y Pérez, *Memoria de gobierno de Amat*, p. 179.
4. *Recopilación*, libro III, título III, ley XIX.

treasurers could not authorize *libranzas* for extraordinary expenses of regidores, unless the payment had been sanctioned by the real audiencia or by the governor residing in the city. It was not necessary to obtain approval for expenses of this nature amounting to less than 3,000 maravedis, it being understood that proper notation of these expenses would be made in the municipal accounts. But in viceregal cities customs established by royal representatives were to take precedence over the above regulations.[5]

Municipal property was to be leased publicly to the highest bidder with no favors being shown to previous renters.[6] Cabildos were required to refrain from making extraordinary expenses for the reception of agents other than the viceroy, under penalty of 1,000 pesos for each infraction and having the act considered as a special indictment during the visita or residencia.[7] In the payment of ordinary debts and expenses the municipalities might act in complete freedom without interference of viceroy or audiencia.[8] By a law of Philip II, in 1573, viceroys, presidents of audiencias, and governors were to be held responsible for the annual auditing of municipal accounts by royal agents and for the dispatch of statements of these to the Council of the Indies for its information.[9] In every town having an audiencia, a member of this body in turn had to check the accounts of the municipal propios.[10] When a leasing by the cabildo of the right to supply provisions to the town or of municipal properties took place, an oidor had to be present and report to the audiencia before the act was made binding on both parties.[11] Before a license to collect fines was renewed by the crown, the municipality was obliged to submit to the royal officials a statement of the income from its propios and rents and of expenditures. Unless these facts were made available, no renewal was to be considered.[12] Finally, a municipality could authorize expenses for the funeral ceremonies of royal persons, provided the amount was not excessive.[13]

Despite its good intentions and its deceptive inclusiveness, this legislation was not enforced nor did it go far enough in conserving and supplementing the meager sources of municipal funds. The pre-

5. *Ibid.*, libro IV, título XIII, ley II.   6. *Ibid.*, ley III.
7. *Ibid.*, ley IV.   8. *Ibid.*, ley V.
9. *Ibid.*, ley VI.   10. *Ibid.*, ley VII.
11. *Ibid.*, ley VIII.   12. *Ibid.*, ley IX.
13. *Ibid.*, ley X.

carious state of Lima's finances, paralleled by that of other cities, shows the existence of a grave but not insoluble problem.

Almost from the beginning of the eighteenth century Lima's financial troubles were apparent. As early as January, 1715, in a discussion over a decreto from the viceroy ordering a reduction in the rent of the *derecho de mojonasgo*, "excise on spirits and wine," it was pointed out that the city could ill afford to lose the income "in view of the fact that the propios and rents of this city are so slight and that there are not sufficient funds for the annual expenses." The council, nevertheless, agreed to accept the will of the viceroy in the matter.[14] Again, in 1737, the majordomo cited the need for additional sources of income, "the propios being so attenuated that they hardly permit payment of required expenses."[15] The disastrous earthquake that destroyed much of Lima and severely damaged the casa de cabildo put a heavy strain on limited resources.[16] Lacking funds for the paving of the plaza mayor in 1759, the cabildo was forced to borrow 2,000 pesos from a citizen at 6 per cent interest.[17] Indebtedness attained the figure of 47,467 pesos in 1764, which necessitated an examination of measures for its reduction.[18] When informed of the approaching marriage of the Prince of Asturias, the ayuntamiento signified its inability to prepare a suitable celebration because of the "condition of its propios and that of its obligations which are more than 50,000 pesos."[19] In deferring payment of salaries to the royal chaplains in 1778, the majordomo alluded to "the poor state of the propios."[20]

Of a similar nature were the difficulties confronting the cabildo of Trujillo. The restricted extent of the propios gave pause for thought to the councilors who hoped to celebrate in an appropriate manner the accession of Charles III. In July, 1760, the cabildo proposed the expenditure of 1,000 pesos for this purpose, with a portion coming from the regular revenues and the rest to be prorated among the

14. Minutes of Jan. 11, 1715, Libros de cabildos de Lima, vol. XXXIV, Biblioteca municipal, Lima.
15. Minutes of April 13, 1737, *ibid.*, vol. XXXIV.
16. Minutes of July 1, 1747, *ibid.*, vol. XXXV.
17. Minutes of Oct. 31, 1759, *ibid.*, vol. XXXVI.
18. Minutes of Nov. 15, 1764, *ibid.*, vol. XXXVI.
19. A viceregal decreto of Oct. 13, 1766, forced compliance on the part of the council. Apparently a loan was negotiated for this purpose. See minutes of Oct. 16, 1766, *ibid.*, vol. XXXVI.
20. Autos que siguen los Capellanos Rs. sobre que se les pague su salario por el majordomo de la ciud. año 1778, Cabildos, legajo 3, Archivo nacional, Lima.

citizenry.[21] Inability to raise the money, "the propios being scanty," forced a postponement of festivities in January, 1761.[22] No fiesta having been given by April, the corregidor lectured the ayuntamiento on its procrastination, with the result that he offered to give 100 pesos and the capitulars offered to give 50 each.[23] A climax in financial straits apparently came in 1775. In that year the deterioration of the propios was such that the council had to suspend the salary of the procurator and contributions to certain fiestas.[24] The arrival of the incoming Viceroy Guirior at Payta, the port for Trujillo, called for preparations for a fitting reception. However, the cabildo, considering the scarcity of propios, was unable to carry out any elaborate ceremony. In order to economize, it was resolved to dispatch the alguacil mayor and the alférez real as commissioners to greet the royal representative.[25] Undoubtedly, other cities and towns felt relatively as much the pinch of insufficient income and increasing expenses.

An analysis of the various items of expenditure and of the diverse sources of income will reveal clearly the unsound financial position of the municipality. Unfortunately, no set of figures showing a complete list of expenses and sources of revenue for any single year prior to the advent of the intendancy is at hand for any city or town in the audiencia.[26] It is possible, however, to estimate general amounts or totals in some cities for certain years. In 1750, when the cabildo of Lima saw the danger of an Indian uprising accompanied by native riots in the city it appealed to the Conde de Superunda to station units of cavalry and infantry in the city. In considering a proposal to turn over a site for the construction of a barracks, it estimated the annual rents at 18,000 pesos, with ordinary expenses at 14,000 pesos, not counting the "extraordinary expenses that occur every year" and the payment of interest on municipal debts. In round figures the indebtedness was 33,000 pesos, 7,000 pesos being owed to the crown without interest but the principal to be repaid periodically at 1,000

21. Minutes of July 16, 1760, Libros de cabildos de Trujillo, vol. XV.
22. Minutes of Jan. 20, 1761, *ibid.*, vol. XV.
23. Minutes of April 10, 1761, *ibid.*, vol. XV.
24. Minutes of Aug. 25, 1775, *ibid.*, vol. XV.
25. Minutes of May 31, 1776, *ibid.*, vol. XV.
26. Accounts and receipts are missing from the Municipal Archives in Lima. The figures given were obtained from the Libros de cabildos and various and sundry legal documents to be found in the National Archives and the Archivo de Ministerio de Hacienda, Lima.

pesos a year. The remaining 26,000 pesos, on which interest was due, were owed to various individuals and bodies. The result was that if the city met with further extraordinary outlays, it would be forced to consider omission of regular expenditures.[27] Nevertheless, in view of the emergency, the council at a later session agreed to offer the sum of 20,000 pesos toward the putting up of a building to house the soldiers, with a contribution of 3,000 pesos each year.[28] Deficit financing was not unknown in colonial days!

An itemized list of ordinary expenses for Lima for the year 1766 is extant. From one standpoint this may be taken as a normal year, no extraordinary expenses having been incurred. Paradoxically, from another viewpoint it may be regarded as abnormal, in view of the frequency of the extraordinary outlays in other years. A breakdown of the expenditures into various categories is as follows:

1. Salaries		
(1) Municipal officials	6,230 ps.	7 rs.
(2) Guards	220	
(3) Other functionaries	1,671	
	8,121	7
2. Interest on loans	565	
3. Other expenses	743	4
4. Endowed fiestas	1,400	
	10,830 ps.	3 rs.[29]

27. Minutes of Oct. 5, 1750, Libros de cabildos de Lima, vol. XXXV, Biblioteca municipal, Lima.

28. Minutes of Oct. 22, 1750, *ibid.*, vol. XXXV.

29. It is interesting to note the salaries paid to members of the cabildo and other municipal functionaries:

2 Alcaldes (55 ps. each)	110	
Alférez	360	2 rs.
Alguacil mayor	55	
6 Regidores (55 ps. each)	330	
Secretario de cartas	300	1
Contador	337	4
Juez de aguas	1,412	4
Escribano mayor	325	
Majordomo	959	4
Procurador-general	437	4
2 Asesores (450 ps. each)	900	
2 Porteros (351 ps. and 2 rs. each)	702	4
Guarda de la caja de agua	100	
Guarda de la alameda	120	
7 Ministros (commissioners)	996	

While the decaying municipality of Piura for 1773-1774 had virtually a balanced budget, the reduced nature of the revenue permitted payment of only minimum salaries to a few officials. The allocation of the sum of just over 500 pesos for the two-year period followed a slightly different pattern from that of Lima:

1. Salaries	52 ps.	4 rs.
2. Fiestas	84	
3. Other expenses	364	7
	501 ps.	3 rs.[30]

A scrutiny of the figures for the two cities discloses the relatively small amount expended annually for ordinary needs in terms of population. On the basis of 40,000 inhabitants for Lima in 1766, this is roughly .25 pesos per person and for Piura in 1773, with 5,000 population (estimated), .05 pesos per capita. Mexico City, with a population at least twice as great as that of Lima, expended .64 pesos per person. Salaries consumed approximately 80 per cent of the Lima budget as opposed to 11 per cent for Piura, reflecting the considerable size of

Procurador	50
Capellan (chaplain)	300
Escribano teniente	100
Contraste	225
8,121 ps.	7 rs.

See Expediente formado con motivo del superior decreto de 25 de enero 1772 . . . por el cual se ordenaba una immediata revisión en las cuentas a cargo de Don Felipe José de Colmenares, mayordomo de los propios y rentas del cabildo, justicia y regimiento de esta muy noble y leal ciudad de los Reyes, Cabildos, legajo 3, Archivo nacional, Lima.

Mexico City made a slightly better showing with an income of around 60,000 pesos and expenses of 64,000 to 69,000, thus incurring a small deficit. A breakdown of expenditures shows the familiar pattern:

1. Salaries	10,612 ps.	
2. Interest on loans	9,665	
3. Fiestas	4,600	
4. Other expenses		
Public works	24,400	
Maintenance of aqueducts	15,000 or 20,000	
	64,277 or 69,277 ps.	

There is no provision made in the Mexican budget for extraordinary expenditures for social festivities, including the viceroy's reception and other gala activities. See Ramón Ezquerra Abadía, "Un presupuesto Americano: el del cabildo de Nueva Orleans al terminar la soberanía española," *Anuario de estudios Americanos*, V (1948), 697, 698.

30. Residencias, legajo 24, Archivo nacional, Lima.

the group of functionaries in the capital. The neglect of public works may emphasize the backwardness of the Lima council compared to the ayuntamiento of Mexico City, which was constantly alert to the upkeep of the aqueducts.[31] However, this is an item that might vary depending on the particular needs of the city. The annual contributions of the municipalities to religious celebrations were generally fixed with little variation from year to year.

Omitted from the list are the extraordinary expenditures to be made on very special occasions. At times these constituted a serious drain on municipal funds. Immemorial custom obligated the citizenry of Lima to honor the incoming viceroy with receptions and demonstrations of fealty and joy. To a lesser degree, the other cities and towns bore the onus of entertainment for a corregidor or governor or of providing accommodations for a zealous viceroy on inspection tour or with a taste for travel. In 1707, the cabildo of Lima made preparations for the reception of the Marqués de Castell dos Rius, ordering a pyrotechnic display at night and the holding of bullfights on three consecutive days. An examination of the *cuentas* revealed that the expenses, "necessary and unavoidable," amounted to more than 12,000 pesos, probably not including certain "extras" to be presented later.[32] As time went on, the tendency was to increase rather than diminish the appropriations.

For the installation of the Viceroy Diego Ladrón de Guevara the cabildo, in a session of December 5, 1719, went on record that it did not know where to obtain "sufficient money." Nevertheless, an alcalde was authorized to make every effort to this end.[33] Celebrations for the Marqués de Villagarcía in 1736 were planned on a more elaborate scale, the costs being estimated at 16,800 pesos.[34] In 1761, the cabildo assigned approximately 17,000 pesos for the recibimiento of Amat.[35] If the appointee was a popular personality, the sum expended might be four or five times greater than the limit imposed by the Laws of the Indies. In such cases the ayuntamiento appealed for permission to the audiencia, usually citing as a pretext the high prices for food and

31. Ezquerra, "Un presupuesto Americano," p. 698.
32. Minutes of Sept. 12, 1707, Libros de cabildos de Lima, vol. XXXIV, Biblioteca municipal, Lima.
33. Minutes of Dec. 5, 1719, *ibid.*, vol. XXXIV.
34. Minutes of Oct. 11, 1735, *ibid.*, vol. XXXV.
35. Minutes of May 21, 1761, *ibid.*, vol. XXXVI.

articles of dress. Thus the outlay for Manuel de Guirior, one of the best-liked administrators, was more than 63,000 pesos.[36]

Beside the considerable appropriations to honor a newly designated viceroy, there were other unforeseen demands that taxed the slender treasury. Events associated with the royal family required an overt expression of jubilation or sorrow. A long list of public works necessitated the allocation of funds: construction of aqueducts, digging of canals, repairing the casa de cabildo and bridges, paving of streets, maintenance of an agent at the court at Madrid, and the prosecution of municipal lawsuits. The terrible catastrophe of 1746, leveling shops and buildings owned by the cabildo and disrupting streets and plazas, called for unusual measures to accomplish rehabilitation.[37]

Municipal revenue came from a variety of sources. The most significant of these were the leasing of the right to collect the mojonasgo, the renting of the seats and stalls on the plaza mayor, and the collecting of censos, or dues, from lots and other municipal properties. In addition, the municipality sold a number of offices, which permitted the holder to collect fees, among these being the inspectorship of weights and measures, the offices of crier, supplier of beef, and exchange broker.

The right to dispose by lease of the mojonasgo had been intermittently in the possession of the cabildo since the first quarter of the century.[38] From this source the city obtained, during the period from 1753 to 1762, 6,550 pesos annually, and from 1762-1765, 7,500 pesos annually. In view of the needs of the treasury and the increased value of the right to the purchaser, the cabildo entered into a five-year contract in 1771, stipulating the payment of 12,900 pesos a year. Subsequently, this source produced over 15,500 pesos annually.[39]

36. Bromley, "Los recibimientos de virreyes," p. 39.
37. In this instance the cabildo resorted to economies, reducing temporarily salaries and appropriations for fiestas. The schedule adopted lowered the salary of the water inspector from 1,412 pesos 4 reales to 1,112 pesos 4 reales, that of the alférez from 300 to 200 pesos, that of a guard from 300 to 200 pesos. Savings were effected also through reduction of appropriations for fiestas and through a voluntary cut of 10 per cent in the salaries for the majordomo, contador, and other functionaries. Alleging that their only emolument was the paltry sum of 50 pesos, the capitulars left their own salaries untouched. See minutes of July 1, 1747, Libros de cabildos de Lima, vol. XXXV, Biblioteca municipal, Lima.
38. Minutes of Jan. 11, 1715, ibid., vol. XXXIV.
39. It might be inferred from the memoria of Teodoro de Croix that this source of revenue was first made available to the municipality in 1757. See Memorias de los virreyes que han gobernado el Perú, V, 174. References to this concession by the crown

The crown usually denied this tax to all but the most outstanding municipalities or to those desperately in need of funds.[40]

Renting of space on the plaza mayor afforded another means of revenue to Lima. Instead of leasing each facility separately, the ayuntamiento gave the concession for the entire area to an individual, who in turn might sublease various sections. In 1774, in return for an annual payment of 5,000 pesos, a lessee had full use of the large area, obligating him, among other things, to clean up the square after the celebrations, including the corridas de toros, to replace broken paving stones, to keep the aqueducts free, and on the days appointed for the "tribunal and court of the alcaldes to set up the desk, chairs, and benches in rows."[41] Renting of municipal-owned sites on the banks of the Rimac and along the bridge brought in a considerable amount annually. Other rented property, consisting of a few fincas, "farms," and lots, scattered throughout the city or on its edge, classified as censos activos, contributed a smaller sum. This last-named source represented the remnant of property once held by the municipality in the form of commons, pasture land, and woodlands donated by the crown at the time of founding. Since the early days, the town had sold or granted its holdings to private citizens or had permitted illegal occupation. No further allotment of land had been made by the crown.[42]

A final source of revenue was the auctioning for a year or longer of offices having fees attached. The returns were generally unchanged from year to year though in a few cases higher profits for the holders enabled the city to arrange the leasing at new, more substantial figures.

It is obvious that while these sources were possibly adequate to meet ordinary expenses, they could not produce sufficient income for the extraordinary expenditures with which the councils were con-

go back much earlier. See Remate del dro. de mojonasgo hecho en Don Lorenzo de la Rosa, por cinco años por 15,500 pesos cada año, en 21 de mayo de 1776, Cabildos, legajo 3, Archivo nacional, Lima.

40. It was asserted in the council that other municipalities of the audiencia, notably Trujillo, Saña, Piura, had resorted to this right to the detriment of Lima, "without permission of the king or the Superior Government," See minutes of June 9, 1780, Libros de cabildos de Lima, vol. XXXVI, Biblioteca municipal, Lima.

41. Autos que sigue Dn. Juan Domingo Taron sobre la rebaja del arrendto. de la plaza mayor, año de 1774, Cabildos, legajo 3, Archivo nacional, Lima.

42. There are no references to extensive land grants made by the crown to the settlements of Galveztown, Fort Miro, and Lake Charles, founded by the Spanish in Lousiana, possibly in conformity with French procedure.

stantly faced. The 18,000 pesos, estimated for Lima in 1750, did not suffice to implement a program of public works or cover the costs of public ceremonies. Similarly, the propios of Trujillo in 1761 were described by the ex-corregidor as "very limited," consisting principally of a slaughterhouse and the *almojarifazgo*, "duty on wine and spirits," and bringing in annually about 950 pesos. The result was a growing indebtedness and an inability to fulfil many normal municipal functions.[43]

In order to raise extra money the cabildo had recourse to various expedients. The most common practice was to negotiate a loan from a religious community or some wealthy citizen, the propios being pledged for its repayment. In 1717, when fiestas were deemed necessary for the reception of the Viceroy Prince of Santo Buono, the Lima council was compelled to accept the offer of 4,000 pesos from one of the capitularies at the exorbitant interest rate of 8 per cent.[44] The number and diversity of debts, amounting to 24,277 pesos 6 reales, with interest rates of 5 and 6 per cent, induced the municipal accountant in 1756 to suggest to the council that the debts be consolidated and a refunding operation be carried out at a lower rate of interest.[45] At the next meeting of the council it was decided to empower the major-domo to solicit from the tribunal of the Inquisition or from some other source the sum of 30,000 pesos, essential for the refunding and payment of certain expenditures.[46] Prospective lenders were sometimes men holding special concessions and contracts from the municipality. For example, in 1737, acting on a petition from the majordomo, the council designated a commission to secure an advance from the holder

43. Relación de la ciudad y provincia de Truxillo, legajo 819, Audiencia de Lima, A. G. I.

Revenues of Mexico City in 1743 were similar to those of Lima but more extensive in view of the larger population and the necessity of maintaining an expensive system of lakes and aqueducts. The total income of 60,000 to 65,000 pesos was divided as follows: mojonasgo, 15,000 to 20,000 pesos; rentas de propios, 31,750 pesos; censos, 999 pesos, 4 reales; and offices, 14,950 pesos. In 1775, Santiago de Chile containing 15,000 to 20,000 people had an income of only 3,537 pesos, coming chiefly from rent of shops and fields and from the sale of snow. See Ezquerra, "Un presupuesto Americano," pp. 696-699.

44. Minutes of Oct. 6, 1717, Libros de cabildos de Lima, vol. XXXIV, Biblioteca municipal, Lima.

45. Minutes of Dec. 2, 1756, *ibid.*, vol. XXXV.

46. Minutes of Dec. 7, 1756, *ibid.*, vol. XXXV.

of the lucrative mojonasgo to the amount of 288 pesos 2 reales for the purchase of 210 pounds of wax.[47]

Outside of loans, there were few effective ways of supplementing the regular revenue. Spasmodically, and usually with little success, appeals were made to the crown to assign the proceeds from the *sisa,* "impost," on merchandise, livestock, and agricultural commodities entering or leaving the district. It was not unusual for the cabildo to request the crown to assume a portion of the expenses of a public work. If the municipality still held landed real estate, it might arrange a sale illegally.[48] The cabildo imposed few direct levies on the citizenry. It is clear that this recourse would have solved most of the difficulties, but opposition to this expedient from the vecinos was strong and only in emergencies could enough public spirit be mustered to overcome the aversion. Thrift was seldom practiced. But, in order to recover from the calamitous effects of the earthquake in 1746, the council reduced the remuneration of many officials for a two-year period. It may be to the credit of the cabildos that salaries remained virtually unchanged throughout the rest of the century so that no additional strain was put on the limited propios. On the other hand, an increase in compensation might have engendered among the councilors greater interest in civic affairs with perhaps more efficient administration.

A further financial responsibility of the cabildos was oversight of the assessment and collection of the alcabala. With the approval of the audiencia, the councils fixed the amounts to be paid annually by the individual guilds and submitted reports on receipts. The sales tax brought in a substantial sum to the royal exchequer.[49] One may obtain some idea of the relative importance of the various corporations from the size of their assessments. Although the gremios were often in arrears, the crown did not hold the councils accountable or expect them to make up the deficits. Complaints and remonstrances

47. Minutes of April 13, 1737, *ibid.,* vol. XXXV.
The special conditions sometimes attached to municipal borrowing are illustrated in a loan negotiated by the cabildo in 1780. See minutes of Dec. 20, 1780, *ibid.,* vol. XXXVI.
48. Rare instances of the sale of land are recorded in the council book. In 1748 the viceroy declared null and void a sale of lots to Juan Baptista Vidaurre. See minutes of Sept. 5, 1748, *ibid.,* vol. XXXV.
49. See chap. ii, "Revitalization of Old Concepts in America."

against the rate and amount of the payments to the crown were registered with the councils in the Audiencia of Lima, but the imposition did not lead to acts of open resistance encountered in other audiencias and viceroyalties.

In addition to limited sources and the extraordinary expenditures, shortage of municipal funds resulted from other circumstances. Favoritism and graft in financial transactions existed to a considerable extent. Numerous lawsuits directed by individuals against the cabildo suggest an element of truth in the charge that partiality and nepotism determined the awarding of contracts. The regidores themselves were not above suspicion as profiteers in municipal business. No satisfactory system of collecting and disbursing funds was in operation. It was customary for the majordomo to have conciliar approval for the negotiating of loans and for the payment of extraordinary expenses and, at the end of the year, for him to submit the accounts to a member of the audiencia for approval. Although a great deal of time in conciliar sessions was devoted to debate over finances, the bursar still enjoyed considerable leeway and was sometimes tempted to engage in peculation.

It is probable that the crown did not realize fully the plight of the Lima council until the middle of the century. The inability of the ayuntamiento to raise funds for the reconstruction and repairs of buildings and streets in 1746 must have brought home to the Viceroy Superunda the need for the allocation of other sources of income and for the supervision of the use of funds. Nevertheless, nothing was done. In view of the cabildo's difficulty in arranging payment for his recibimiento, the Viceroy Amat appointed in January, 1762, a special judge to investigate the accounts of the majordomo.[50] The failure of the council to co-operate in the inquiry led to the issuance of a second decreto, admonishing it to produce the necessary records and accounts "with the greatest speed."[51] The subsequent examination of the papers by royal officials led to the indictment and eventual removal of the

50. In the 1760's Lima had a celebrated case involving alleged malversation by its majordomo, José de Colmares. Judges appointed by the ayuntamiento charged him with being short of funds to the amount of 2,387 pesos 3 reales during a long tenure of office. The resultant suit dragged out over a number of years, eventually going against the treasurer. See Expediente sobre los propios del cabildo de Lima, Cabildos, 3, Archivo nacional, Lima. See also minutes of Jan. 11, 1762, Libros de cabildos de Lima, vol. XXXVI, Biblioteca municipal, Lima.
51. Minutes of Jan. 12, 1764, *ibid.*, vol. XXXVI.

guilty individual. Despite the obvious need, Amat judged that no other step was feasible or urgent.

Deeming that municipal finances like almost everything else came within his purview, the Visitor-General José de Areche intervened in conciliar matters. In January, 1778, he peremptorily ordered the cabildo to prepare and submit to him a comprehensive report of financial transactions.[52] In time this was followed by the appointment of a *juez conservador*, "inspector" of *propios y rentas*, from the audiencia.[53] Neither of these two measures bore fruit.[54] The reasons for Areche's failure are examined in a subsequent chapter. It was evident that firmer, more resolute action by the crown was necessary.

The condition of municipal exchequers was symptomatic of the general unprogressiveness of local regimes. For the most part income remained the same and, thus, did not keep abreast of expenses which were steadily increasing. There was no consistent effort on the part of the crown to make available further sources, either in the form of land or excises, which might have afforded relief for pressing needs. Nevertheless, in a rough comparison of municipal per capita income, Lima's rating of .45 pesos in 1750 was above average among the following colonial cities: Santiago de Chile .14 pesos in 1775, Buenos Aires .17 in 1784, and Mexico City .60 in 1743.[55]

Could expenditures have been limited to normal outlays for salaries and fiestas, a balanced budget would not have been impossible, despite rising prices. However, with no provision for additional funds the cabildo was forced to incur indebtedness to pay for public works that could not be postponed and for extraordinary ceremonies and celebrations connected with the arrival and departure of royal officials. Over a long period the trend was to neglect any worthwhile program of civic development. The lack of a uniform system of collection and disbursement created confusion in keeping accurate accounts and encouraged embezzlement of public funds. Rigid supervision of municipal finances, though making the cabildo more dependent on the crown, was a justifiable function of the intendancy. Accompanying this reform should have been the access to other sources of revenue, a remedy for which countless appeals had been fruitless.

52. Minutes of Jan. 13, 1778, *ibid.*, vol. XXXVI.
53. Minutes of Feb. 10, 1778, Dec. 11, 1781, *ibid.*, vol. XXXVI.
54. Minutes of April 27, 1782, *ibid.*, vol. XXXVII.
55. See Ezquerra, "Un presupuesto Americano," pp. 675-702.

CHAPTER VII

Procurators, Petitions, and Popular Assemblies

Colonial cabildos in the eighteenth century realized the vital need of remonstrance and appeal to the crown for the relief of grievances and for the grant of beneficial concessions. The most effective means of making the Council of the Indies aware of municipal conditions was the maintenance of procurators and agents at the court in Madrid and at the viceregal capital. The dispatch of memorials and petitions was a common practice dating from the earliest days of colonization. A device that might have served as a powerful lever in relations with the crown was the cabildo abierto, the open assembly of citizens. But the potentialities of this organ were never realized until the revolutionary era.

The conciliar agent was the instrument best suited to keeping the crown informed as to what was transpiring in the American municipalities. Like the English settlers, the Spanish colonists had no right of representation in the assembly of the kingdom, the Cortes of Castile, of which the transatlantic region was an appendage. Advancement of civic interests could be most efficaciously assured through agents sent to Europe or through the designation of Spanish officials or persons in residence at the court for this purpose. In exceptional circumstances, lesser cities, through payment of a fee, might avail themselves of the services of agents sent from America by the wealthier municipalities. Thus Cuzco, having no regular agent abroad, was accustomed to employ the talents of the representative maintained by Lima. Unable to finance procurators in Spain, small localities sometimes hired lawyers or clerks residing in Lima or Mexico City to look after their interests in the viceregal centers.

At the beginning of the Bourbon era the right of the local council to dispatch procurators freely to the court at Madrid was open to question. Existing legislation apparently favored the cabildo. By a cédula of June 11, 1621, neither a city, town, place, religious, or secular community, nor university might send procurators to the court to plead its cause without permission of the viceroy or audiencia, and then only for matters "serious and unusual."[1] There was no objection to cartas written by these groups in their own behalf. A later law, issued on September 28, 1625, granted cities the authority to nominate agents at the court without restrictions or limitations from the viceroy or audiencia. Neither a relative of an oidor, nor alcalde ordinario, nor a fiscal of the audiencia might be elected to this position.[2] Although these laws empowered councils to dispatch procurators, the regidores of Lima in about 1700 entertained misgivings as to the privilege of representation at the court through special, elected individuals. Doubt on this score had been enhanced by the fact that the practice of sending agents had been discontinued after 1687 because of the general confusion in civic administration that ensued after the earthquake of that year. Hence it was believed essential to secure the king's approval for resumption of this custom. Accordingly, in 1701, the cabildo resolved to petition the king "to grant to the said city of Lima the authority, which according to law all the cities and places of these kingdoms possess in order that they may send to this court a procurator-general whenever it recognizes it to be suitable to the royal service and to the relief of that kingdom, speaking for itself and for the other cities of it [kingdom] as head of those provinces."[3] It was also requested that the city be allowed to pay its *apoderado*, "agent," an annual salary of 500 pesos, which had been provided in bygone years. The fiscal of the consejo, in a parecer of March 3, 1702, recommended approval of the petition on the grounds that the right had been given in the past to all secular and religious communities. In accepting this opinion, an acuerdo of the council on November 29, 1702, stated that henceforth the cabildo "might name its agent to the court and assign from its propios and rents 500 pesos as salary, without fear of interference or obstruction by the viceroy or audiencia."[4]

1. *Recopilación*, libro IV, título XI, ley V.
2. *Ibid.*, ley IV.
3. Cartas y expedientes de varios cabildos, legajo 428, Audiencia de Lima, A. G. I.
4. *Ibid.*

It is clear that conciliar motivation for the confirmation of this right came also from an apprehension of further interference by the higher colonial authorities in local matters.

The appointment of a new agent necessitated the dispatch of credentials and testimonials of his qualifications. In 1707, Lima proposed the name of Martín Zamudio to replace Nicolás de Mansilla. His dossier contained among other things a letter from the city, calling attention to his connections with the oldest families in the city and his experience as alcalde ordinario, and a commendation from the viceroy, with reference to his noble birth and his military service.[5] Upon his resignation another agent was quickly appointed. That the post was never allowed to remain vacant for any length of time is evidence of a realization by the cabildo of the importance of having a spokesman and advocate at the seat of power.[6]

Procurators were guided by general powers and by specific instructions incorporated in cartas drawn up by the local councils. Illustrative of the broad character of a *poder*, "power of attorney," granted by a city in the eighteenth century is one dictated by the cabildo of Lima for two individuals to serve simultaneously in this capacity:

> Each one in the position to which he is named or which he represents before His Majesty and other councils and tribunals, that he may with full legality handle those petitions and businesses, thus to solicit concessions and grants from His Majesty as well as appeals to justice contained in letters, and everything else that may present itself, without any defect in authority or lack of right to execute it [as procurator], and that 200 pesos de renta be paid him each year . . . on condition that the apoderado render an account of it [to the city] in two years.[7]

Memorials and petitions from the cabildos supplemented the activity of the agents in Madrid. Few restrictions were placed by the viceroy and the audiencia on the right of written communication

5. His instructions included a plea for the appointment to the Audiencia of Lima of educated limeños, many of whom had studied at the University of San Marcos "in the hope of becoming oidores in their own land." His nomination was approved by the consejo on Jan. 18, 1709. See Cartas y expedientes de varios cabildos, legajo 420, Audiencia de Lima, A. G. I.

6. The libros de cabildos of Lima contain many references to arrangements for the transfer of funds to agents at the court. Payment of salaries evidently enjoyed high priority.

7. Minutes of April 5, 1739, Libros de cabildos de Lima, vol. XXXV, Biblioteca municipal, Lima.

with the Council of the Indies. Hundreds of cartas dealing with a wide variety of matters were thus drawn up. Some asked for the preservation of fundamental rights and liberties or the elimination of inequities and discriminations. Thus the council of Lima petitioned the crown to allot corregimientos on the basis of individual merit without regard for place of birth, "the accident of the natal soil."[8] Another memorial condemned the contemptuous, disdainful attitude of the Viceroy toward the caballeros of Peru, revealed "in word and in correspondence," and requested that the regidores be shown the respect that was accorded to the aldermen of Mexico City.[9] Others protested the imposition of taxes and special levies and illegal interference by crown officials in conciliar elections. In 1754 the ayuntamiento of Cuzco appealed to the King against the continuance by the Viceroy as juez de naturales of a man whose term of office had expired, an act in contravention of Francisco de Toledo's famous ordinances of the sixteenth century. Since the office was elective, the Viceroy's act was considered as a limitation on the power of the council. The fiscal, in his parecer of January 24, 1756, recommended that a cédula be dispatched to Peru, requiring the king's representative to "carry out punctually the aforementioned ordinance and not allow the judge of the natives of the City of Cuzco to serve, unless he deems it vital for the public weal." The consejo's decision conformed to the fiscal's advice.[10] Through *informes de méritos* to the crown, the ayuntamientos could promote the careers of deserving public servants.[11]

Conversely, the right of petition might be abused by the conciliar bodies. Favors for influential citizens could be secured. These were by no means few in number. Almost no matter was regarded as too insignificant for referral to Spain. Trivial details of protocol involving the cabildo and governmental officials plagued the sessions of the Council of the Indies. For example, the city of Cuzco in 1756 demanded that equality in the seating arrangements for public ceremonies between the secular and ecclesiastical cabildos be enforced. In the opinion of the

8. Cartas y expedientes de varios cabildos, legajo 428, Audiencia de Lima, A. G. I.
9. Cartas y expedientes de cabildos, legajo 802, Audiencia de Lima, A. G. I.
10. *Ibid.*
11. In an informe of Dec. 20, 1756, the council of Cuzco lauded the character and ability of the archdeacon of the cathedral of Cuzco Don Pedro de Orellana. See expediente, Cuzco, legajo 428, Audiencia de Lima, A. G. I.

fiscal there was nothing in the Laws of the Indies that stipulated complete parity in these matters. Unwilling to render a decision in such a
trifling question, the consejo returned the dispute to the Viceroy for
settlement.[12] Through petitionary action the cabildo of Lima in 1704
obtained from the crown a promise that regidores judged guilty of
infraction of law should be confined to a jail, suitable for "noble
and honorable persons."[13]

Towns less influential and prosperous than Lima and Mexico
City looked to the viceroy rather than to the Council of the Indies as
a source of concessions and favors. Out of respect for the newly
appointed official and at the same time in hopes of currying favor
by flattery, some cities customarily dispatched "ambassadors" to Lima
to participate in the ceremonies of the recibimiento. On July 31, 1745,
the city of Cuzco named the Marqués de Salinas, vecino of Lima, as
its representative in the reception of the Conde de Superunda:

> Be it resolved that the city nominate an ambassador, as is the
> custom—since the ayuntamiento, composed of alcaldes ordinarios, a
> juez de naturales, alférez real, depositario, cannot go down in person
> to the City of the Kings because of their duties—a person with the
> qualifications necessary for this service, and who should be the
> Marqués de Salinas y de Torrebermeja, secretary of the district, a
> citizen of the City of the Kings, who may in the name of you and the
> cabildo and the city of Cuzco, of the Kingdom and provinces of
> Peru, act in this capacity and extend greetings to His Excellency,
> manifesting the joy of the city at his having been made Viceroy of
> this Kingdom ... with power to speak for the city in all pleas and
> cases that may offer themselves . . . giving special attention to the
> preservation and extension of the prerogatives, usages, customs, and
> privileges [of the city] ... and keeping secret those matters referred
> to him by us....[14]

On October 11, 1745, the cabildo received a friendly carta from the
new Viceroy in response to its congratulatory message. In this same
packet was a letter from the Marqués de Salinas, giving an account
of his activities in behalf of the city.[15]

12. Expediente, Cuzco, legajo 802, Audiencia de Lima, A. G. I.
13. Expediente, Lima, legajo 802, Audiencia de Lima, A. G. I.
14. Minutes of July 31, 1745, Libro de actas del cabildo de Cuzco, vol. XXI, Archivo
de la Universidad de Cuzco.
15. Minutes of Oct. 11, 1745, *ibid.*
The pay was not excessive. In 1776 Cuzco remunerated its apoderado with the
annual salary of 100 pesos.

While some municipalities sent envoys to greet the incoming viceroy, they sometimes employed attorneys or notaries resident in the capital for the implementation of particular transactions. Thus Cuzco in 1780 utilized the talents of Dr. Francisco Xavier de Olleta, abogado of the Audiencia of Lima, who was to be guided in "the matters that are pending in the city of Lima" by the following instructions:

> The expediente that advocates the reduction of the censos from five to three percent is in the final stage of argument [recibirse la causa a prueba], according to the latest news of the apoderado.
>
> Item, in the same subject concerning the special expediente, in order that in the interim the reduction be concluded and fixed, let those who collect the censos give a fianza, which is asked by the fiscal, and have it returned with the papers presently in the possession of the apoderado that have not been presented in court. . . .
>
> Item, that [attention should be given to] the expediente submitted to the Customs Administration, with an informe of the Treasury officials of Cuzco, concerning the prohibition of the establishment of a ramo de sisa on the meat from Castile, in which many papers should be drawn up, in order that this tax should not be introduced because it is harmful to the trade of the Indians, as well as injurious to the general public, with the serious considerations that this subject offers.
>
> Item, that there should be enforced the decrees exempting from the alcabala the maiz, wheat, and other food that are to be found in the storehouses, which are exempted by law, but including in it those articles [of food] belonging to the vecinos, whose granaries are sometimes considered as warehouses, with the reflections that are offered concerning the Indians, the most interested group in this business.
>
> Item, that there should be maintained the privilege held by the Indians of not paying the alcabala, except on foodstuffs and meats brought by the mestizos and Spaniards, listing those commodities enjoying this exemption and those that are subject to it, alleging that the present increase of two percent amounts to more than these foods and articles bring in profit.
>
> Item, that it should be urged that whenever a tax or monopoly is proposed this matter should be discussed before the cabildo . . . so that when a levy is declared nothing unusual will perturb the people of the town, which is numerous, and arouse the inhabitants from roundabout.
>
> Item, that in everything else that benefits the republic and contributes to its welfare, you will proceed as the matter presents itself,

with the zeal and diligence that confidence, faithfulness, and patriotic love prescribe.

Item, that concerning the privileges of the cabildo, you will bear in mind to solicit the power of the regidores to elect the alcaldes ordinarios when convenient, as they always did, as is proved by the books of the cabildo dealing with elections of alcaldes and officers of the republic, and above all, do not overlook what is the practice in the cabildo of Lima and others of the Kingdom concerning their fueros, and you will notify [us] as to what is offered.[16]

Representation of the cabildos in Spain by means of agents and cartas achieved only partial success. Although in a surprisingly large number of cases the Council of the Indies listened sympathetically to the pleas of the cabildos against the encroachment upon their liberties by the crown officials in America, it did not devise an operative method for curbing the excesses of the viceroy, audiencias, and corregidores. Compared to the agents employed by the North American settlers to adjust colonial differences in London, the Spanish American procurators had patently less freedom of expression and action. The formal autocracy of the court at Madrid was less conducive to bold utterances than the undemocratic but freer atmosphere of the court of St. James and the houses of Parliament. More favorable circumstances for the attainment of objectives developed when the throne was occupied by a weak ruler and when Spain itself was faced with dire financial problems. Through firmness and donations to the crown, colonial cities, particularly Lima, saw a way of regaining certain lost privileges and even of acquiring a limited number of new ones. The improved status of the capital did not, however, signify a return to the self-governing status that it had enjoyed for a short time in the sixteenth century.

In addition to the use of agents and memorials, the cabildo might strengthen its position vis-à-vis the crown by still another course of action. This was the summoning of extraordinary assemblies of the citizens, or the cabildos abiertos. They were destined ultimately to play a far more consequential role in the separation of the colonies from the mother country. In these assemblies the concept of popular representation remained alive throughout the colonial period.

Although the convocation might well have become a potent lever

16. Minutes of March 2, 1780, *ibid.* vol. XXV.

in prying concessions from the king, the ayuntamiento preferred to employ it in the solution of difficult local issues facing the citizenry. In actual practice, the major purpose of the assembly was the consideration of special taxes levied by the crown or of donations by the cabildo to the king for the defense of the realm. At least five cabildos abiertos were noted for Lima, three for Trujillo, and one for Piura in the period from 1700 to 1784, the year in which the intendancies appeared in Peru.[17] Until the dynastic crisis in Spain in 1808, there was no marked increase in the number of these assemblies. In the first three-quarters of the eighteenth century the normal hostility of the crown to a citizen assembly and the aristocratic character of the cabildo itself might explain the reluctance regarding more extensive use of this powerful instrument of the popular will. Under the more restrictive intendancy there was little opportunity or occasion for the utilization of a representative process.

To understand more clearly the nature of the cabildo abierto in this period, typical examples are selected for examination from the history of Lima, Trujillo, and Piura. The circumstances of their summoning and the import of their decisions will be noted.

A majority of these convocations discussed financial matters. Illustrative of this in Lima is a meeting called by the cabildo for November 20, 1762, to consider the advisability of a monetary gift to the king in the war with England. Earlier in the year the Viceroy Amat, a vigorous soldier as well as a capable administrator, had ordered all able-bodied men in the capital from the ages of fourteen to sixty to be drafted for the militia. During the first two weeks of November the companies drilled and underwent inspection. Since they lacked proper equipment, the Viceroy offered to provide from funds at his disposal uniforms and arms for four companies of grenadiers. Not to be outdone in patriotism, the audiencia, the Consulado, and the Society of Jesus made similar proposals.[18] On November 19, the cabildo resolved to give 11,000 pesos for this purpose, the amount to be raised through voluntary contributions made in an open assembly. The resultant cabildo abierto, meeting the next day and attended by the

17. Doubtless the institution—if it can be called such—operated in most of the cities and towns, though the records are not sufficiently complete to provide other examples than those given above. Assuredly, the tradition of a wider representation in civic government than the vendible cabildo did not die out.

18. Vargas Ugarte, *Historia del Perú, virreinato, 1700-1790*, pp. 301, 302.

regimiento and many of the nobility of the city, denied the appeal, "alleging various motives for not complying with it." To offset the unpatriotic spirit of the influential citizens, the cabildo begrudgingly borrowed the money from the Caja de Indios at 4 per cent interest, "since it lacked ready money."[19]

Several cabildos abiertos were called to ascertain public opinion toward changing the system of operation of the aqueducts of the city. An assembly of September 23, 1769, comprising the *jueces de barrios*, "judges of the districts of the city," important property owners, and members of the cabildo, twenty-four individuals in all, voted that "it was not suitable to replace private aqueducts" with a municipally owned and run network of canals and ditches. Other convocations of October 16, 1769, February 16, 1770, and March 5, 1770, supported this view. Consequently, no action was taken by the council at this time.[20]

In Trujillo similar assemblies treated the question of raising money for the protection of the city against Spain's rivals. A cabildo abierto of August 31, 1742, protested the imposition by the crown of a tax of 4 reales per arroba of sugar for the prosecution of the war with England, as being harmful to the vecinos and the owners of the plantations.[21] The assembly's act evoked a strong letter from the Viceroy, which was discussed at a second cabildo abierto in November of that year.[22] Some years later members of the cabildo, prelates of the various orders, and certain influential citizens met to consider a decreto, or order, from the Viceroy, proposing a quota from the vecinos, religious houses, and the owners of the fincas for the financing of necessary repairs on and of maintenance of the city walls. It was resolved to take proper steps to this end.[23]

The only instance of a cabildo abierto for Piura in the period for which records exist occurred in 1740 when preparations for hostilities with England required contributions from the vecinos and *moradores*, "non-householders" of the city. In this case, contrary to regular procedure, the formal initiative came from the corregidor at the behest of the Viceroy. A fine was to be imposed on those refusing to par-

19. Minutes of Nov. 18, 19, 20, 1762, Libros de cabildo de Lima, vol. XXXVI, Biblioteca municipal, Lima.
20. Minutes of Sept. 23, Oct. 16, 1769, and Feb. 16, and March 5, 1770, *ibid.*
21. Minutes of Aug. 31, 1742, Libros de cabildos de Trujillo, vol. XIV.
22. Minutes of Nov. 16, 1742, *ibid.*   23. Minutes of Jan. 16, 1746, *ibid.*

ticipate.[24] On September 19 of that year the ayuntamiento and prominent citizens came together in the town hall to hear an entreaty for funds "for the most urgent need in which the city of Lima finds itself for the support of the regiments raised at the king's command for the defense of the capital." Despite the corregidor's fervent exhortation the assembled group refused to contribute money to this end, alleging "bad crops, scarcity of livestock, and low prices for meat." As loyal vassals of His Majesty, the citizenry swore to defend the port of Payta, "because it was the jugular part of the Kingdom."[25]

A study of the above instances reveals relatively few procedural modifications from the preceding era.[26] Called by the cabildo, they were attended by a selected few, the wealthiest citizens and the clerical dignitaries. Decisions were generally advisory in nature. The dearth of these assemblies in the pre-intendancy period and their virtual disappearance during the regime of the new crown official corroborate the decline of local institutions.

During the eighteenth century the cabildo exercised the right of petition for redress of grievances and for new concessions. By subsidizing a procurator in Madrid, Lima sought to protect and advance the interests of its citizens. Secondary cities and towns had to be content with the dispatch of letters to Spain and with maintaining agents at the viceregal capital. Cabildos abiertos were held on infrequent occasions, usually to deal with royal taxes or voluntary donations from the citizens. The rejection of crown requests from time to time shows that the creole assembly was not a rubber stamp for the viceroy in financial matters. In truth, the open assembly was a political organ in being, one of much potentiality. Were a crisis to develop involving the basic interests of the powerful creole class, the cabildo abierto might guide public opinion and form a legal foundation for independence. But despite these diverse recourses the local councils were unable to contain the encroachment of royal authority. A still greater loss in municipal power came from the establishment of the intendancies.

24. Minutes of Sept. 15, 1740, Libro del cabildo de Piura.
25. Minutes of Sept. 19, 1740, ibid.
26. Moore, Cabildo in Peru, pp. 125-135.

CHAPTER VIII

Founding of the
Intendancy

In most of its ramifications local administration in the Audiencia of Lima was sharply affected by the establishment of the indendancy. After the issuance of Philip II's famous Ordinance for the Founding of New Towns it was the most important single influence exerted upon municipal development.[1] Had Charles III been followed upon the throne by an equally able monarch, disposed to govern energetically and with foresight, its imprint would have been deeper. But the son did not inherit the firmness and persistence of the elder Bourbon. However, that the effect of the intendancy was entirely wholesome and beneficial for municipal growth and functioning is dubious.

Before proceeding to assess the working of the intendant system and the results at the local level, the circumstances of its origin and inauguration in America must be considered. Adopted by Philip V in Spain in 1718 from French practices, it was abandoned the following year because of its apparent inapplicability and remained in disuse until 1749 when it again became a part of the administrative machinery.[2] Like his Gallic prototype, the Iberian official had extensive attributes in the judicial, financial, administrative, and military spheres. But considering that the faculties of this agent were too ample, Charles III in 1766 deprived him of judicial authority.[3] Despite an

1. Moore, *Cabildo in Peru under the Hapsburgs,* pp. 45-47.
2. Lillian E. Fisher, *The Intendant System in Spanish America* (Berkeley, Calif., 1929), p. 7.
   A recent authority maintains that its establishment was foreshadowed by the appointment by Charles II in 1687 of a *superintendente-general de hacienda* and in 1691 of superintendentes for the twenty-one Castilian provinces. See Luis Navarro García, *Intendencias en Indias* (Sevilla, 1959), pp. 7, 8.
3. Ballesteros, *Historia de España,* VI, 25.

inauspicious start the institution attained success in centralizing governmental power and augmenting the revenue available to the crown.

Prior to the planting of this agency in America there was a growing belief among many high bureaucrats in Spain that the system of colonial government was outmoded and badly in need of revamping. In 1743 José Campillo, Philip V's chief minister, wrote the *Nuevo sistema de gobierno económico para la América*, in which he advocated radical changes beginning with a thorough investigation of all phases of colonial administration by special judges.[4] While nothing came of it, the monarchy had another chance to be enlightened as to general conditions in America by the secret report of Ulloa and Juan, dictated from first-hand experiences. Another Spanish minister, Bernard Ward, of Irish birth, whose chief concern was the improvement of the national economy, reiterated the idea of a general visitation for the colonies to bring into clearer perspective the flaws in political and economic policy and to furnish the Council of the Indies with suggestions for a remedial course.[5] The upshot was the dispatch of José de Gálvez to New Spain and José de Areche to Peru, a preliminary step in the introduction of reforms. The informes of these visitors, in particular the one dealing with the Mexican viceroyalty, had great weight in inducing the crown to undertake the innovation.

Trial of the intendancy in the transatlantic possessions began on the island of Cuba, a small and relatively unimportant region. The Spanish Ordinance of 1749 furnished the outline and basis for the new laws.[6] The Spanish code contained 146 articles, providing governmental power for the intendant in four significant areas: finance, war, judiciary, and police. Periodically, changes and additions were made by royal decree in order to give sufficient flexibility to the system.

Because of its primacy the Cuban ordinance of October 31, 1764, deserves further attention. In the main, modeled after the Spanish law of 1749, it had, however, fewer articles—124 in all. Instead of covering four departments of government, it gave cognizance to the intendant only in matters relating to the treasury and to war and hence was definitely more restrictive in character.[7] The article defining his authority in these fields closely resembled those in the later Ordi-

4. John Lynch, *Spanish Colonial Administration*, p. 12.
5. *Ibid.*, pp. 12, 13.   6. Fisher, *Intendant System*, p. 9.
7. Haring, *Spanish Empire in America*, p. 144.

nance of 1786 for New Spain. However, the law applicable to the possessions on the mainland and to the Philippines was extended, like the Ordinance of 1749, to provide some jurisdiction in all four branches.[8]

Once appointed, the Cuban intendant became an important cog in the administrative machinery. He had a rank comparable to that of the captain-general. Over questions of finance, including those involving the church, the department of war, and civil administration, he possessed exclusive authority. His assent was essential in the making of decisions for the movement of troops, the building of fortifications, suppression of contraband, and supervision of crown lands. The captain-general was ordered to work harmoniously with the new official, but friction and resentment, generated by the natural jealousy of the older official, arose almost at once, a circumstance that repeated itself time and again in the establishment of intendancies elsewhere.[9]

Having convinced himself of the viability of the administrative reform in the West Indies, Charles III applied the intendancy system to other regions. If his vision materialized, colonial government would be more tightly organized and more uniform than ever before. Since this move involved many officials and a huge area with a dense population, it was the better part of wisdom to act with circumspection. Accordingly, the King in 1767 dispatched José de Gálvez as visitor-general and intendant of the army to New Spain. After conferring with the co-operative and sympathetic Viceroy Marqués de Croix, Gálvez submitted in 1768 a plan for the introduction of the system to Mexico.[10] The advantages of the office, he stated, were marked for both the crown and the colonists. It was to be expected that many in America would be in the opposition, preferring the old system because it had the weight of tradition behind it and because the belief was common that evils were too deeply rooted to be eradicated by any bureaucratic reorganization. The Indians would be exploited to a lesser extent through the abolition of the office of alcalde mayor, the equivalent of the corregidor in Peru. But of all the officials in America the most over-worked was the viceroy, for which the Laws of the

8. Ballesteros, *Historia de España*, VI, 670.

9. Fisher, *Intendant System*, pp. 10, 11.

10. As will be discovered by the reader later on, the Marqués' nephew Teodoro de Croix, viceroy of Peru, 1784-1790, became one of the most virulent opponents of the system.

Indies by assigning to him a bewildering multiplicity of duties was mainly responsible. By turning over to the intendant many minor details, the king's alter ego might concentrate on the chief problems in the kingdom. As the functions of the intendant in Spain and those of the American official were in many respects similar, progress would be made toward the realization of the ultimate goal, the assimilation of the colonial political system to its European progenitor.[11]

Gálvez' plan dealt likewise with specific issues existing in New Spain. Varying salaries were arranged for the eleven intendancies which were to be set up in Guadalajara, Durango, Sonora, Valladolid, Guanajuato, Californias, Mexico City, Puebla, Oaxaca, Yuacatan, and San Luis Potosí. To avoid extra expense on the treasury, provision would be made for the assignment of a portion of municipal revenues with the exception of those from Oaxaca and Campeche, provinces in such a wretched economic state that they could not afford the levy. Collection of the taxes due the crown was to be carried out by subdelegates, designated by the intendant, men who would take over the duties of the alcaldes mayores. Alcaldes ordinarios were to retain jurisdiction in the first instance and, moreover, furnish aid in the handling of the tribute. The scheme offered solutions for some vexatious matters, such as the elimination of illegal, compulsory purchases by the natives from the alcaldes mayores of unnecessary tools and clothing at exorbitant prices.[12]

With what appeared to be an acceptable and feasible plan in hand, the crown nevertheless proceeded cautiously to extend the system of the intendancies to the continent. In 1768 Visitor-General Gálvez and Viceroy de Croix were instructed to create provisional intendancies in Sonora and Sinaloa and to authorize the governor of Vera Cruz to exercise some of the general powers of an intendant.[13] The crown followed this with an order of March 1, 1777, to the Viceroy, requiring him to force the alcaldes mayores to submit lists of their employees and to suggest ways of simplifying the procedure for fixing the boundaries of the new districts. A junta, appointed by the Viceroy, was to meet in Mexico City to examine the reports made by the alcaldes mayores. This body, assembling in the capital in October, 1777,

11. Fisher, *Intendant System*, p. 12; see also Lynch, *Spanish Colonial Administration*, pp. 52, 53.
12. Fisher, *Intendant System*, pp. 12-15.
13. *Ibid.*, p. 15; see also Lynch, *Spanish Colonial Administration*, pp. 54, 55.

decided upon the limits of the alcaldías, after which it agreed upon the boundaries of the intendancies.[14]

Parallel steps to plant the intendancy system in South America were likewise being taken. In September, 1777, the crown designated an intendant for Venezuela, with authority also over Cumaná, Guayana, Maracaibo, and the insular territories of Margarita and Trinidad. Buenos Aires received an intendant in 1779.[15] A similar official was appointed for the provinces of Córdoba and Tucumán.

As Minister of the Indies, a post to which he had been elevated in 1775 for his outstanding work in Mexico, José de Gálvez soon realized some of the inadequacies of his initial labors. He saw the need for the issuance of additional legislation to spell out in greater detail the actual powers of the intendants. He therefore made many recommendations, later embodied in the Ordinances for Intendants for Buenos Aires and Mexico.[16] Some of these affected the status and duties of the alcaldes in the towns with a Spanish population. In order to stop up the loopholes in the system of taxation, Gálvez declared that provision should be made for the collection of the tribute in districts having neither alcaldes ordinarios nor subdelegates. It was his suggestion also that alcaldes be held to strict accountability for the security of the tribute, with the penalty of confiscation of personal property imposed on these officials for procrastination in gathering the tax on the Indians. From the subdelegates the crown would stipulate bonds placed with the treasury against theft or dishonesty in the handling of funds.[17] Gálvez' keen mind comprehended the importance of preserving government at the lowest level. Hence he urged the inclusion of ways and means of electing alcaldes and regidores in towns without municipal regimes.

Prior to the promulgation of an ordinance for intendants for Buenos Aires and Peru, the Minister of the Indies ordered a visitor-general to Lima to determine the state of the government and the general economy. More than ever before basic, far-reaching reforms were necessary in the oldest South American viceroyalty. As recent authorities have put it: "Peru was one of the colonies most punished by the laziness of its governors. . . . Life in Lima—as it happened and happens in all colonial systems—was more relaxed than that of the Peninsula. It

14. Fisher, *Intendant System*, pp. 16, 17.
15. *Ibid.*, p. 17.   16. *Ibid.*, p. 18.
17. *Ibid.*, p. 19.

was not rare to find judicial officers, employees of the Real Hacienda, and heads of other tribunals committing illegalities without count and taking for themselves not only income, but delaying matters committed to them with the object of getting their hands on more money."[18] Particularly urgent, even critical, was the depletion of royal revenues which had sunk to a low point. The wealth from the mines reaching the Cajas Reales of Trujillo, for example, averaged in the period from 1774 to 1802 only 67, 193 marcos, a far cry indeed from the returns of an earlier period.[19] To these were added other ills of economic and social nature.

It was hoped that the mission would be attended with the same results that had ensued from Gálvez' own visit to New Spain. "Unfortunately, the person selected did not possess the qualities of the former."[20] But it must be admitted that José Antonio de Areche was not without some experience in affairs of the colonies. Originally appointed by Charles III in 1766 as oidor of Manila, he found his orders countermanded while in Mexico en route to the Far East and, in consequence, accepted from the Viceroy the offer of the position of criminal prosecutor of the Audiencia of Mexico and later that of civil prosecutor of the same body.[21] On June 14, 1777, he reached Lima, with orders to increase the royal revenue by reforming the various branches of the treasury and to restore the administration of justice consonant with the principles of honesty and equity. His pettiness and lack of tact were soon revealed, however, in his sharp criticism of the well-liked, easy-going Viceroy Manuel de Guirior.[22] Areche's constant complaints induced the crown to remove Guirior, who was replaced on July 22, 1780, by Agustín de Jáuregui, captain-general of Chile.

18. Vicente Rodríguez Casado and José Antonio Calderón Quijano, *Memoria de gobierno de José Fernando de Abascal y Sousa* (Sevilla, 1944), I, XLIV, XLIX.
19. Some of the financial woes of Peru, however, were caused by the creation of the Viceroyalty of Buenos Aires, with the resultant prohibition of the exportation of gold and silver to Lima from districts attached to the new administrative area. See Vargas Ugarte, *Historia del Perú, virreinato, 1700-1790*, pp. 378, 379.
20. *Ibid.*, p. 378.
21. Areche had an opportunity to become well-informed on nearly all aspects of life in the viceroyalty. One of the extant copies of the *Noticias secretas* now in the Biblioteca de Palacio, Madrid, was set aside for his perusal and use, and the notations and underlining indicate that either he or his secretary probably consulted it.
22. Vicente Palacio Atard's *Areche y Guirior: Observaciones sobre el fracaso de una visita al Perú* (Sevilla, 1946) is a scholarly study, based on records in the Archives of the Indies, of the long feud between the two men.

Already intensely disliked by the limeños for his persecution of their favorite, Areche crowned his unpopularity by intervention in conciliar matters. On November 27, 1777, the visitador, acting under *Reales Instrucciones Reservadas*, requested that the Viceroy have the ayuntamiento turn over to him as soon as possible all important records, including among other items the following: a list of the rentas and censos, with exact information about the commons, rural and town properties; a *razón* of the taxes or branches of revenue that were alienated or were in litigation; a statement of the salaries, pensions, and of the normal and foreseeable expenses; a summary of *oficios vendibles y renunciables* of the cabildo, with the number and names of the holders and their salaries; and an account of the procedure followed in the choosing of the alcaldes, "the circumstances of their election," and the jurisdiction enjoyed by them in the absence of a corregidor or governor, "whose presence is customary in all other cities of the other kingdoms of our nation." On November 28, 1777, Guirior remitted the order to the cabildo, with a formal demand for compliance.[23] In part because of the secret opposition of the councilors to the visitor and partly because of the difficulty of assembling the information, the documents and papers were not in Areche's possession until March 31 of the following year.[24]

That the Spanish investigator was aware of the politically unhealthy conditions in Lima is evident from his correspondence with Fernando Manzino, general superintendant of the Hacienda of Mexico. Comparing the local regimes in the Peruvian capital and Mexico City, he inferred that the former was much inferior: "the capital of the Kingdom, instead of having a single head [a corregidor], was governed by two alcaldes ordinarios elected annually. Its abastos had no regulation. Its sanitation depended on the arbitrary decisions of an alguacil mayor. Nobody had authority over its customs. . . . The collection of the tribute, alcabala, and the fifth was in scandalous confusion and uncertainty."[25]

Areche's evaluation of the municipal government of Lima, in particular the careless handling of finances, led him to appoint by order of November 29, 1781, a *conservador de propios y rentas* in the

23. Minutes of Nov. 28, 1777, Libros de cabildos de Lima, vol. XXXVI, Biblioteca municipal, Lima.
24. Minutes of March 31, 1778, *ibid.*
25. Quoted in Vargas, *Historia del Perú, virreinato, 1700-1790*, p. 380.

person of Benito de la Mata Linares. After passing a resolution approving the designation and extending the full co-operation of its members, the cabildo formally received the new judge on December 17, 1781.[26] Friction soon developed in conciliar sessions. The cabildo, annoyed by the infringement upon its liberties, remonstrated to the visitador that the judge refrained for no good reason from attending meetings devoted to a discussion of civic ordinances, thus slowing down the work to be done. Added to this was the charge that the judge was unduly sensitive to adverse remarks about the visitor.[27] For his part the conservador, faced with the basically uncompromising attitude of the capitulars, replied that no reorganization of finances was possible through the efforts of one man, and in a short time he resigned his post.[28]

Areche's zealousness in another field created new enemies. His attempts to eliminate the inadequacies of the tax system aroused ill will throughout the viceroyalty and eventually led to a short-lived rebellion in certain provincial cities. The establishment of a customs house in Arequipa brought on a tumult, necessitating the dispatch of troops to the city. The example of Arequipa encouraged the creoles in Tarma, Huailas, and finally in Cuzco to demonstrate, though unsuccessfully, against the efforts at financial reform.[29] "The riots of this year served to clarify many things, among them being the irreconcilable hatred of the creole element for the Spaniards and the yearning for separation from the mother country that stirred many Peruvian hearts, as was soon revealed more clearly in the uprising of the Inca pretender."[30] In administrative reform much had been sought for, little accomplished.

As a municipal reformer and tax investigator, Areche could point to only a few successes. His general failure may be attributed to a combination of personal factors and fortuitous events. "Primarily, he lacked the capacity for the formidable enterprise that he had undertaken."[31] But his energies were partly absorbed by the uprising of the Inca descendant Túpac-Amaru and by his constant rivalry with

26. See chap. vi on municipal exchequer.
27. Informe al cabildo de Lima de la contaduría general, July 17, 1784, legajo 1223, Audiencia de Lima, A. G. I.
28. Vargas, *Historia del Perú, virreinato, 1700-1790*, p. 424.
29. Palacio Atard, *Areche y Guirior*, pp. 39-42.
30. *Ibid.*, p. 43.   31. *Ibid.*, p. 79.

Guirior.[32] Had he attempted further civic improvements, it is doubtful whether he could have achieved them because of the stubborn resistance of the creoles, aided by his other enemies, and because of his imprudence. To his credit were his rigid—perhaps too strict—devotion to duty and his clear understanding of the need for vital changes. Just before his replacement as visitor-general, he fired a final volley at the cabildo by announcing that he intended to "give an account to His Majesty of the conduct of the ayuntamiento, which did not observe the providencias that were contemplated for the public benefit and the conservation of its propios."[33] Undoubtedly, his reports, both written and oral, reinforced the crown's resolve to obtain more knowledge of Peru and, if results warranted it, to extend the intendancy system to the region as rapidly as possible.

From another viewpoint his unhappy sojourn may have militated against the interests of the monarchy. A Peruvian historian states that it "consolidated the criollo group and created a force anticipating the constitutionalism of the early nineteenth century."[34] Perhaps it was a further stimulus to the growing self-consciousness of the creole class.

Areche's replacement, the new visitor-general, was Jorge de Escobedo, a man with superior qualifications for the task that lay ahead. In this instance Gálvez made no mistake in his choice. Escobedo, who had been appointed as oidor of Charcas in 1776 and was at the moment of nomination governor of Potosí, was "the prototype of one who might be the ideal American administrator."[35] It was left to him to continue the reforms initiated by his predecessor. His greatest claim to recognition rests, however, on the implementation of the Peruvian intendancy.

Before ordering the installation of the intendants in Peru and Buenos Aires, the crown sought further advice on the feasibility of the new procedure. By order of July 29, 1782, it solicited informes

32. Vargas, *Historia del Perú, virreinato, 1700-1790*, p. 424.

33. Minutes of April 27, 1782, Libro de cabildos de Lima, vol. XXXVII, Biblioteca municipal, Lima. A more sympathetic treatment of him is to be found in Eunice J. Gates, "Don José Antonio de Areche: His Own Defense," *Hispanic American Historical Review*, VIII (Feb., 1928), 14-42.

34. Valcárcel, "Perú borbónico y emancipación," *Revista de historia de América*, p. 354.

35. Viellard-Baron, "L'Etablissement des Intendants aux Indes par Charles III," p. 545; see also Manuel de Mendiburu, *Diccionario histórico-biográfico del Perú* (2nd. ed.; 11 tomos; Lima, 1931-1934), IV, 417, 418.

from important royal officials in the two viceroyalties on the problems and difficulties likely to be encountered in the enforcement of the *Ordenanza* of January 28, 1782. Those consulted at first were the Visitor-General of Peru; the President of the Audiencia of Charcas, Ignacio Flores; the teniente asesor of the same audiencia, Juan José de Segovia; the Viceroy of Buenos Aires, Juan José de Vértiz; and the Intendant of Buenos Aires, Manuel Ignacio Fernández. Their replies agreed on the utility of the administrative enactment, though they differed on the effect and value of various articles.

Since Escobedo probably knew more about actual conditions in Peru than any of the others, his views on the application of the ordenanza to the localities must be carefully weighed. The extinction of the corregidores, he declared, would not be followed by greatly improved government in the towns (Article 8). A major hindrance was the strife attending the election of alcaldes, occasioned by the ambitions of

> haughty persons of these towns, whose birth is distinguished only by color of skin and by the name of chapetones (so the Europeans are called), those in whom adulation, connections, and desire for gain exist alongside vanity[36]....who in the ayuntamiento and in the elections wish to choose alcaldes from their own faction and if they succeed regard justice as something bought and sold, but if their party loses, they turn to discord, framing appeals that have been so frequent as to nullify elections, with all the scandals, intrigues, and plots.[37]

In most cases officials of the cabildo, he said, gave primacy to personal interests over those of the public. This was a danger in towns where the councils retained some authority.

Jurisdictional rivalry between the alcaldes and the *tenientes letrados,* "legal advisors of the intendants," had to be avoided (Article 12). To lessen friction, he advised the delimitation of areas of legal cognizance and the admonishment of alcaldes "to be prompt" in their decisions, so as to preclude the need for intervention by the tenientes. While the salary of the legal advisor was less than desirable, "to assign 1,000 pesos from the propios and arbitrios [of the towns] is very much a mistake, since in most of the cities, except Lima, the income is any-

36. Escobedo echoes Ulloa's denunciation of the inordinate desire for power and the self-esteem of European-born colonists.

37. Extracto de los informes dados por varios gefes del Perú y Buenos Aires sobre la ordenanza expedida por S. M. en 28 de enero de 1782 para el establecimiento, é instrucción de Intendencias en dhos virreynatos y sus provincias, legajo 1118, Audiencia de Lima, A. G. I.

where from 3,000 to 4,000 pesos, and is drawn from uncertain sources."

Escobedo foresaw conflict between the intendant and the viceroy over the status of each vis-à-vis the cabildo (Article 15). Should the intendant preside over the ayuntamiento in public and private sessions and, in addition, have a vote in conciliar elections? If the viceroy retained his present authority over the cabildo, the intendant would be ignored or despised by the capitulars. Unless the intendant's power was augmented, he would lose face in the mind of the populace by the obsequious position he would have to assume in the ceremonies for the entrada of the viceroy.

Examination and revision of the sources of municipal income were "indispensable" (Articles 23-29). "In the appraisal of the budget," he asserted, "the Real Hacienda should not take past expenditures as a guide . . . few are the cabildos in which many disorders and irregularities do not occur and in Lima those resulting from the entradas of the viceroys would not be inconsiderable." A regulation to fix a proper and suitable amount to be expended on these occasions had to be drawn up. For the public tranquility, the intendant was to have oversight of the propios and abastos (Articles 30-33). But this would bring on disputes with the cabildos, "who will resist the arrangement that is wisely devised" (Articles 34-47). Trustworthy notaries and clerks were hard to find. "There is no fabrication that they will not make, so that together with their ignorance, malice, and poverty no one is entirely sure of his obligations and transaction."

Pósitos, or public granaries, were unnecessary, because "rarely is there a shortage [of food] in Peru, or a steep rise in the price of flour and grain" (Article 68, 69). Arequipa, it was true, had a place of storage for the public, but its operation was "very unsatisfactory and beset with disorders."

Finally, Escobedo predicted trouble in the collection of the tribute by the alcaldes and the subdelegates (Article 116). Despite the remuneration of 3 per cent of the amount taken in, many would shirk their responsibility, since they had to furnish security in their persons and possessions.[38]

38. Informe sobre la ynstruccion de Intendentes, que a ella acompañava, manifestando todas las utilidades que ofrece aquel sabio establecimiento, las dificultades que pueden entorpecer su execucion, y los medios con que juzga se vencerian para no retardar la resolucion que recomienda como mui urgente . . . por visitador general del Perú, Jorge Escobedo y Alarcón, Lima, June 16, 1783, legajo 1117, Audiencia de Lima, A. G. I.

The unfavorable picture of civic administration painted by Escobedo does not take on a brighter hue in the informe of February 16,
1783, from the Governor of Potosí, Juan de Pino Manriques, solicited
by Gálvez:

> The conquest of Peru was due to men outstanding in valor, but
> so lacking in culture and education that their crudeness was noted
> even in a backward age, and with the difference that in the enter-
> prises of Hernando Cortes are reflected his understanding, wisdom,
> and prudence and a worthy respect for cultural matters and piety;
> [but] in this Kingdom only these conquerors made names for them-
> selves through their notorious bands, in which Almagro and Pizarro,
> shamefully involved, filled the land that they trod with deaths and
> barbarous acts that humanity cannot condone, nearly all perishing
> in this same effort. It may well be concluded that that unhappy
> epoch was the one that gave to the Kingdom a tone so dismal and
> tragic that its unfortunate influence has come down to our times,
> since you can scarcely read about any event in Peru in which civil or
> political happenings are not tinged with bloodshed, only a few ex-
> amples being needed to prove the truth of this....[39]

No one would deny the need for revitalizing the municipal government in Peru, but that corruption and turbulence had reached the
degree alluded to by Escobedo and Pino is doubtful. It is not impossible that both administrators were unduly influenced by the disturbances among the cities in 1780, a tendency that had manifested
itself sporadically in the history of the first South American viceroyalty. Thus the desire to suppress future signs of sedition and violence
may have provided additional motivation for the reform program of
Charles III and his ministers.

The crown's concern over the nature of local administration in
this region was revealed in the instructions of June 19, 1783, written
for the incoming Viceroy Teodoro de Croix. Three articles in particular dealt with the relations of the Viceroy and the municipalities.
He was to found new cities on good sites and allocate land and *solares*,

39. Informe del Gobernador de Potosí, Juan de Pino Manriques a D. José de
Gálvez, Potosí, Feb. 16, 1783, legajo 1118, Audiencia de Lima, A. G. I.
    Another letter from Pino to Gálvez re-emphasizes the inclination of the inhabitants
of the sierras toward rebellious acts and suggests that the large towns and villages
have "an intermediary authority, a judge who can deal with the first abuse that
occurs in these towns, the appearance of rival bands, and other features of the
elections." See Carta del Gobernador de Potosí a D. José de Gálvez, Dec. 16, 1783,
legajo 1118, Audiencia de Lima, A. G. I.

provided "it is not at the expense of my Royal Treasury nor with injury or prejudice to a third party, and chiefly to the Indians." It was his duty also to encourage the construction of highways and public works in the cities and to see that hospitals under the crown or cabildos were well run. As for the functioning of the local councils, the Viceroy was specifically enjoined from interfering in elections:

> I am informed that some regulations are not obeyed, those which have no other end than to leave in liberty the electors of the ayuntamiento to choose alcaldes and other officials of the republic; and as to the non-observance this has been noted chiefly in the capital of Lima, where the annual election of the cabildo is only a brief ceremony, which is an immediate cause of their degradation and the vacancy of many varas of regidores of my ayuntamiento, doing injury to the public in their [lack of] service, to my royal treasury in its interests, and to the electors in the right of election that they obtained with their offices; I charge you strictly to do away with this fault, occasioned by the viceroys your predecessors, not mixing in such elections, except to approve them or command reforms when it can be proved that they are required, leaving the care of the propios and the arbitrios to my Visitor-General and Superintendant of my Real Hacienda.[40]

On July 7, 1784, the Viceroy de Croix, at the suggestion of the Visitor-General, began the enforcement of the Real Ordenanza of Intendants in Peru.[41] The region was divided into seven intendancies: Lima, Trujillo, Tarma, Huancavelica, Guamanga, Cuzco, and Arequipa. With the annexation of Puno by a royal order of February 1, 1796, another intendancy was created, thus bringing the total to eight. These districts were subdivided into partidos, governed by subdelegates.[42]

Many regulations of the ordinance applied to local government.[43] A primary objective being the augmentation of royal revenue, a number

40. Correspondencia con los virreyes, legajo 640, Audiencia de Lima, A. G. I.
41. Vargas, *Historia del Perú, virreinato, 1700-1790*, p. 437; see also Fisher, *Intendant System in America*, pp. 21, 22.
42. Vargas, *Historia del Perú, virreinato, 1700-1790*, p. 438.
43. The Ordinance of 1782 contained 276 articles as opposed to 306 in the Ordinance for New Spain. Of this number, 108 correspond exactly with those of the later code, while 111 vary only in insignificant details of wording made for greater clarity and understanding. Because of the very close similarity of the two documents, Fisher's excellent translation of the Mexican code is used for summarizing the provisions concerning the Peruvian municipalities. A valuable appendix to this work compares the two ordinances with a complete notation of differences.

of sections treated financial reform through the adoption of new agencies and expedients. Cognizant of the impoverishment of municipal treasuries and the ineptitude of officials, the crown supervised the collection and disbursement of local funds. Moreover, the intendant had the authority to order construction of public works and the repair of bridges and streets. With the abolition of the office of corregidor, the king looked to the alcaldes ordinarios, in the capacity of deputies, to assist in the collection of certain taxes. Whether these measures benefited only the crown or meant in the long run a general improvement of municipal regimes will be examined in the next chapter.

According to the provisions of the ordinance, the intendant replaced the corregidor as head of the local council. This was to be done "without prejudice to the authority belonging to the alcaldes ordinarios." Power to confirm elections was in the hands of the intendant. Where the ayuntamiento was non-existent, he might appoint for the first year one or two alcaldes depending on the size and status of the town. If there were two officials, in elections subsequent to the installation of the intendant only one alcalde was to be chosen annually, but with a two-year term, so that tenures of office for the chief magistrate would be overlapping.[44] In the major Indian towns, the subdelegates, and in the smaller native settlements, the alcaldes were to have responsibility for good government and the protection of life and property. When elections took place, the subdelegates or alcaldes had to render a report of proceedings to the intendant or governor.[45]

The intendant was to preside over the cabildo of the capital. In his absence, this function had to be performed by his assistant, the teniente asesor, who was to be paid a salary of 1,000 pesos by the municipality. When no royal official was available, an alcalde ordinario might take over, with the proviso that an account of what occurred had to be given to the intendant. As superior judge in the district, the intendant was to be charged with the impartial administration of justice, summoning the lesser agents "to notify them of their obligations and exhort them to fulfill them." Unnecessary delays in the handling of cases was to be investigated and proper action taken. Officials dispatched by the Council of the Indies for the purpose of conducting residencias were to be given every encouragement by

44. Fisher, *Intendant System in America*, pp. 106, 107.
45. *Ibid.*, pp. 107-111.

the intendant to look into all aspects of municipal office-holding. To assure justice and the well-being of the citizens of the towns, he had to carry out an annual inspection "without imposing any burdens upon the towns."[46]

With the solvency of the municipal treasuries and the status of the communal funds of the Indians the crown expressed much concern. It entrusted general oversight in these matters to a *junta superior de hacienda*, located in the capital. Attached to this body was a special accountant for municipal funds who was obliged to be present at all meetings.[47] In order to ascertain the present condition of finances in the towns of Spanish founding and in the Indian villages, officials of both types of municipalities were to give to the intendant an account "concerning the grant and origin of them, the perpetual or temporary dues that they pay, the necessary or extraordinary expenses to which they are subject, the surplus or deficit that occurs every year, and concerning the actual location and custody of, and the accounting for these funds."[48] Special scrutiny was to be made of the arbitrios, their origin and legality, and any taxes being collected without royal sanction were to be suppressed. Having gathered the essential data regarding finances, the intendant had to devise for each town a *reglamento*, "ordinance," governing the use of civic revenue and community funds, which was to be submitted to the junta superior for its approval. Expenditures were to be divided into four classes: (*a*) salaries and traveling expenses for municipal officials; (*b*) payment of the censos, due from the towns, or lumped into a single sum; (*c*) appropriations for fiestas and charity; (*d*) "extraordinary and incidental expenses, which may not have a fixed quota."[49] In the towns of Spanish origin warrants for expenses up to 40 pesos might be approved by the intendant, any amount beyond that requiring the consent of the junta superior. In the Indian settlements the limit was 20 pesos.[50]

To supervise finances there was to be established in every Spanish municipality a junta comprising the alcalde ordinario of the first vote, two regidores, and the procurador-general, or síndico, who had no power of vote. The principal function of this body was to conduct annually the auctioning of the collectorships of the taxes. Unusual

46. *Ibid.*, p. 118.
48. *Ibid.*, p. 120.
50. *Ibid.*, p. 123.

47. *Ibid.*, pp. 118, 119.
49. *Ibid.*, p. 122.

care was to be taken of the leasing of municipal revenues and the conservation of the public supplies, "since the communities are interested
that the former shall be auctioned at just value, and that the second
may possess the greatest advantage of prices."[51] With the approval of
the intendant and the junta superior, the municipal junta might
enter into contracts for a period of five years. Every year it was to designate a majordomo "who shall have charge of precisely all the funds
of municipal finance, and of their exact account and calculation,"
for which he was to be remunerated with $1\frac{1}{2}$ per cent of the amount
collected.[52] At the end of the year he had to draw up a statement of
accounts to be submitted to the junta for its approval. Funds left over
after the payment of expenses and debts were to be deposited by the
treasurer in a strong box with three keys in full view of the junta.
When the account had been certified by the junta, it was to go to the
cabildo and, after a scrutiny there, returned to the junta for dispatch
to the intendant.[53] Any surplus in the strong box had to be transmitted
to the central treasury, where it was to be kept until the junta superior
made provision for its disposition. The additional revenue to be saved
by this procedure might permit the withdrawal of irksome arbitrios
or repayment of censos. When debts had been extinguished, the money
might be used for the establishment of manufactures.[54] Subdelegates
would have control over use of lands, properties, and funds of the
Indian communities and in January of each year had to render to the
intendant a strict accounting of revenues and expenditures of the
preceding year.[55] In order to pay the salaries and traveling expenses
of the accountants, treasurers, and officials connected with this business,
the intendant was to authorize the deduction of 4 per cent of the
entire revenue of each Spanish town and 2 per cent of the annual
proceeds from the communal funds of the Indians.[56] It was his duty
to see that alcaldes ordinarios and subdelegates did not misappro-
priate sums obtained from fines and penalties.[57]

In the department of policía, or general administration, the intendant must exercise some authority. He might distribute unused
royal and private property to bring about greater cultivation of
certain crops, provided this could be done without hurt to the com-

51. *Ibid.*, p. 124.
53. *Ibid.*, pp. 126, 127.
55. *Ibid.*, pp. 128, 129.
57. *Ibid.*, p. 135.

52. *Ibid.*, p. 125.
54. *Ibid.*, pp. 127, 128, 130.
56. *Ibid.*, p. 132.

mons and the communal property and with the sanction of the junta superior. Inns and lodgings had to be operated for the comfort of travelers and to the profit of innkeepers. At his instigation and with the approval of the junta superior, additional resting places might be constructed with the use of the surplus from the municipal funds. The intendant was to check on the work of the Santa Hermandad so that these officials would keep the roads and countryside safe from bandits and robbers. He had to take pains to see that the local officers kept the avenues and squares clean, paved, and free from obstructions. Cities and large towns, particularly the capitals of the provinces, were to be surrounded by a wall. No church or public building might be put up without submission of the plans to the junta superior, which might make suggestions for its greater solidity and beauty.[58]

In the department of finance the intendant's responsibilities were linked with the fiscal activities of the alcaldes. He had to "inquire whether the contribution [of the alcabala] is levied on the inhabitants with due consideration for the property, contracts, business, and profits of each, and whether they lease or administer the public markets honestly wherever they are found, in order that the profits therefrom may serve the common welfare."[59] Upon the extinction of the corregimientos, the alcaldes, under the direction of the intendants, were to assume charge of the collection of the tribute and the transfer of the funds to the royal treasury. In the Indian towns the subdelegates, who had to give bonds for their probity, should have this obligation.[60] For the alcaldes and the subdelegates the remuneration would be 4 per cent of the amount collected and for the Indian alcaldes 1 per cent.

The intendant was to abide by the regulations and decrees governing the sale of municipal and royal offices. When bids for an office were made and valuation decided upon by the junta superior, the papers pertaining were to be returned to the intendant, who had to certify the deposit of funds for the sale in the treasury.[61] To the viceroy went, however, the power of issuing titles to office.[62]

Local regimes were only slightly affected by regulations relating to the department of war. The intendant was to require the alcaldes of the towns where troops were to be quartered to draw up a list of

58. *Ibid.*, pp. 142-144.
60. *Ibid.*, pp. 186-189, 195.
62. *Ibid.*, p. 214

59. *Ibid.*, p. 182.
61. *Ibid.*, p. 213.

all private residences to be used for this purpose. Before the soldiers could be withdrawn the *sargentos mayores* had to obtain a statement from the ordinary justices that there had been no injuries to citizens nor damage to premises. Payment to individuals for theft or destruction of property might be authorized by the intendant.[63]

A review of these functions leads to several conclusions. The most important departments outlined in the ordinance were those of the treasury and justice. The intendant was the indispensable key to the entire operation of the system. Much would depend therefore on his personal qualifications, in particular on his initiative. "That he should propose" was indicated again and again with purposeful insistence.[64]

By royal command the enforcement of the ordinance was assigned to the visitor-general rather than to the viceroy. Naturally, this led to animosity and ill will between the two officials. Escobedo perforce had the responsibility for drawing up instructions for the subordinate intendants. An order of July 1, 1784, from the Visitor-General directed them to take special care in the selection of the subdelegates and alcaldes ordinarios, as these were the individuals who would collect the tribute. It was preferable that each official name as bondsmen persons resident in the capital of the intendancy to minimize the risk of theft and peculation. Moreover, each was required to have in his possession a ledger for recording the sums of money, usually gathered in thirds from each village or town, with receipts signed by the collectors.[65]

A series of secret instructions, sent out prior to July 1, called to the attention of the intendants specific political and economic problems that the Visitor-General believed might be encountered in the particular districts. José Menendez Escalada, the appointee for Arequipa, was warned that his capital had been the focal point in the disorders of 1780. The ayuntamiento constituted a "powerful party, because the majority of its members, according to what I understand, are related to each other and those who enter this body get what they want." The city had propios, "but they are disorganized and limited in scope like all those of the Kingdom." Another question was the expeditious

63. *Ibid.*, pp. 313, 314.
64. Navarro, *Intendencias en Indias*, p. 85.
65. Ynstrucción origl. sobre aprovación de matrículas, y demás puntos q. explica, Lima, July 1, 1784, legajo 1117, Audiencia de Lima, A. G. I.

handling of the alcabala by the Real Hacienda, but the re-establishment
of the customs house, a serious issue in 1779, was assured.[66]

In Cuzco the royal agent had to see that the tenientes and asesores
letrados did not abuse the trust reposed in them by involving the crown
in jurisdictional disputes "under pretext of points of law." What was
true in the remainder of the kingdom applied to the former Inca
capital in regard to the sale of offices. There was perhaps not a single
cabildo in Peru without a vacant aldermancy as a result of the poverty
of the region and the unfortunate policy of the corregidores, who admitted unsuitable persons to the councils and who failed to preserve
the municipal fueros. It was Escobedo's conviction that this traditional branch of the treasury could again supply revenue if "the intendants, respecting these bodies and not interfering in their annual
elections, would restore to the citizens the honor and good name of
the capitular."[67]

Guamanga, though not a center of riots against the government,
posed problems of a financial nature. The exhausted condition of the
propios had already resulted in the issuance of *providencias*, "orders,"
for their increase. Consideration had to be given to the imposition
of a sisa for the construction of the fort at Callao, a tax obtained until
then only from Guanta and Piura. As to the collection of the alcabala,
Escobedo asserted:

> no other [tax] costs me as much fatigue nor requires of me more
> diligence in its management....It is necessary that the intendants
> exercise the greatest efficacy, effort, and zeal in reconciling a fair
> collection with the public convenience and take precaution against
> frauds, bearing in mind that they do not have to believe the clamors
> that are continually heard from the contributors nor that they must
> give in to the administrators and officials, against whom one should
> preserve no little vigilance lest they incur popular displeasure through
> their imprudence or lose respect through omission, misdeed, and
> ignorance.[68]

For the intendant of Trujillo there were questions of the improvement in government and finance. The corregidor of the city had imposed for seven years "an incredible despotism." Hence it was rec-

66. Ynstrucción práctica que para adaptar la nueva Rl. de Yntendencias se da por
el tribunal de visita á el Sor. D. José Menendez Escalada que va a servir la de Arequipa, Lima, Oct. 4, 1784, *ibid.*
67. Ynstrucción práctica . . . a la de Cuzco, Lima, Oct. 4, 1784, *ibid.*
68. Ynstrucción práctica . . . a la de Guamanga, Lima, Oct. 4, 1784, *ibid.*

ommended that the alcaldes be allowed to remain in office "because they will resist and not be cowed." An illustration of his tyranny is that he "has imposed many fines, on slightest pretext, without giving an account of them." In the matter of the possible transference of the cabildo from Saña to Lambayeque the intendant was to proceed cautiously and deliberately, keeping in mind that the former place might be ruined by the non-existence of a council. Attention was to be directed to the enforcement of providencias relating to the propios, and, if possible, the officials in charge of the alcabala were also to collect the sisa.[69]

The intendant of Huancavelica, like other intendants, had to prevent his assistant and his legal counselors from extending royal prerogatives at the expense of municipal rights. Providencias to remedy the lack of propios having been prepared by the Visitor-General, the intendant had to see to their execution. The alcabala and the sisa were to be collected earnestly and honestly.[70]

Tarma, the Visitor-General wrote to the intendant, had only one city, Leon de Huánuco. Its cabildo had many unfilled posts, such as those of the alguacil mayor, alcalde de hermandad, and escribano, partly because of the attitude of the corregidores who refused to permit the exercise of these positions and hampered officials in the discharge of their regular duties. It was to be his aim to raise the esteem in which these offices were held. Huánuco was without propios because of its removal from one site to another; the intendant was to find ways to provide revenues. It was thought wise to consider founding pósitos there in view of the occasional scarcity of food.[71]

While devoting much effort to making recommendations to the provincial intendants, Escobedo was not oblivious to the latent envy and pique of the Viceroy, whose uncle had been a collaborator of Gálvez in the preparation of the first plan for the intendancies in Mexico. He sought therefore to take De Croix into his confidence by disclosing some of the difficulties involved in applying the system. On the identical day in which he ordered the enforcement of the ordinance, he transmitted an informe to the Viceroy, noting some of the thorny problems that could arise in the viceroyalty, in particular

69. Ynstrucción práctica . . . a la de Trujillo, Lima, Oct. 4, 1784, *ibid.*
70. Ynstrucción práctica . . . a la de Huancavelica, Lima, Oct. 4, 1784, *ibid.*
71. Ynstrucción práctica . . . a la de Tarma, Lima, Oct. 4, 1784, *ibid.*

in Lima. In his estimation an important mistake was the insufficient compensation to the subdelegates and alcaldes for the collection of the tribute, which might create temptation to misappropriation. In order to avoid incurring the hostility of the ayuntamiento of Lima, always sensitive to an encroachment on its privileges, he was not to designate a teniente for himself. It was an exception to Article 12 of the ordinance. In the absence of the Visitor the alcaldes would preside as they had in the past, "so as to give inspiration and dignity to this honor." Of all the councils whose affairs required investigation, none needed it more than that of Lima, "which is superior to the rest in income and standing." A providencia would have to be issued, removing the obstacles that many had encountered in aspiring to become regidores. The Viceroy would be made cognizant of all reforms intended for the capital.[72] In spite of this conciliatory gesture De Croix remained adamant in his opposition to what he realized was a deprivation of authority for himself as the chief executive officer of the region.

With his customary energy, Escobedo set out at once to put the governmental machinery into operation. He informed the cabildo of Lima in an oficio of July 12 of his intention to be the intendant-general and preside over that body. Flatteringly, the cabildo replied the same day, avowing its pleasure in having as its chief official a person "who has given to the Kingdom the most striking proof of his distinguished talent, his consummate wisdom, love of the king, and ceaseless attention to the public welfare."[73] On the next day, July 13, all of the intendants took their oaths of office. Later in the same day the Visitor-General entered the sala de cabildo and designated ten men among the prominent citizens to fill out the regular complement of the ayuntamiento.[74] Although contrary to custom and practice, there was no outward protest by the council against this act.[75] Measures

72. Informe de Jorge Escobedo al Virrey Teodoro de Croix, July 1, 1784, *ibid.*

73. Carta del ayuntamiento de Lima, 12 julio, 1784 al Vist. Super. de Rl. Hacienda Jorge Escobedo, *ibid.*

74. Since 1748 there had been vacant conciliar posts. The most recent purchase, taking place several years prior to 1784, had been at 4,000 pesos, almost one-third of the amount exacted for the office in the first half of the eighteenth century. See minutes of July 13, 1784, Libros de cabildos de Lima, vol. XXXVIII, Biblioteca municipal, Lima.

75. Escobedo was undoubtedly pleased that "this body did not offer the resistance that it has shown on other occasions." See Informe (n. 306) del visitador genl. al Señor D. Jph. de Gálvez, Lima, 16 julio, 1784, legajo 1117, Audiencia de Lima, A. G. I.

aimed at the improvement of public services and finance were soon enacted.[76] To facilitate municipal administration and to insure full enforcement of the ordinances, the Visitor-General in an order of April 17, 1785, redivided the city into *cuarteles*, "districts," and barrios, or wards, thus changing the decrees of 1768 and 1770. Thereafter Lima had four cuarteles, each composed of ten barrios, a geographical arrangement that lasted until May, 1821. Alcaldes de barrios, appointed by the Visitor, were assigned to the smaller units and held accountable for public order and maintenance of the streets.[77]

In erecting the mechanism of the intendancy in the Peruvian kingdom and putting the wheels in motion, the second visitor-general deserves high praise. It was "a crushing assignment," executed equitably and comprehensively.[78] Escobedo's understanding of local problems was thorough and well grounded. His sincerity in wishing to restore efficiency, honesty, and self-respect to municipal regimes through paternalism cannot be challenged. But, as he confessed, it was necessary for him to act at times contrary to the letter of the ordinance.[79] De Croix's jealousy and resentment were a portent of things to come in the relations of top crown officials. Would the vision of Gálvez and Escobedo assume form and substance? Only time might tell. Unhappily for the reformers, an insufficiency of this precious element doomed to failure their cherished aims.

76. On Nov. 29, 1781, it will be recalled, the first visitor-general had appointed a member of the Audiencia of Lima as juez conservador de sus propios y rentas, with authority to reform the policía of the city government. The cabildo received the new official on Dec. 17, and he then took the unprecedented step of presiding over the election of Jan. 1. Relations between the judge and the cabildo were unsatisfactory almost from the beginning, the latter's dislike reflecting in part Areche's unpopularity. Several appeals made by the cabildo to the Consejo de Indias helped to bring about his suspension. See Informe al cabildo de Lima de la Cont. gral., Madrid, 17 julio, 1784, legajo 1223, Audiencia de Lima, A. G. I.

77. For a description of the urban areas comprising the various barrios in 1785 and again in 1821, see Fernando Gamio Palacio, *La municipalidad de Lima y la emancipación, 1821* (Lima, 1944), pp. 239-251.

78. Viellard-Baron, L'Etablissement des Intendants aux Indes par Charles III," p. 545.

79. He had to curb the aggressiveness of the tenientes asesores, who caused disputes by pushing too vigorously royal jurisdiction in the localities. See Informe acerca el establecimiento de Yntendencias en Perú, Jorge Escobedo a José de Gálvez, Lima, 20 agosto, 1784, legajo 1117, Audiencia de Lima, A. G. I.

CHAPTER IX

The Immediate Effects of the Intendancies

In retrospect, it is hardly imaginable that the intendancy could have fulfilled all of the expectations of Charles III and his advisors even if fate had granted a greater life span to this colonial empire. Problems were too complex and too deeply implanted, and solutions had been postponed too long. In this chapter the preliminary impact of the administrative change on municipal development will be observed. What was accomplished by crown officials in this area in the first decade of the functioning of the new government? What was the attitude of the local councils toward the activities of the new officials? These are the major questions for which answers are sought.[1]

Before treating the actual work of the intendants it would be well to pause and recall the salient reasons leading to the adaptation of the seventeenth-century French form of government to the American colonies. Foremost was the hope of augmenting the crown's revenue from America. The royal coffers required replenishing with gold and silver so that Spain might again take her rightful place under the aegis of Charles III as a world power of the first magnitude. An aggressive foreign policy to stem the imperial designs of Great Britain and an elaborate court at Madrid to recapture royal prestige dictated the need for additional funds. It was only too clear that a reversal of the trend of smaller shipments of bullion which had been noted since the seventeenth century had to be brought about. The application of various stimuli to the colonial economy, such as the adoption of free trade between Spain and her transatlantic colonies and the removal of

1. John Lynch's *Spanish Colonial Administration* is enlightening for the effects of the system in the Viceroyalty of Buenos Aires.

restrictions on intercolonial commerce, might result in greater prosperity and indirectly make possible the collection of larger revenues. A second aim was the bolstering of overseas defenses through improvement in the organization of the military forces and in the spirit and physical comforts of the troops stationed in America. It was to be the intendant's duty to see to the prompt payment of the soldiers and their proper provisioning. Measures to better the training and quality of the troops and the type of fortifications supplemented his efforts. There was also a limited consciousness on the part of the crown of an obligation for the welfare of natives and colonists, as the oppression of the Indians by unscrupulous corregidores and alcaldes mayores had been condemned by the Council of the Indies. The rebellion of Túpac-Amaru brought home the necessity of curing a festering sore in the body politic by the transference of the duties of older officials to intendants, subdelegates, and alcaldes ordinarios, all of whom, it was believed, would be more submissive than their predecessors to directives from Europe. The lassitude and decay of municipal regimes pointed to the indispensability of reinvigorating the cabildos through investigation of corrupt practices, correction of evils, and supervision and expansion of civic services.

In the area of local government some of these aims were partly realized in the years immediately following the inception of the intendancy. In the augmenting of revenues from municipal sources the crown did not achieve unqualified success. The following table of accounts of salable offices of the Real Hacienda of Lima for five-year periods, from 1770-1795, is revealing:

OFICIOS

	Collected in Lima		Collected outside		Total	
1770	10,470 ps.	½ rs.	11,549 ps.	6½ rs.	22,020 ps.	7 rs.*
1775	12,168	3½	11,341	5¾	28,504	¾
1780	9,993	6	12,529	⅞	23,621	3**
1785	4,128	2	5,751	7-21¼	9,880	1-21¼***

*The returns from the provincial cities and towns were as follows: Huancavelica, 1,449 ps.; Saña, 970 ps. 6½ rs.; Chancito (Chancay?), 143 ps. 2½ rs.; Piura, 3,178 ps. 7¾ rs.; Arequipa, 921 ps. 7½ rs.; Cailloma, 583 ps.; Arica, 976 ps.; Cuzco, 672 ps. 4¾ rs.
**The total includes some amounts from the previous year.
***Apparently, sums left over from the preceding period were counted.

Collected in Lima and
in other treasuries   *To be collected†*

| 1790 | 5,640 ps. | 7 rs. | 7,622 ps. | 3 rs. |
| 1795 | 7,179 | 2 | 16,900 | 3†† |

†This would not include the area of Cuzco, as will be evident.

††The offices sold or rented at this time include those of regidor, escribano público, escribano de provincia, escribano de naturales, alcalde provincial, procurator, and receptor.

Source. Cuentas de la real caja de Lima de los ministros de Real Hacienda, legajos 1141, 1143, 1146, 1151, 1156, 1161, Audiencia de Lima, A. G. I.

From an examination of the above it is obvious that the amounts secured from oficios after the installation of the intendancy were markedly less. The decline after 1787 resulted in part from the creation in the same year of the Audiencia of Cuzco which had a royal treasury of its own. More important, there was the lessened esteem in which municipal officeholding was regarded.[2] The Viceroy Abascal testified to a reduction of returns from this source in the period from 1806-1816, which he attributed in part to the smaller number of aldermen and escribanos de cabildo.[3]

Other revenues associated with municipal prosperity gave more promising results. An upward movement in the sums collected from the alcabala and stamped paper is noted. In 1770 the sales tax produced 468,698-2½; in 1775, 233,221-5½; in 1780, 502,440-7½; in 1785, 559,034 (including some amounts from the previous year); in 1787, 678,775-6½ (including returns from all areas of the viceroyalty). A sampling of income from stamped paper in the same period indicates a parallel tendency: 1770, 12,584-6¾; 1775, 11,494-7¼; 1780, 17,789-6; 1785, 33,890-7-30 (including sums from the previous year); 1787, 33,012-3½ (collected from the viceroyalty); and 1790, 93,938-7 (from the vice-

2. The most valuable offices were those of escribano de cabildo and alcalde provincial, to which were attached the right to collect fees. In Lima the position of alférez real, though carrying no remuneration, continued to be highly prized for the social prestige that it gave to its holder. The regular price of an aldermanic post in the capital from 1790 to 1800 was 2,000 pesos.

3. The crown had made some slight efforts to give the office more attraction by lowering the cost of confirmation and by allowing an inheritor to take over a position whose former holder had not lived the necessary twenty days required by law upon payment of one-sixth of its value. The limit of exemption from the media anata was raised by 1806 to 300 pesos, thus removing the application of this tax from most municipal salaries. See Rodríguez and Calderón, *Memoria de gobierno de Abascal y Sousa*, I, 276-278.

royalty?).[4] These figures reflect the increased commercial and mining activities resulting from other reform measures as well as attesting to the efficiency and probity of the intendants.

To assess fully the timely contribution of the intendants to the welfare and well-being of the municipalities, it is worthwhile to explore the conduct and activities of several of these officials in their respective districts. These intendants are perhaps unusual exemplars of the new bureaucracy, but what they did may be regarded as in part typical of the work of the intendant. In many significant areas of local administration the official came directly into contact with the ayuntamiento, since his role was a dual one of reactivating old functions and of devising new services. This might embrace a program of public works for the benefit of the community. On the other hand, in his capacity as quartermaster-bursar he had little to do with the municipal bodies. Contracts for supplies of meat, bread, and clothing were generally made with individual merchants or firms operating outside the purview of the local councils.

Of all the intendants, Escobedo deserves special attention for his accomplishments in the capital. Having assumed the headship of the cabildo in July, 1784, he undertook almost at once an attack on its economic problems.[5] On August 13 he issued an oficio authorizing the location of the aqueducts and the cleaning of the streets. In rapid succession other orders of a similar nature were drawn up and sent to the council for execution. But in March, 1785, he complained to the cabildo of its inaction and procrastination. Prodded by this criticism, the council gave fresh consideration to the work of the alcaldes de barrios and to construction of the aqueducts. When zeal slackened once more, he instituted measures to force the attendance of the capitulars at ordinary sessions; and, to inspire the alcaldes de barrios, he invited them to his residence to explain carefully the nature of their duties. Dissatisfaction of the Intendant with the cabildo for "doing nothing and limiting its efforts to a few ideas and conferences" continued.

4. Cuentas de la real caja de Lima de los ministros de la Real Hacienda, legajos 1141, 1143, 1146, 1151, 1156, Audiencia de Lima, A. G. I.

5. In an oficio of Dec. 14, 1785, to the cabildo, he represented himself as a "father and head [of the corporation], who looks out for its honor and wishes to avoid the stigma of a stern judge." See Cabildo secular de Lima, año, 1786, folio 1, legajo 802, Audiencia de Lima, A. G. I.

In a communication to the cabildo in December, 1785, Escobedo summed up his accomplishments in Lima:

> Let us say that the propios have been augmented by many thousand [pesos] and freed of their former confusion and disorder. I mention the establishment of the alcaldes de barrios that you desired and I approved immediately. I mention the real bodegaje that was scarcely thought of, but finally suggested by the cabildo, which received in the junta superior the strongest support; you requested the sisa for certain public works and the urgencies of the public treasury did not prevent me from assigning increased sums and thus dissipate the badly founded opinion which was held in regard to the application of this tax; you sought to repair the sala capitular which has always been in an indecorous and pitiful condition, and you see it already having the appearance and commodiousness fitting for the distinguished body that assembles there; an appeal was made for money for uniforms and other articles for the processions and for the alférez real with the standard; and without delay all was granted; and finally, tell me what you have grumbled about, asked for, and desired that I have not attempted to aid with my providencias.

In concluding his thinly disguised effort to spur the cabildo on in its labors, the Intendant requested that body to peruse his message attentively and prepare a full reply to the charges, to which should be attached a complete list of the expedientes initiated since July of 1784 and their present state.[6] Despite Escobedo's demand for a prompt response, the cabildo took its good time in submitting the report. It was not until January 18 that the razón of autos y expedientes was transmitted to the Intendant, to be followed a few days later by a list of the oficios dispatched by the Superintendente General de Real Hacienda.

But the attempted refutation of Escobedo's criticism did not come until April 6, 1786.[7] With a touch of sarcasm, the ayuntamiento acknowledged at the outset its debt to the wisdom and resolution of its presiding officer: "There has always been recognized the scrupulous devotion of Your Excellency and the great providencias issued in

6. *Ibid.*, folios 1-10.

7. Prior to the dispatch of this rejoinder, the escribano and the archivist, who asserted that they knew more about the city's affairs than the council, drew up a most flattering informe for the Intendant, crediting him with the complete reformation of the city's government. It is hard to believe that civic affairs could have reached the depths described in this report. Needless to say, it was given without the approbation of the ayuntamiento. See *ibid.*, folios 20-30.

order to reach certain goals that concern this body whose most worshipful head, dedicated to the innumerable cares that surround him, has tried and has succeeded where similar efforts in several centuries have failed to impose regulations which, if observed, would make this city a replica of the court of Madrid." Though inwardly resentful, the cabildo begrudgingly admitted the usefulness of certain ordinances. The *Bando* of October 14, 1785, contained twenty-one articles "of the greatest importance for the public health and well-being." The number of alcaldes de barrios was increased to forty, "because the perspicacity of Your Excellency saw that two alcaldes ordinarios were not sufficient to discharge so many duties" of a varying nature. To these officials were assigned the cleaning of the streets and garbage disposal. But although responsible to the alcaldes de crimen, they did little to fulfil their duties. How was it possible for the cabildo to compel them to perform their tasks if the guidance of Escobedo was not sufficient to infuse them with the proper spirit? Finally, those in charge of cleaning the streets were summoned to the cabildo; and, when reprimanded for their remissness, they declared that the owners of the shops had failed to pay necessary costs. While the destruction of the old aqueducts was a commendable act, the city had to await the building of the underground conduits, a "work that requires time." Of all the measures proposed by the Intendant, the cabildo regarded the establishment of the *acordada* as "the most useful." Its agents were to be disposed to prosecute the "numerous highwaymen who live in this capital, stealing in its churches and in its shops, even in the middle of the day."

To cope successfully with these matters, the council needed more financial resources than were available from the present propios. Diverse sources of revenue were suggested: among others, a tax on carts and wagons transporting goods from Callao to the city, "a very old and legitimate tax;" an increase in the rent of the fincas; a part of the mojonasgo, or a contribution from the residents of the Valles of Vitor Mages, "as did Guamanga and other provinces to the real caja belonging today to Buenos Aires"; a tax of ½ real on pigs driven into the city to pay for the damage to the streets; a levy on corridas de toros, held on special occasions; and an increase in the tax on gambling. The municipality was grateful for the allotment of funds from the sisa for the rebuilding of the upper works of the bridge, without which great havoc would have occurred during floods, and for the construction of ditches to bring additional water to the city.

Not only did the city wish to express its gratitude to the Intendant for the grant of funds, but it was thankful for his assistance in the closer regulation of prices on articles of sustenance. Food was plentiful. The price of potatoes, at one time 16 pesos a load, was down to a little more than 20 reales because of the penalties and fines imposed on the hucksters and the execution of royal orders by the guards at the gates.

In other matters the ayuntamiento was dutifully carrying out its responsibilities to the citizenry. On the first of every month the junior alcalde received notices of purchases of wheat and wax and instructed the buyers to fix a fair price on bread and candles. The sale of articles in the plaza mayor was rendered easier by the assignment of sections to the various types of vendors. For the discussion of civic questions the cabildo met on the days set aside for this purpose. When public fiestas were held, all of the members were present, with the natural exception of those absent by permission because of the exigencies of the haciendas and those ill.[8]

The citation by the cabildo of its own accomplishments should not belittle what Escobedo had done for the city. The extensive program of public works, including repairs of the bridges and aqueducts, the beautification of the town hall, and the augmentation of the propios were major contributions.

Helpful also was the issuance of a *Reglamento de policía*, "municipal code."[9] Containing eighty articles and drafted by Escobedo to put an end to the disorders and confusion in the handling of civic affairs, the new regulations prescribed the appointment of a *teniente de policía*, with a salary of 2,000 pesos annually, of two deputies at 600 pesos each, of four alguaciles at 300 pesos each, and an overseer of public works at 500 pesos. Under the teniente were the alcaldes de barrios, who were responsible for the execution of bandos and orders. Excluded from civil and criminal jurisdiction, they were to see primarily to the cleaning, lighting, and repair of the streets. Weekly meetings of the alcaldes de barrios of each cuartel were to be held

8. *Ibid.*, folios 30-42.

9. The laudatory informe of the escribano and the archivist refers to Escobedo's regulations as "fixed, well-accepted, and so comprehensively drawn that they do not overlook any case." See *ibid*, folio 29.

under the supervision of the teniente for the discussion of particular problems encountered. To pay for the costs of removing garbage and refuse and keeping the streets free of rubbish, the alcaldes were to inspect their districts and draw up a razón of expenditures. When this was done, a regidor, designated by the alcalde for each barrio, was to summon to his home a junta, composed of twenty-four citizens and the alcalde de barrio, to prorate the costs among the citizens.[10]

Lastly, the reglamento rectified negligent practices of the guilds. Article 14 provided for better supervision by the cabildo of the activities of the business establishments and labor organizations. A shop or store could not open for business without a license from the ayuntamiento, which had to keep a separate book in its archives for each gremio. The election of alcaldes of the guilds was to be held in the residence of the senior alcalde ordinario at the beginning of each year. Should a guild lack a set of rules for its government, one had to be drafted immediately by the procurator-general and approved by the cabildo and the intendant.[11]

The execution of measures for the improvement of transportation, communication, and the water supply was entrusted initially to José María Egaña, the first teniente de policía. To make it easier to locate the streets and houses, he ordered signs with names of streets to be put up and the houses in each block numbered. To the denizens of a modern city confronted by the intricate multiplicity of buildings and blocks, the absence of these simple expedients is incomprehensible. In addition to the paving of a large section of the street of Santa Clara, the large fountain in the plaza mayor as well as those in the less important squares were repaired or rebuilt under his direction. The people of Lima might well be grateful to him for the purity and abundance of their drinking water. In view of the limited finances of the municipality, he persuaded the Junta General de Hacienda to turn over the proceeds of the excise on wheat sold in Bellavista for the cleaning of the public buildings.[12]

As was evident, the immediate effect of the intendancy in Lima

10. *Nuevo reglamento de policía agregado a la instrucción de alcaldes de barrio* (Lima, 1786).

11. *Ibid.*; see also Expediente promobido en el exmo cabildo por D. Francisco Yampaez sobre que se le conceda licencia para abrir una pulpería (año 1817), legajo 10 (cabildos), 1809-1817, Archivo nacional (Lima).

12. Vargas Ugarte, *Historia del Perú, virreinato, 1700-1790*, pp. 450, 451.

was a curtailment of the authority and prestige of the regidores and alcaldes. While the membership of the council was increased to sixteen, the number of meetings recorded in the libro de cabildo significantly declined to an average of six a year for the period from 1785-1788. During this interval the teniente asesor of the intendant regularly presided over the conciliar elections. But, alleging that the presence of the crown official was contrary to immemorial privilege, the cabildo managed to obtain a cedula in March, 1788, abolishing the practice. On January 1, 1789, the ayuntamiento resumed its custom of selecting by "secret vote" an alcalde for a two-year term and a juez de aguas for a single year.[13] Following the election, the capitulars trooped to the Viceroy's palace for his approval of proceedings and later received confirmation of the act from the Intendant. The list of elective secondary officials remained strictly limited to the procurator and the two judges of the municipal junta, many offices having been extinguished or suspended at the Intendant's orders. The cabildo relinquished completely its time-honored custom of receiving and registering the credentials of important officials associated with local government. The exclusion of the Intendant's representative from elections may have been responsible for the holding of numerous conciliar sessions in the years following 1788.

Further loss of the alcalde's judicial and administrative powers was not taken supinely by the cabildo of Lima. It remonstrated against the teniente de policía, who was accused of "becoming a juez de la Hermandad" under the pretext of rounding up vagrants and other undesirables in the city. The indignant council resolved to inform the Viceroy that no good had come from the appointment of an official who had four deputies "notoriously employed in tasks unconnected with their supposed duties," and in addition, two subordinates drawing 600 pesos annually but presently residing on haciendas at some distance from the city.[14] It seems clear also that the alcaldes de barrios, encouraged by the Intendant, had overstepped their rightful bounds of authority. For in 1793 the ayuntamiento dispatched a consulta to the Viceroy, asking for a copy of an earlier decree directed against the abuses of these officials so that means might be found to

13. Minutes of Sept. 22, 1789, Libros de cabildos de Lima, vol. XXXVIII, Biblioteca municipal, Lima.
14. Minutes of Oct. 13, 1791, *ibid.*

prevent them "from deciding everything, even an agreement over debts, although the amount be small, or making judicial appeals and executions, or putting anyone in prison for debt."[15]

The designation by the Intendant of officials for the government of Indian villages situated near the cities and formerly subject to their jurisdiction was not to the liking of Lima and other cities. Arequipa's protest was typical. In a representación of October 10, 1785, the cabildo expostulated vigorously to the Viceroy against the encroachment, as contrary to "its oldest and immemorial custom . . . of choosing alcaldes ordinarios for the municipal district. . . ." Not only had no obstacle been put in its way in the past by the corregidor, but the ayuntamiento had selected a deputy from its membership to preside over native cabildos in settlements not administered directly by the royal agent. The council agreed to recognize the Intendant's right under the ordinance to name judges for some villages, but, with the qualification that they be "of proven citizenship." It was observed that certain judges, appointees of the Intendant, were "men of little or no education and who are only good at obeying orders." While the outcome of the petition is unknown, it is unlikely that the Intendant's power, so recently instituted, was checked.[16]

Measures aimed at reform of the local councils did not cease with the promulgation of the Ordinance of Intendants. To prevent office-holders from looking upon their positions as outright property to be disposed of as they pleased and likewise to safeguard his own financial interests, the king issued a general cédula, dated October 15, 1787, at San Lorenzo, applying to Peru and other areas of the empire:

> Although the occupants of vendible offices have the right of possession with the limitation that the laws prescribe, they are not authorized to dispose of them at will, as if it were some finca of their inheritance, since my crown retains always direct ownership, with a future right of reversion to it, for different reasons that may develop; and wishing to reconcile the valuation of these offices to the welfare of my Royal Treasury, to the common good, and to particular in-

15. Minutes of April 19, 1793, *ibid.*
As the procurator general of Lima expressed it many years later, "the alcaldes de barrios are not judges, but simply commissioners as they were designated in the first articles of their establishment in the years 1768 and 1770 . . . and in the Instructions of 1785." See Expediente sobre establecer dos serenos barrio de Monserrate a expensas de sus vecinos, 1807, legajo 8 (cabildos), Archivo nacional (Lima).
16. Representación de Arequipa, *ibid.*

terests, and that they be filled by persons fit for employment . . . I have resolved to forbid by general decree any imposition of a censo or other obligation on the salable offices of my Kingdoms of the Indies, so that with respect to the law in the event of a substitution or leasing [full ownership] must be reserved to its possessors concerning the function and the emoluments of the same offices. . . .

As a general regulation, I so declare that in all cases of substitution or leasing of notarial offices, salable and disposable, the balance should be divided, after satisfying he who uses it, between my Real Hacienda and particular interests, in the same proportion that the principal sum would be assigned in the case of a sale, according to the spirit of the laws, but with the precaution that putting these vacant offices up for leasing should be avoided as far as possible, acording to the disposition of various real cedulas. And finally, I declare that no more than one third of the emoluments and salaries of such offices can be attached by reason of debts of their possessors.[17]

Control of the city's finances had passed to a large degree to the newly created municipal junta. Comprising two regidores chosen by the council, the senior alcalde, the procurator-general, and the intendant, it was a small body, more readily held accountable to the crown. But since the membership was mainly conciliar it might continue to voice the sentiments of the cabildo. To provide figures and facts for the junta in the capital, Escobedo ordered the cabildo of Lima by an oficio of September 22, 1784, to draw up a statement of its propios y arbitrios and *bienes de comunidad*. When the estimate was turned over to the Intendant, it was amended with the hope of increasing the income by the addition of new sources and elimination of unnecessary expenditures. From this information the contaduría general de propios y arbitrios prepared a list of sources of income and items of expenditure from November, 1784, to December, 1787. This was to be the basis of a budget, calculated to produce annually a surplus instead of a deficit.[18] In time, strict supervision of the finances and the

17. Cédula general, San Lorenzo, Oct. 15, 1787, legajo 1802, Papeles de Cuba, A. G. I.

18. The revenues amounted to 39,929 pesos 1½ reales; expenditures, 22,218 pesos 2 reales, with the ramo of the mojonasgo bringing in 20,674 pesos. This figure did not include the returns from the ramo de sisa on Castilian beef, for which the cabildo had petitioned the Junta Superior, nor the ramo de bodegaje on each fenega of wheat, amounting to 25,000 to 30,000 pesos, but obligated to the expenses of policía. On the other hand, the annual list of expenditures omitted extraordinary outlays, which in the three years from Nov. 16, 1784, to the end of 1787 came to 103,730 pesos, spent mainly for the construction of the bridge, the digging of a canal, and other public

well-intentioned measures of thrift aroused the cabildo's displeasure. Virtually no payment, it was declared, could be made without authorization of the municipal junta. The ayuntamiento finally complained that frugality was enforced to such a ridiculous point that even the ancient right of the capitulars to purchase large tapers at conciliar expense for the procession of Santa Cruz on Holy Thursday had been suppressed. But protests were unavailing.[19]

Efforts similar to those in Lima were made by the crown to determine the financial condition of municipal treasuries in the remaining intendancies. In fulfilment of Article 47 of the ordinance, the contaduría on June 2, 1787, submitted to Escobedo as superintendant of the royal treasury a statement of the propios and arbitrios and of expenditures of the chief cities and towns of the Audiencia of Lima, based on razones furnished by the various councils, with modifications applied by the Intendant, down to December, 1786. Essentially, this was to serve as a financial guide or directive to hold municipal expenditures in line with income.

In submitting the proposed budgets, the contaduría noted that those for Lima, Cuzco, Huancavelica, Guamanga, and Tarma had already been approved. Nearly all of the statements, it will be observed, disclosed a surplus, which could not in reality be considered as such since no provision was made for the inevitable extraordinary expenses coming from repairs of buildings and other public works. The arbitrios to supplement regular income, proposed by the Junta Superior, comprised three types: the first being that of the mojonasgo on spirits and wine, introduced into Tarma and Jauja; the second, 1 real on each fanega of pepper from Palpa for the benefit of Yca; and the third, 1 real on each fanega of wheat and fodder from Chile in favor of Lima. Only the first was introduced, however, as appeals were presented to the crown by those groups disadvantageously affected by the excises. It was impossible to present at that time, the contaduría pointed out, a statement of the bienes de comunidad of the Indians, because of the "sparse and mixed up" figures secured

---

works. These were to be partly defrayed by the income from the sisa and from the regular propios. See Estado general que demuestra los productos y gastos efectibos, y eventuales, que anualmente tienen las rentas de propios y arbitrios de esta capital de Lima, Lima, 1 abril, 1789, legajo 14, Archivo histórico de hacienda y comercio, Lima.

19. Minutes of Nov. 28, 1786, Libros de cabildos de Lima, vol. XXXVIII, Biblioteca municipal, Lima.

Income

Intendancies	Cities	Types of income				
		Renting of fincas and haciendas	Censos activos	Ramo mojonasgo	Sisa	Total
Lima	Lima	13,494 ps. 4 rs.	2,210 ps. 4 rs.	20,674 ps. ½ r.		36,379 ps. ½ r.
	Yca	284 2				284 2
Trujillo	Trujillo	573 5½		859 6	946 ps. 6½ rs.	2,380 2
	Lambayeque	360		1,100		1,460
	Piura	412			258	670
Cuzco	Cuzco	1,038 4	1,100			2,138 4
Huancavelica	Huancavelica			1,199 6½		1,199 6½
Guamanga	Guamanga	801	15	1,639 7½		2,455 7½
Arequipa	Arequipa	4,255	1,387 5			5,642 5
Tarma	Huánuco	481		350		831
	Tarma			1,050		1,050
	Totals	21,699 ps. 7½ rs.	4,713 ps. 1 r.	26,873 ps. 4½ rs.	1,204 ps. 6½ rs.	54,491 ps. 3½ rs.

EXPENDITURES

Intendancies	Cities	Types of expenses					
		Salaries and stipends	Censos pasivos	Fiestas	Fixed	Total	Balance
Lima	Lima	8,410 ps.	5,742 ps.	1,658 ps. 4 rs.	1,576 ps. 6 rs.	17,387 ps. 2 rs.	18,991 ps. 6½ rs.
	Yca			98 2½	32 1	130 3½	153 6½
Trujillo	Trujillo	1,304	39 3	150	258	1,778 3	601 7
	Lambayeque	660			80	740	720
	Piura	251		100	80	431	239
Cuzco	Cuzco	812		416	50	1,278	860 4
Huancavelica	Huancavelica	1,000		200	100	1,300	
Guamanga	Guamanga	1,234 2	50	227	40	1,551 2	904 5½
Arequipa	Arequipa	4,539 ½	252	66 4	250	5,107 4½	535 ½
Tarma	Huánuco	200		162	50	412	69
	Tarma	200			50	250	100
	Jauja	800			100	900	150
	Totals	19,410 ps. 2½ rs.	6,083 ps. 3 rs.	3,078 ps. 2½ rs.	2,693 ps. 7 rs	31,265 ps. 7 rs.	23,325 ps. 6 rs.

NOTE. There are some discrepancies in the calculations of the accountants, but these figures reveal the general sources of income and types of expenditures of the municipalities.

SOURCE. Estado general que manifesta las rentas de propios y arbitrios que igualmente gozan las ciudades del Reyno del Peru, segun consta de las razones dadas por sus respectivos cabildos...in Expediente sobre la averiguacion de las rentas de propios, arbitrios y bienes de comunidad de las ciudades, y villas del distrito, cuaderno 14, legajo 14, Archivo histórico de hacienda y comercio, Lima.

from the subdelegates, who were handicapped by lack of proper documents in determining the origin and disposition of funds.[20] Although undoubtedly aware of the major defect of the budgets, the inability to provide for the extraordinary expenditures, Escobedo nonetheless on June 12, 1787, temporarily approved the revisions and modifications and ordered copies distributed to the various municipalities. Much store was set by their release.

Numerous visitas in the audiencia underline the initial display of energy and imagination by the lesser intendants in tackling municipal problems. Notable for its thoroughness is an inspection of the southern province of Arequipa by the second intendant, Antonio Alvarez y Jiménez, from 1785-1793. On August 12, 1785, he addressed a letter to the cabildo of Arequipa, informing that body of his arrival in Lima and his imminent departure for the post. By November 10 he was in the city and had begun to issue orders requisite for the execution of the administrative changes.[21] In twelve months all preparations had been completed for the visit to the city and to the settlements of the seven partidos comprising the province.[22]

Alvarez' reforms for Arequipa were well planned, inclusive, and of enduring benefit. Realizing the importance of solvency for a well-ordered municipality, he drew up by February 12, 1787, a reglamento of income and expenses. The bridge over the river requiring further maintenance, the Intendant recommended to the Junta Superior de Real Hacienda the use of funds from an increase in the tax on maize of a certain type and quality. This was sanctioned by an auto of December 12, 1787.[23] When unusually heavy flooding in 1790 necessitated additional repairs to the bridge, the Intendant summoned a cabildo público of all the citizens to obtain approval for a special levy.[24] Among other public works undertaken were the widening and straightening of the streets, the rebuilding of the casa de cabildo and the pósito, the repairing of the city walls and the aqueducts, and the establishment of two inns on roads leading to the city.[25]

20. Expediente sobre la averiguación de las rentas de propios, cuaderno 14, legajo 14, Archivo histórico de hacienda y comercio, Lima.
21. He succeeded José Menéndez de Escalada, who had withdrawn for some inexplicable reason. See Victor M. Barriaga (ed.), Memorias para la historia de Arequipa, 1786-96 (3 tomos; Arequipa, 1941-1948), III, pp. 282 note, 283, 284.
22. Ibid., I, 125-127.   23. Ibid., I, 44.
24. Ibid., I, 64, 65.   25. Ibid., I, 124.

To instil vigor into the functioning of the cabildo was likewise an objective of the Intendant. Enough citizens were appointed to the ayuntamiento to give it the prescribed number of sixteen. He encouraged, also, the purchase of offices that were vacant, in particular that of the escribano. As he declared in his report, "In effect my urging has brought about advantageous sales, and even at the present time numerous expedientes are being drafted in my office, which I shall not put aside until I see each one of the ayuntamientos with its proper number of capitulars in order that the Real Hacienda receive what legally belongs to it."[26] Thus municipal government was stimulated with profit to the citizenry and to the crown as well.

Alvarez spared neither physical strength nor patience in his examination of the remaining towns, villas, and pueblos in the intendancy. Outside of the capital, the European settlements that merited his attention were the city of Arica and the villas of Camaná and Moquegua. His visit to Moquegua may be regarded as typical of his painstaking scrutiny of secondary communities.

In general, his accomplishments in the outlying localities followed the same lines of action set forth for the capital. The aims were just and efficient government and the diligent assessment of royal taxes. What he did for Moquegua well illustrates the pattern of his policy for the lesser towns. Alcaldes ordinarios were ordered to keep a record of their fines to make certain that the treasury got its proper share.[27] The Intendant appointed a ward commissioner to aid the alcaldes in the care of the streets, without any authority to institute legal suits or to imprison criminals.[28] Construction of a suitable town hall was obligatory. To ascertain the extent of the propios and to adopt measures to supplement those in existence, the Intendant held a cabildo abierto, with forty-two persons present, at which it was agreed to impose a small tax on each bottle of wine. From this excise it was estimated that 15,607 pesos, 6 reales would be realized. Of this amount 12,000 pesos would constitute the propios, which lent at 5 per cent would bring in an annual income of about 600 pesos. The remainder was to be

26. *Ibid.*, I, 87.

27. Seis quadernos, los 5 q. contienen las relaciones legalizadas de visita en el partido de Moq. y el 6º y ultimo el reconocimto. del Puerto de Yca del partido de Arica en dha. Prov. 7 enero, 1793, por don Antonio Alvarez y Ximenez a Excmo. sr. dn. Pedro de Acuña y Malbar, folio 2, legajo 805, Audiencia de Lima, A. G. I.

28. *Ibid.*, folio 20.

allotted to meet the cost of a building containing a hall for the conciliar sessions, a jail, and chapel.[29] Measures were taken for the paving of streets and keeping them free of refuse and obstructions. To this end citizens and residents had to assist in the transporting of stones for the foundation of the roads. All householders possessing dwellings damaged by fire or earthquake were required to rebuild their homes within three months, under penalty of seeing their lots put up at public auction. Whoever should fail to "clean, pave, whitewash what belongs to him shall be forced to pay for the cost of this work."[30] As for the aqueducts, those who threw stones or garbage into the channels would be punished. Particular care was taken to rectify certain "pernicious abuses concerning excessive profits of the proprietors of grocery stores, which have developed to the injury of the public."[31] The trouble lay with the "owners who traveled along the highway, as far as the pueblo of Torata, or even farther, to buy up all the goods and provisions brought by merchants and which by law should be exhibited on the principal square." To eliminate the monopoly, the Intendant issued a series of bandos, carrying heavy fines for violation of their provisions.[32] It was forbidden for owners of shops, hucksters, and other individuals to purchase any objects of gold or silver, jewelry, or clothing from a servant, without full assurance that this was done with his master's consent. The occasional scarcity of fish in the market place was not so much the result of the indolence of fishermen in the nearby port as it was of the greediness of shopkeepers. Accordingly, it was stipulated that all fish destined for the city "be transported to the public square for sale and for no claim, reason, or pretext to private homes, unless it was especially ordered for them."[33] Other decrees point to the fine care for the well-being and security of the citizenry.

A thorough inspection was ordered also for the Indian villages and *doctrinas* in the province, in accordance with the instructions to intendants. In this case procedure was uniform, the examination being made in the four categories of administration: *real patronato*, justice,

29. *Ibid.*, folios 77-83.
30. Oficios pasados a los sugetos que de ellos constan, en la visita de la villa de Moquegua, cabezera del partido de su nombre y son los mismos que en la relacion legalizada de dha visita se mencionan, *ibid.*, folio 46.
31. *Ibid.*, folio 48.   32. *Ibid.*, folios 49-51.
33. *Ibid.*, folio 52.

policía, and war. Reference will be made here chiefly to the formation of the local council and the disposal of public property and services, as these constituted areas in which the inhabitants had some authority over their own affairs.

A typical pueblo and doctrina that submitted to a visitation by the Intendant was Paucarpata in the partido of Arequipa. Between June 7, and 11, 1788, Alvárez investigated fully its administration. In a scrutiny of its government the first step was an examination of the probity and impartiality of the Spanish and native alcaldes. Depositions and oral affirmations cleared the officials of serious charges, though this was by no means universally true in such inquiries.[34] The doctrina having no funds, the Intendant instructed the officials of the village to locate unclaimed land that might provide future income. The Indians were to hold no conciliar session without the presence of the Spanish alcaldes.[35] To solve disputes over water rights, Alvarez assigned jurisdiction to the alcalde de aguas of Arequipa.[36] In planning for the future growth of the pueblo, he lamented the difficulty in extending the streets "owing to the gullies and declivities that are to be found a few steps from the main square."[37] Owners of unoccupied solares were to utilize their land to public advantage. While the town possessed a casa de cabildo, the building was small and in need of repairs. The plaza itself had been reduced in size by the encroachment on it of Indian huts. To pay for the legal costs of removing the squatters and to arrange for additional public structures, the Intendant secured donations from the Spanish alcalde and several landowners, with the cacique of the village directing the operations.[38] In many other villages it was necessary for Alvarez to order the native cabildo to build a casa for the capitulars.

Further exemplification of an intendant's zealousness exists in the report of October 17, 1786, to the crown from the administrator of Tarma, Juan María de Gálvez. The capital of the intendancy presented a picture of desolation and neglect, lacking propios and even a local council. The Intendant installed a cabildo with the regular number of regidores, and this body proceeded forthwith to the election of alcaldes. When it was discovered that the village had no

34. Barriaga, *Memorias para la historia de Arequipa, 1786-96*, I, 206.
35. *Ibid.*, p. 207.   36. *Ibid.*, p. 208.
37. *Ibid.*, p. 210.   38. *Ibid.*, p. 211.

propios, he authorized for the local treasury an excise of 4 reales on each bottle of spirits, a tax that enjoyed a precedent in the case of Lima. Other improvements included the remodeling of the parish church, establishment of a slaughterhouse, and the beautification of the cemetery.[39] To the neighboring city of Jauja he dispatched an engineer to rebuild the aqueduct and construct a bridge over the Yanama, a stream dangerous for travelers when in flood. Similarly, Huánuco, an old settlement, whose privileges were granted by Charles V after the uprising of Francisco Hernando Girón, had suffered an economic decline since the seventeenth century, with many of its citizens removing their residence to Lima. The cabildo comprised a few regidores, who "were so in name only, but not in the exercise of their offices." So remiss were they in their duties that the sala of the ayuntamiento was opened only once a year, and then for the election of the alcaldes. What propios the municipality once held had been dissipated through "omission and carelessness of the capitulars." For this sorry state of affairs the remedy was to fill the unoccupied seats in the cabildo and institute biweekly sessions on Tuesday and Saturday, with a definite agenda for discussion. An inspection of municipal assets having revealed civic property illegally in the hands of private citizens, the Intendant ordered the restoration of the lands to the rightful owner. In this way the annual rent from town holdings was doubled.[40]

If additional evidence is needed of the enterprise and resourcefulness of the royal incumbents in the first stage of the intendancy, such may be found in the petitions and memorials addressed by the cabildos to the crown. Many municipalities recognized the foresight, the disinterestedness, and the industry of these officials, which were reflected in the number of material improvements and in the rehabilitation of civic esprit. In cartas to the king they expressed their gratitude for the appointment of wise and able administrators.

It is not surprising that the cabildo of Arequipa eulogized the civic contributions of the Intendant Alvarez. In a conciliar session of May 7, 1787, it was resolved to remit an informe to the King in appreciation of the designation:

39. Informe extensamente quanto le ha parecido digno de noticiar a V. E. p. que se sirba trasladarlo a los pies del Soberano . . ., Tarma, 17 octubre, 1786, legajo 646, Audiencia de Lima, A. G. I.
40. *Ibid.*

For since he [Alvarez] entered office in the year 1785 he has labored with all strength and zeal in the service of His Majesty and in fulfillment of royal orders, but also for the well-being of the republic. It is well known that he has aided the crown in finding tracts of land held under false title in some partidos and in augmenting the royal treasury. His ardor in the administration of justice is likewise understood and also the kindness that he reveals towards the poor and especially to the Indians, forcing the caciques to return property that they have usurped. His impartiality is outstanding, for he listens to the pleas of the poor without charging fees. He has labored long in the restoration of the city and in the cleanliness of its streets. He has looked after those committed to prison, helping them with money from his own income. He has visited all the pueblos in the vicinity, settling their affairs without the slightest charge to Spaniard or Indian. He has given his attention to an increase in the municipal propios, to the construction of schools for children of both sexes, with provision for the teaching of the rudiments of education and of Latin. He has laid out a beautiful mall for the pleasure of the citizens in order that they may entertain themselves publicly. He has employed all of his intelligence in stimulating mining and everything else that may serve the cause of His Majesty and the public weal.[41]

A further gauge of conciliar feeling is an informe of November 27, 1785, from the ayuntamiento of Trujillo to the Minister of the Indies, José de Gálvez:

> The cabildo of Trujillo . . . renders its due thanks for the immense benefits that it has received from the royal hand in the establishment of the intendancies and for having nominated for this province D. Fernando Saavedra....[42]

Likewise, cartas from Piura (March 15, 1788) and Huancavelica (April 11, 1788) reaffirmed the sentiments of gratitude and indebtedness.[43]

It is to be observed that most of the favorable expressions came in the period from 1785 to 1788. Thereafter enthusiasm for the system waned. This change of attitude may be attributable to factors and developments of the subsequent era: a full realization by the conciliar bodies of the further curtailment of their liberties; the demise of

41. Barriaga, *Memorias para la historia de Arequipa, 1786-96*, III, 295.
42. Carta del cabildo de Trujillo a D. José de Gálvez, 27 noviembre, 1785, legajo 1117, Audiencia de Lima, A. G. I.
43. Informes de Piura, 15 marzo, 1788, y de Huancavelica, 11 abril, 1788, legajo 802, Audiencia de Lima, A. G. I.

Charles III, who was succeeded by a son of mediocre talent, less concerned with imperial reform; the return to Spain of the aggressive administrator and implementer of the system, Jorge de Escobedo; the outbreak of foreign wars; and lastly, the emergence of a latent national consciousness. All of these factors will be examined in greater detail later on.

Indisputably, from the standpoint of municipal evolution, the immediate advantages of the innovation outweighed the drawbacks. Material improvements of all sorts were numerous and necessary. Public buildings, bridges, highways, and streets were constructed at the orders of the crown officials, who were not loath to authorize new taxes and levies. In cities where propios had been lost through misappropriation of land or structures by individual citizens or through excessive expenditures, the intendants made efforts to supply much-needed funds from other sources.[44] Revitalization of the municipal spirit and the elevation of morale were a direct consequence. Cabildos, which had ceased to exist or which functioned in a desolutory manner, were reorganized and restored to operation. But in the long run was the price paid for these benefits too high? The cost for the local councils was a reduction of rights and privileges—a condition that would lead to dissatisfaction among the creoles, who regarded the cabildo as their own institution. It could safely be predicted that demands for its abolition or modification would be pressed by conciliar bodies and by jealous officials of the old order. To lessen the criticism the crown might permit a partial restoration of the pre-intendancy administration.

44. Close supervision of municipal finances by a series of energetic governors plus co-operation of the cabildo made New Orleans in Louisiana an exemplar among Spanish colonial cities. Between 1782 and 1801 the income, obtained chiefly from sale of solares on the *plaza de armas*, leasing of the meat supply, and from duty on brandy, rose from 4,389 pesos 2 reales to 11,653 pesos 5½ reales. The city's per capita income was roughly five times higher than that of Mexico City, twelve times that of Santiago de Chile, and twenty times that of Buenos Aires. See Ezquerra "Un presupuesto americano," pp. 691-700.

CHAPTER X

Limited Resurgence
of Municipal Rights

Circumstances by 1790 were more conducive to the resumption of some
of the earlier authority of the cabildos in the Audiencia of Lima.
The full effect of the oppressiveness of the intendancy lasted only
six to eight years. Like preceding reforms in the Spanish Empire,
it lost momentum after a few years of trial and adoption. A series of
propitious events also tipped the scales in favor of the local councils.

The demise of Charles III on December 14, 1788, under whose
auspices the changes had been initiated, played into the hands of the
creoles. Likewise, the passing from the scene of the great Minister
of the Indies, José de Gálvez, a year and a half earlier removed the
chief inspiration for reform among the King's advisors. The new
ruler, Charles IV, cast in a lesser mold than his celebrated father,
was little concerned with matters of state, foreign affairs, and colonial
policies. His ineptitude and indifference meant the selection of less
energetic personalities for office and a general lowering of morale in
the bureaucracy. Celebration of the advent of the fifth Bourbon
sovereign took place in Lima on October 10, 1789, an event marked
by the unfurling of royal pennants with customary fanfare and processions. The guild of the grocers, though little accustomed to versifica-
tion, composed a short poem in honor of the King. Crowds of creoles
and Indians gathered in the streets for the occasion, which was described by the official in charge in a book, *The Sun at Noontime: Oh
Happy Year.*[1]

Almost coincidental with the shift in monarchs was the departure

1. Vargas Ugarte, *Historia del Perú, virreinato, 1700-1790*, pp. 463, 464.

from Peruvian soil of one of the most alert and energetic figures in the history of the viceroyalty, the visitador Escobedo. Lackadaisical royal and municipal officials breathed easier with his return to the Peninsula. For his efforts in America he was rewarded with a seat in the Council of the Indies, where for a number of years he continued to have a voice in policy-making decisions.

In 1789 the occurrence of the French Revolution set in motion a train of events that would eventually lead to the independence of the Spanish colonies. Ideas of liberty, equality, and fraternity appealed to prominent creoles in many parts of the empire. Intellectual horizons were broadened and new visions appeared. The philosophy of the Revolution was well able to serve as a vindication of the colonial criticism of Spanish policies and Spanish-born administrators. But it was unlikely that Peruvian creoles, cognizant of the huge Indian population and the dire consequences of class warfare, would travel far or quickly along the dangerous path. Aristocratic in outlook, they would preserve ties with the crown longer than many other sections. Nevertheless, the involvement of Spain in 1793 in war with France created opportunities for the conciliar bodies, enabling them to secure limited concessions from a hard-pressed monarch. A few high-ranking officials in Spain were not oblivious to the possibility of the loosening of colonial ties as an aftermath of the conflict. The Minister of State Conde de Aranda, whose uncanny prophesies verged on clairvoyance, counseled neutrality as late as February 23, 1793. In his mind an important consideration was the effect of the war on America.[2] The die had already been cast, however, for secret aid had been furnished Louis XVI in September, 1792. Consequently, on March 7, 1793, the

2. His advice to Charles IV deserves recording: "Armed neutrality is not only suitable with respect to the conflict in Europe, but also is more politic for our states in America. Let us have no illusions as to this fact. It should not be thought that our America is as innocent as in past centuries or so unpopulated, nor should we believe that there are lacking informed persons who see that those colonists are forgotten on their own soil, that they are treated with severity, and that those born in the Peninsula devour their sustenance [;] nor are they ignorant of the fact that in various parts of that continent there have been insurrections requiring expenditures of men and money for their suppression; for this it has been necessary to send forces from Europe. No one should be blind to what goes on, that they have books expressing new doctrines of liberty and that propagandists will not fail to be there to persuade them if the proper moment arrives. Part of the region of the South Sea is already contaminated; that of the North Sea has not only the example but also the influence of the English colonies which are close enough to provide aid." See Modesto La Fuente, *Historia general de España* (22 tomos; Madrid, 1850-1859), XXI, 414 note.

Convention broke off relations with Charles IV and declared war. The exigencies of the conflict, paramount among them the need for funds, would render the Spanish government less adamant in its opposition to redress of municipal grievances.

Accountable in part for the revival of local rights was a burgeoning spirit of nationalism. It was reinforced by a realization by the cabildos of the loss of their privileges. This intangible phenomenon, inspired to some extent by foreign concepts and happenings, was a rational development of the colonial environment. The interaction of natural forces had shaken the English colonies free of the mother country. The sight of North American ships in the South Seas emphasized the stark reality of liberty. Somewhat belatedly, parallel conditions would evoke a demand by the creoles for satisfaction of grievances and subsequently for independence. The last decade of the eighteenth century was a preparatory period, the matrix of the revolution. "The events taking place at the beginning of the nineteenth century," declares the eminent Peruvian historian Jorge Basadre, "cannot be understood if they are considered as a sudden seismic shock. They only accelerated and made more violent a process already under-way, which had manifested itself from the middle of the eighteenth century, at first by a modest cultural and scientific consciousness. In reality, the process was the logical consequence of American colonization and settlement."[3] Aware of the decadence of Spain, creoles aimed at a greater portion of self-government. Once in control of their destiny, they might modify the merchantile system to their advantage and make certain that taxes collected in America would be expended on colonial terrain rather than for the dynastic aspirations of the Bourbons in Europe. It was inevitable that the Peruvian cabildos, particularly that of the capital, would reflect through their acts and resolutions the apprehensiveness of the times and the wish that an organ of local origin should assume responsibility alongside the representatives of a decaying throne.

The growth of nationalism was accompanied by an eagerness for

3. Jorge Basadre, "Notas sobre la experiencia histórica peruana," *Revista histórica*, XIX, 22.

To Victor Belaúnde the rise of nationalities was the real explanation for revolution: "The fundamental cause of the independence of the Americas was that Spain, in her glorious fecundity, had created a multitude of national consciences." See *Causas y caracteres de la independencia hispano-americana* (Congreso hispanoamericano de historia, Madrid, 1953), p. 37.

knowledge of the outside world and by the spirit of scientific inquiry. To many rationalism became the approach to the solution of problems. Symptomatic of the cultural trend was the flowering of periodicals in Lima. Specifically, there were many causes for their appearance in the 1790's. To a greater extent than in the past, the demand was widely felt for the dissemination of information about the bewildering episodes transpiring in revolutionary France and their repercussions in other parts of Europe. At the same time the improved communication of the west coast of South America with Europe and the United States by more frequent voyages through the Straits of Magellan made available more news for editors. In October, 1790, with the permission of the Viceroy, the first newspaper, *El diario curioso, erudito, económico y comercial* appeared. It was a daily of four pages, containing a few scholarly articles, in addition to commercial news.[4] Unfortunately, the *Diario* expired after two years. Vastly more important was the *Mercurio Peruano*, which saw the light of day in January, 1791. It was sponsored by the Sociedad de Amantes del País, whose motto was fittingly enough *Patriae et Immortalitati*, "symbolizing admirably the objective of this periodical."[5] Its pages were filled with literary and scientific articles contributed by the best talent in the viceroyalty. Like the *Diario*, its appeal was basically nationalistic, reflecting native pride and feeling. Despite this bias, the *Mercurio* enjoyed a circulation beyond the confines of Peru until its demise in August of 1794.[6] A third publication, *El seminario crítico*, was started in June, 1791, by the Franciscans with the avowed aim of improving the education of youth and raising the standards of literary appreciation. It too had a short life. The *Gaceta*, or official daily, founded in 1793, was published for a number of years in the capital, but the quality of its articles was far below that of the *Mercurio*.[7] Indubitably, these newsheets and reviews, together with occasional broadsides, revealed the awakening of creole nationalism. Simultaneously, they permitted this sentiment to have a broader base

4. The editor in a memorial to the Viceroy, March 16, 1791, stressed its local or regional character, declaring that "the physical description and the history of these kingdoms are the chief topics in my paper. . . ." Quoted in Carlos A. Romero, "Los orígenes del periodismo en el Perú. De la relación al diario, 1594-1790," *Revista histórica*, XII, 306.

5. Vargas Ugarte, *Historia del Perú, virreinato, siglo XVIII*, pp. 36-39.

6. There is no evidence that the Viceroy took definite steps to bring about its extinction. See *ibid.*, p. 38.

7. *Ibid.*, p. 37.

by making converts of the literate section of the populace hitherto unaffected.

Even before the historic session of the Estates-General at Versailles, there is evidence of a quickening interest by creoles in local affairs in Peru. In Lima the annual election of January 1, 1789, was characterized by greater freedom for the capitulars, that is they were without the presence of the teniente asesor of the superintendant of the royal treasury.[8] Disputes over conciliar selection were revived. The number of meetings was augmented, thus evincing greater zest on the part of the councilors for tackling everyday problems of municipal administration. Between the years 1785-1788 there had been only thirty-three sessions. But starting in 1789, the cabildo assembled for the next four years on an average of forty-two times per year. This does not mean that all sessions were fully attended; in many instances only three or four out of a possible ten to twelve members were present. Lesser cities experienced a similar upsurge in the number of meetings, the cabildo of Trujillo being in session thirty times in 1798 and the same number of times in 1799. But non-attendance again became a serious problem in many localities. In Moquegua the Viceroy, on the complaint of the subdelegate, issued an order threatening the regidores missing more than six successive sessions with deprivation of the right to vote in conciliar elections. This penalty, in addition to the regular fine imposed by the cabildo itself, was seemingly ineffective.[9]

Conciliar sessions in Lima were denoted as ordinary or pleno. The latter type became of more frequent occurrence during the period from 1790-1810, when events of the day, affected by the outbreak of war and the English blockade, called for grave thought and reflection. A conciliar resolution prescribed the conditions necessary for the holding of a cabildo pleno and the authority that it might exercise:

8. In other localities intendants and subdelegates presided over conciliar meetings. Electoral abuses still prevailed. For example, the citizenry of Tauli in the province of Chachapoyas protested to the Viceroy against the tyranny of one Bernabe Ximenes, who, they alleged, had held the office of chief magistrate for nine years. Appropriate action for his removal was forthwith authorized by the Superior Government. See Expediente, Alcalde de Tauli, Cabildos, legajo 10, Archivo nacional, Lima.

9. Objecting to the viceregal provisión, the ayuntamiento of Trujillo averred that regidores were often engaged in their haciendas, "some of which lay in the partidos of Huamachuco and Lambayeque and others at a long distance from the capital," and that it would obey the order of His Excellency "only in the matter of the fine levied on regidores, who, being in the capital, failed to attend the cabildos." See minutes of April 2, 1799, *Anales de cabildo, Ciudad de Trujillo, del 8 de octubre de 1794 al 17 de setiembre de 1802*, ed. Alberto Larco Herrera (Lima, n.d.).

No payment beyond 100 pesos can be authorized except in cabildo pleno; nor can any matters guiding decisions [in cabildo pleno] be brought up for examination or discussion nor any resolution taken be reversed in a regular session; no meeting can be regarded as a cabildo pleno, unless twelve señores with right to vote are present; and if the assembly is not attended by twelve individuals, it should be classified as a cabildo ordinario. . . .[10]

To a minor degree registration of titles was resumed as a pre-rogative of the cabildo. Among the offices noted in the Lima records were those of regidor, escribano mayor, escribano de provincia, *familiar del Santo Oficio*, contador de propios, *maestro mayor de los gremios*, and alguacil mayor. In addition, it was customary to list titles of nobility and certificates of naturalization. Intendants and subdelegates were not required to submit their letters of appointment for formal approval and acceptance by the ayuntamiento.

An increase in the number of capitulars comprising the cabildo indicates somewhat wider participation in the possession and exercise of town office by the citizenry. In the case of Lima the expanded membership is partly ascribed to a steady reduction in the cost of a regimiento from 4,000 pesos in 1776 to 2,000 pesos by 1790. Neverthe-less, exacerbation over the size of the body prompted the cabildo in 1797 to draw up a consulta to the Viceroy to the effect "that no bids for further sales be authorized," inasmuch as the regidores already counted twenty, eight more than the number set by the Laws of the Indies.[11] Also in the minds of the councilors must have been the thought that their social prestige would be diminished by an enlarge-ment of personnel. The viceregal reply was that steps would be taken to forestall further sales.[12] Conversely, in a few places the price of a regimiento rose, the office in Moquegua in 1742 having sold for 400 pesos, but in 1808 for 800 pesos.[13]

10. Minutes of July 23, 1805, Libros de cabildos de Lima, vol. XLI, Biblioteca municipal, Lima.

11. Minutes of Nov. 17, 1797, *ibid.*, vol. XXXIX.

12. Minutes of Feb. 6, 1798, *ibid.*

13. Those who aspired to the purchase of aldermancies generally belonged to the local aristocracy. In claiming eligibility for the office in Moquegua, one Lorenzo Fernando Maldonado in 1807 gave proof of his legitimate birth, *limpieza de sangre*, general fitness, and additionally, of the nobility of his ancestors, "who had held the most honorable positions in the state as corregidores and in the militia as colonels, captains. . . ." See Expediente sobre el remate de la vara de regidor perpetuo del cavildo de Moquegua, Cabildo, legajo 10 (1805-1808), Archivo nacional, Lima.

Because of the incipient nationalism in Peru and the debilitated status of Spain it is not remarkable that this period witnessed the presentation of numerous petitions by the local councils to the crown for redress of wrongs. The mounting costs of the war for the Spanish exchequer became the pragmatic means for the attainment of certain colonial objectives. Generous donations by the councils resulted in grants and concessions. As the wealthiest city in the viceroyalty, Lima was in the best position to offer funds, thereby securing the return of some coveted privileges and even the possession of new rights.

Remonstrances were formally presented to the crown by an apoderado, or procurator resident, in Madrid. In the eighteenth century Lima was seldom without a spokesman for its interests. In 1796, because of the ominous tidings from Europe, Trujillo designated two procurators, one for Madrid and the other for Lima.[14] The cabildo in the capital customarily paid its agent the annual salary of 500 pesos, above certain expenditures for bribes, clerical aid, fees, and supplies. The installation of the intendancy in no serious way hampered the exercise of the prerogative of petition, save that the remittance to Spain of a large sum, usually 2,000 pesos, required the sanction of the junta municipal and the Junta Superior de Real Hacienda. Rarely was authorization for Lima refused or delayed. In January, 1793, in view of the impending conflict between Spain and France, the cabildo resolved to appoint a special representative, or deputy, in the person of an able limeño, José Baquíjano y Carrillo, attorney for the audiencia and professor of canonical law at San Marcos.[15] Baquíjano journeyed to Europe in that year, but resigned his appointment and by the latter part of 1795 had returned to Peru.

Beginning in 1791, the cabildo of Lima directed its agent and later its deputy to draft a series of memorials seeking new privileges and the restoration of some which had been withdrawn in the past. Important among them was the request for the title of "Metropolis," already conceded to Mexico City.[16] In September, 1795, the ayun-

14. Minutes of Aug. 6, 1796, *Anales de cabildo de Trujillo.*
  It was usually the custom of smaller municipalities to have agents only at the viceregal capital.
  15. Minutes of Jan. 2, 1793, Libros de cabildos de Lima, vol. XXXVIII, Biblioteca municipal, Lima.
  He was replaced by Tadeo Bravo de Rivera y Zavala, who was unremitting in his efforts in behalf of the city.
  16. At the same time the cabildo authorized the dispatch of an oficio to Mexico

tamiento authorized a formal appeal at the court against the excessive ecclesiastical aranceles which bore a hardship on the public, on the grounds that the audiencia had refused to entertain any recourse against them.[17] Two months later the cabildo resolved to protest against the assumption of the judicature of water rights by the audiencia to the detriment of the municipal officials.[18] In 1798, there was an appeal to the King against an increase in the cost of stamped paper.[19]

While consideration of these memorials was pending in Madrid, a sure way of winning the good will of the crown presented itself to the cabildo. Extraordinarily heavy outlays for military and naval preparations for the war against England made imperative an appeal to the colonies for funds. The response of the cabildo of Lima was generous. At the outbreak of the general European conflict in 1793, the council voted the sum of 12,000 pesos with an addition of 4,000 a year for the remainder of the war. In November, 1798, "in view of the indispensable and unusual expenses for the defense and happiness of the realm," the ayuntamiento doubled the original donation.[20] The prospect of further gifts in the offing was not without effect on the crown. By 1805 approximately 150,000 pesos had been contributed to the royal treasury.

Earlier, in January, 1793, the cabildo had drawn up detailed instructions for the guidance of the deputy Baquíjano and his successor in negotiations with the crown. For a number of years the efforts of the agents bore no fruit. In view of the crown's indifference these points were repeated, with some modifications and additions, in a new set of instructions, adopted in a session of the council in March, 1799. A summary of their significant provisions is desirable for an explanation of the attitude of the cabildo toward the crown at this moment.[21] Although they stressed the immediate demands of this body, they contained also the basic creole aspirations that had existed throughout the eighteenth century.

City, requesting the officials of that municipality to send a copy of all the "gracias recently received concerning salaries of regidores, informes, everything that may contribute to its greater honor and prestige." See minutes of May 20, 1791, *ibid.*, vol. XXXVIII.

17. Minutes of Sept. 4, 1795, *ibid.*, vol. XXXIX.
18. Minutes of Nov. 12, 1795, *ibid.*, vol. XXXIX.
19. Minutes of May 22, 1798, *ibid.*, vol. XXXIX.
20. Minutes of Nov. 12, 1798, *ibid.*, vol. XXXIX.
21. Minutes of March 1, 1799, *ibid.*, vol. XXXIX.

Conciliar grievances or pleas embraced a broad spectrum of subjects. Representation in the political machinery for the colonies was not foreign to the thinking of the creoles. It was urged that one-third of the seats in the Audiencia of Lima be assigned to native-born Peruvians, for "it is obvious that no American should have an impediment preventing him from holding a plaza togada in his own patria, as happens in Navarre" (Item 20). To avoid a monopoly of offices in the Consulado by European-born Spaniards, the posts of prior and consul should be rotated between criollos and those from the Peninsula (Item 19). The two alcaldes ordinarios ought to be elected annually according to past custom, since, it was alleged, the office was burdensome and busy citizens would be reluctant to be absent more than one year from their own professions and occupations (Item 15).

Many points dealt with the judicial attributes of the magistrates and the council. This had been a sore spot in crown-cabildo relations throughout the eighteenth century. It was requested that the viceroy and the audiencia refrain from overstepping the bounds of their jurisdictions: Appeals from the regular sentences of the alcaldes should proceed directly to the audiencia and not to the juez de provincia or any other royal judge (Item 8). "His Majesty must deny to the viceroys such power [cognizance of appeals], except for the consideration of recursos that indicate criminal and unjust acts by the judges" (Item 16). The jurisdiction over water rights must be removed from the viceroy's commissioner and restored to the cabildo (Item 10). The teniente de policía should not be permitted to set himself up as a judge "to the complete confusion in the jurisdiction of the alcalde ordinario, alcalde de la Hermandad, and the juez de aguas" (Item 11). The magistrates must be free "to give lashes or castigate with whips minor delinquencies or infractions," without having to give an accounting to the Sala del Crimen (Item 9). Moreover, to facilitate the course of true justice, the crown should authorize a school for the training of lawyers, to be governed by the regulations devised for a similar academy in Madrid (Item 23).

In the economic field there were ample reasons for conciliar dissatisfaction. The ayuntamiento petitioned that the control of the propios be lodged once again in its hands, with approval for certain disbursements to be given by the audiencia rather than by the viceroy or his agents (Item 7). The council should be empowered to spend 3,000 pesos each year for public works without the sanction of the viceroy or audiencia and over 10,000 pesos for the implementation of matters at the court (Items 24 and 25). If the cabildo must participate in the receptions for the viceroy, the the ramo de sisa ought to be assigned to it for this purpose (Item 28). For the settlement of accounts the cabildo should elect an official from its own membership (Item 13). Full supervision of the guilds, of their elections and other activities, should be returned to the cabildo (Item 26).

Commercial regulations were a subject of remonstrance. The council requested that the system of free trade be modified to convert Callao into the sole port for final registration of vessels bound from Europe to the west coast of South America, as Lima could not afford the loss of commerce (Item 29). If freedom of trade meant what was proclaimed, Peru should be authorized to export products to the western coast of New Spain without hindrance (Item 30). The importation of goods manufactured by the Five Guilds of Madrid should be limited as injurious to the local business interests (Item 35).

Features of the system of royal taxation and monopoly came in for a round of criticism. The cabildo complained that the rate of the alcabala, fixed at 6 per cent, was too high and that in consequence merchants were forced to sell goods and merchandise with little profit or at actual loss (Item 33).[22] Negro slaves should be allowed entry free of duty, "as has been granted in other regions of America" (Item 36). The establishment by the crown of the *estanco de aguardiente* in Guayaquil and throughout the Viceroyalty of Santa Fe was "detrimental to the King, to its inhabitants, and to the group of hacendados [Peru]," and should be abolished. The cabildo admonished its deputy to urge this with firmness and persistence, "for all the haciendas de viñas are heavily in debt because of the estanco" (Item 37).

Injured pride and feelings of social inferiority were likewise reflected in the instructions to Madrid. Inasmuch as the cabildo "not only represents the city, but is a body whose members come from its first families," it seeks the title of "Excellency," with the honors of *Teniente General*, and similar favors for the capitulars (Item 2). If a

22. That the tax was so unpopular that care had to be exercised in its collection is attested by the Viceroy Abascal. See Rodríguez Casado and Calderón Quijano, *Memoria de gobierno del Virrey Abascal*, p. 293.

viceroy or oidor adopted a condescending and rude posture or used insulting language toward an alderman, this act must be cited in the residencia (Item 5). Out of fairness the cabildo of Lima should enjoy the same privileges as the ayuntamiento of Mexico City (Item 3). Ironically, in its demand for social equality with the Peninsulares, the council opposed the participation of the subdelegates and the Indian alcaldes in the parades for the fiestas reales as derogatory to the solemnity of the occasion (Item 12).

The character of the instructions bespeaks the circumscribed outlook of the landed and commercial oligarchy. Municipal exclusiveness prevented a disinterested consideration of the economic prosperity of the citizens of Guayaquil, Santiago de Chile, and Santa Fe de Bogotá. There was little attention to popular demands nor could much be expected of this nature from the aristocratic milieu of the viceregal capital. From a dignified plea for representation in the audiencia the creoles sank to the petty insistence on velvet lining for the benches and chairs used by the cabildo for public ceremonies. Notwithstanding, despite the undemocratic tone of the articles, the capitulars regarded themselves as advocates of the true interests of the region comprising the Audiencia of Lima. The more than occasional use of the term "patria" is symbolic of the future.

Before long the results of new conciliar solicitation became apparent. Beginning in 1799, there were a number of concessions made by the crown. Some were more important than others. A royal order of August 24, 1799, eliminated the residence for tenientes letrados, alcaldes, regidores, procurators, and other local officials, the crown asserting that these positions would henceforth be "less burdensome" and "more sought-after." None of these officials might accept any other appointment "without his presenting before the tribunal, the cabildo, or his superior, who must have possession of it, a notarized certificate from the Consejo or the audiencia in whose district he might have served, from which it may be shown that he has no unfilled obligations in his previous employment."[23] In reality, the crown was

23. Real orden, Aug. 24, 1799, legajo 1119, Audiencia de Lima, A. G. I.
Mariluz Urquijo's contention that "as much in Spain as in the Indies the residencia appeared to be the best defense for collective interests"—and as such was popular with municipalities—is not borne out in Peru. The author of this monograph has found no letters or petitions from the cabildos seeking its restoration. While it was a counterweight to viceregal tyranny, it might from the alderman's point of view

legally recognizing what was already a fact, for in many regions the residencia had been abandoned as time-consuming and costly. Another aldermanic grievance was answered in 1800 with the restoration of the annual elections of alcaldes ordinarios by the cabildos everywhere in the colonies.[24] Although the cabildo objected that in practice the incumbent did not have the time to instruct an incoming official, it is likely that the real opposition stemmed from a growing dislike for the arbitrary character of the intendancy.

In addition, the crown authorized in the period from 1799 to 1802 other *gracias* for the relief of the cabildos. The judicial power of the alcaldes was upheld when it was decreed in 1802 that appeals from the magistrates should go to the audiencias and under no circumstances to the juez de provincia. Cognizance of the wills of members of the urban militia in time of peace (1801) and of suits involving alleged violation by soldiers of municipal regulations concerning the abasto (1799) belonged to the local judges. The cabildo might impose fines on any person violating the aranceles or establishing a monopoly. No body, secular or ecclesiastical, was exempted from the mojonasgo, an important source of municipal revenue.[25]

Out of recognition of its services and donations, the King authorized special favors to Lima in a real cédula of September 15, 1802:

> I wish to remain suspended and unexecuted whatever illegal and wrongful interpretation that might have been given to every instruction or act of instruction contrary to my sovereign resolve; that the new Contaduría de propios be extinguished at once and at the same time the salary of 3,500 pesos, as was done in Santiago de Chile, the members of the cabildo occupying the office in turns; that the aforesaid My Viceroy and Real Audiencia consider and give preference to conciliar matters, eliminate continual appeals, so that the interested parties may speed up recourse to My Real Audiencia; that a colegio de abogados like that of Madrid be erected for the more efficient handling of commercial and judicial appeals; and lastly that the caudal de propios y arbitrios, in which are included the ramos of sisa and bodegaje, be under the oversight of the cabildo and not of jueces comisionados because [they] destined for public utility should be

seem tedious, burdensome, and restrictive. See José María Mariluz Urquijo, *Ensayo sobre los juicios de residencia indianos* (Sevilla, 1952), p. 293.

24. Que los cabildos de América elijan alcaldes ordinarios por solo un año (1800), Cédulas y provisiones del cabildo de Lima, libro XXIX, Biblioteca municipal, Lima.

25. Cédula sobre que ningún cuerpo secular esté exceptuado del derecho de mojonasgo (1800), *ibid.*, libro XXVII.

regarded as part of the treasury [municipality] and to be spent for its purposes without more interference than that of My Real Audiencia, the latter leaving to the cabildo the power of spending [but giving an account] from its funds the necessary quantity for those ends of urgent and public need, without having to prepare petitions that increase the expenses and slow down operations [;] and that in those cases in which the city wishes to make demonstrations of its loyalty in gracious gifts to the crown, it may also utilize its propios and arbitrios, and even encumber them if necessary with the court. To avoid doubts and objections in the exact fulfillment of the above, particularly in regard to the ramo of bodegaje, applied to the expenses of policía, I have resolved to declare in accord with a consulta of My Consejo de Indias [July 3, 1802], that the said ramo and that of the sisa must be incorporated with the remaining propios and arbitrios under the supervision of the cabildo, and that royal approval not having been given to its establishment, the juzgado de policía and its regulations are suppressed at once, the regidores assuming the duties, and as was determined for the contaduría de propios y arbitrios the salary of 2,000 pesos assigned to the teniente de policía be struck out, his position being taken over by the capitulars without any salary, but with the sole prudent gratuity ordered by the ayuntamiento and approved by My Real Audiencia, concerning which the cabildo will give an account of the disbursement of its funds . . . annually to the Tribunal Superior de Justicia for certification and afterwards to My Consejo for its examination. . . .[26]

The adroitness and perseverance of the deputy Tadeo Bravo de Rivera in presenting the municipality's petition to the consejo were rewarded. On October 19, 1802, the cabildo received a jubilant letter from Madrid, in which it was declared that the crown had decreed "virtual restitution of all the jurisdictions, fueros, privileges, and the extinction of the contaduria general de propios y arbirios."[27] In recognition of this triumph the council on December 29, 1802, addressed a letter to the deputy, thanking him for "services rendered . . . out of deep love for his country." Following this expression of gratitude was a plea for the abolition of the "onerous and indecorous ceremony of the palio," since it is not in keeping with the distinctions and honors of Grandeza de España conferred upon the cabildo "for its members to carry the canopy through a multitude of streets designated

26. Legajo 801, Audiencia de Lima, A. G. I.
27. Minutes of Oct. 19, 1802, Libros de cabildos de Lima, vol. XL, Biblioteca municipal, Lima.

for the paseo." Included in this carta were other supplications: that the treatment of Señoría be extended to the regidores, "because this distinction comports with the natural dignity of the body and is its due owing to the prompt generosity of its members in rendering aid to His Majesty on opportune occasions"; and that no special group have exemption from important taxes, in particular from the sisa, as was permitted by the Visitor Areche. Although the regular and secular clergy made contributions instead, this amount did not equal what otherwise would have been paid to the local treasury.[28]

Between the years 1802 and 1804 there were other cédulas addressed to Lima, marking further royal concessions. The crown wished to make more palatable the continual demands for funds to defray military and naval expenditures that could not be borne at home. A royal order of 1804 abolished the junta municipal.[29] In the same year another decree restored to the cabildo the full exercise of the *judicatura de aguas* and jurisdiction over the shoemaker's guild.[30] By a cédula of July 17, 1804, a colegio of lawyers, a petition for which had been inserted by the council in its instructions of 1793 to the apoderado, came into being in Lima.

The municipality of the capital pressed its advantage to the farthest point. In January, 1805, another carta with supplementary requests was dispatched to the agent in Madrid. If these were acceded to, the cabildo promised a gift of 50,000 pesos, which would have to be repaid upon revocation of any of the favors. Some of the solicitations were familiar ones, others suggested by the occasion.

Unsatisfactory electoral conditions and the allocation of the proceeds of municipal taxes demanded attention: Conciliar offices should be filled by majority vote rather than by unanimity. Rotation in office must no longer be stipulated for many positions. It was urged that the sisa be freed of any encumbrance, except the 6,000 pesos for the orphans of San Andrés, and be paid by all ecclesiastical bodies "without any appeal being admitted in Lima or Spain"; and that the bodegaje, marked for the cleaning and upkeep of the thoroughfares, be collected in its entirety by the cabildo.

Restraint should be imposed by the crown upon the authority of

28. Minutes of Dec. 29, 1802, *ibid.*, vol. XL.
29. Libros de cédulas y provisiones de Lima, vol. XXVII, Biblioteca municipal, Lima.
30. *Ibid.*

the audiencia in its relations with the ayuntamiento. The administrative court must leave the members of the council free and unhampered in the performance of their duties. Regidores should serve as supervisory officials of the guilds, authorizing their assemblies and approving examinations for the admission of new masters, for "the cabildo is the protector of the gremios and it exacts fair treatment for the public."

Creoles sought assurance of proper respect from crown officials for their representatives in the public ceremonies. Unqualified repugnance was expressed toward the use of the palio: "all of this which in early days of the conquest might have been suitable to impress upon the public the lofty idea of the position of the viceroy, and even more of the person of the king whom he represented, appears detestable today, and foreign to circumspection, or inappropriate to a capital of Peru, so cultured and civilized, that it does not require a ceremony and formalities of such a kind." Instead of the *ministros togados,* local officials should preside over the public shows and entertainments, such as the *Plazas de Gallos, de Toros, de Caballos,* and the *Coliseo de Comedias,* "as takes place in all the towns in the Peninsula."[31]

Again, conciliar pleas did not go unanswered. On June 3, 1806, the cabildo of Lima had cause for further rejoicing, for it was in receipt of a communication from Bravo de Rivera in Madrid to the effect that the King had assented to nearly all of the provisions of the petition. The deputy could hardly restrain his enthusiasm:

> The usage of Señoría [is extended] to those having varas; honors and precedence in the Audiencias of Charcas and Chile to the asesores Belon and Yrigoyen; the cabildo restored to its jurisdiction and direction of plazas and theaters; and in everything relative to the guilds with abolition of the appointed judges; the subdelegation of Cercado [district of Lima] to go to regidores in turn . . . the custom of the palio extinguished, with approval of the instructions left by Escobedo concerning the reception of viceroys, whose oath of office and that of the oidores in the Real Acuerdo are to be taken according to the procedure prescribed for the Royal Seal, and in those other acts in which the ministers are seated, the cabildo will occupy its own benches; the ramo de sisa is freed of [exemption] of any privileged bodies, so that, restored in full, it will have no encumbrances other than those for the orphans and San Andres; and as to the bodegaje it

31. Minutes of Jan. 22, 1805, Libros de cabildos de Lima, vol. XL, Biblioteca municipal, Lima.

returns to its original condition, without the discounts and exemptions introduced, and is [to be] collected with respect to the utility that the cargo bears, leaving responsibility to the proprietors of the taverns. The viceroy will collect back debts, although, with permission of the cabildo, accounts can be settled, and all autos are terminated in their present stage, with no appeal except to the Royal Person. . . .

Concluded also are the autos dealing with the Contaduría de propios y arbitrios with as much satisfaction as the cabildo could wish; and you will see in the real cédulas that will be shortly issued that all will be carried out so that 'for no reason nor pretext of doubt or interpretation (these are his words) will be delayed or retarded the rightful fulfillment of the Sovereign Will'. . . . The articles of exequación [equal treatment] with Mexico will be included in separate cédulas, in order that nothing desired by the Ayuntamiento will be omitted.[32]

Out of gratitude to the King's advisor on colonial affairs, Secretario de Estado, Antonio Caballero, the cabildo bestowed upon him the title of *Regidor de cano proprietario* and ordered his portrait hung in the assembly hall. In a fitting gesture of appreciation it awarded Bravo de Rivera the rank of honorary regidor.[33] The cost in terms of a donation to the royal coffers was not inconsiderable.[34] But if promises were fulfilled, important conciliar grievances would be allayed.

It was not until the latter part of January that the cabildo learned of the arrival of four *cédulas de gracias*. Two weeks later an oficio of the Viceroy ordered their enforcement.[35] The deputy's fervor was not belied by the contents of the new decrees. The first cédula recounted the privileges of the capitulars. The palio, now of no further use, was to be donated to the Church of Jesús María, in accord with the wishes of the ayuntamiento. The remaining cédulas assigned to the council control over the sisa and the bodegaje and authorized the adoption of the honors enjoyed by the cabildo of Mexico City.[36]

Royal favors for Lima had not yet ended. The last two years prior to the Napoleonic seizure of power in Spain witnessed the issuance of additional cédulas in the interests of the cabildo. Capitulars were to

32. Minutes of June 3, 1806, *ibid.*, vol. XLI.
33. *Ibid.*
34. The donation to the crown amounted to 149,122 pesos fuertes and 6 reales de plata. See minutes of Jan. 26, 1807, *ibid.*
35. Minutes of Feb. 12, 1807, *ibid.*   36. *Ibid.*

receive impartial treatment at the hands of the intendant.[37] Finally, Ferdinand VII, shortly before his abdication, promulgated a cédula of *gracias y honores* to the ayuntamiento.[38] Although the fortunes of the council were in the ascendancy in 1808, there had not been a recovery of the rights exercised by the cabildos of the sixteenth century. Because of its greater affluence and consequent ability to make contributions, Lima fared better than the provincial towns and cities in bounties from the crown.

The apparent success of the colonial metropolis in its demands from the crown arose from a continuation of the auspicious circumstances in Europe and from its new aggressiveness and self-confidence. Spain's finances, affected by the European war, had deteriorated to the point where monetary contributions were almost certain to induce a favorable hearing. To a considerable degree, the reforms of the intendancy had invigorated the cabildos. Financially, they were better off, being assured of control over steady sources of income and with decreasing debts.[39] The filling of vacant seats at the council table at crown insistence and enforcement of attendance regulations had likewise stimulated the activity of the local bodies. Vitality was reflected in self-reliance and determination.

From the foregoing memorials it will be noticed that relatively few references to the intendancies were made. But it would be a mistake to assume that opposition to the power exercised by these officials had vanished. The truth is that the ayuntamientos had accepted the innovation as a more or less permanent feature of the governmental machinery in spite of its centralizing tendency. But surely, it was clear to the creoles that without a reduction in the authority of these men no substantial gain in self-rule was possible.

While the conciliar bodies were reticent in their criticism of the intendancy, the opposite was true of the old administrative hierarchy. In Peru the harshest denunciation came from the pen of the Viceroy Teodoro de Croix, who has been called the "protesting viceroy" from

37. Libro de cédulas y provisiones de Lima, vol. XXVII, Biblioteca municipal, Lima.
38. Granted by the crown mainly because of Lima's assistance to Buenos Aires and Montevideo during the British invasion, the decree of Feb. 21, 1808, was for the most part a confirmation of earlier cédulas, with an additional provision, stipulating further control by the municipality over its sources of revenue. See carta al cabildo de Lima, April 10, 1808, legajo 801, Audiencia de Lima, A. G. I.
39. Lynch, *Spanish Colonial Administration, 1782-1810*, p. 288.

his chronic habit of censoring personalities and institutions.[40] There
was also condemnation and sharp criticism from the highest agent
of the crown in the Mexican Kingdom.[41] In a representación to the
King of May 16, 1789, de Croix set forth the case against the intendancies. The indictment was complete. The long list of charges
touched on most of the duties of the intendant: Viceregal authority
and prestige had declined to the detriment of Spanish sovereignty
over the region; as vice-patrons, the new officials had failed miserably,
causing enmity among the ecclesiastics, the normal upholders of
royal prerogative. Little improvement in agriculture and commerce
had been brought about; results in the realm of justice did not bear
out expectations; and, finally, even in the department of finance, for
the betterment of which high hopes had been entertained, there were
no signs of increased assessment and collection of taxes.

The welfare of the municipalities, de Croix argued, was affected
adversely by the appointment of intendants. The administration of
justice was replete with acts of arbitrary intervention, frequent and
unnecessary appeals from the lower courts, and unwise delays in the
settlement of cases, all of which added to the malfunctioning of the
judicial system. Intendants hindered the alcaldes in the performance
of their duties as judges. Occasionally, elections of town officials were
annulled in favor of individuals more susceptible to pressure from
above. But it was difficult for citizens to make formal complaints
against the intendants and their asesores because of the intimidation
of witnesses and the ease with which the accused could produce false
evidence.

Local councils were treated with indignity and often with contempt. On this score de Croix was particularly severe:

> The cabildos likewise cannot bear the pride and arrogance of the
> asesores any more than the imperious attitude of the intendants,
> who dispose of favors at will; they trample underfoot the actas of
> the cabildos and perform other unbecoming deeds toward the honor-
> able citizens composing these bodies. Citizens retire to their homes
> or haciendas in displeasure and give up their zeal for the public
> welfare. . . . Certain offices suffer a steep decline in value with loss

40. Quoted in Viellard-Baron's "L'Etablissement des Intendants aux Indes par
Charles III," p. 532.
41. The Viceroy Revillagigedo, nonetheless, confessed that he saw improvement in
many governmental areas. See Fisher, *Intendant System*, pp. 75-82.

to the Real Hacienda; and in consequence, these offices and those of the alcaldes ordinarios will be despised by men of honor and judgment, who are not to be insulted. . . .[42]

Matters concerning the policía and municipal revenues were handled capriciously by the intendants and their assistants, de Croix contended. These officials failed to distribute copies of ordinances affecting the interests of citizens to the cabildos. In the capitals of the intendancies in the past the acts of malversation of the ayuntamientos had been remedied by residencias and through the oversight of the corregidores, who had functioned in this capacity as effectively as the new officials. But these correctives no longer existed. The handling of the ramos of the alcabala, the almojorifazgo, and the sisa had resulted "in widespread popular displeasure."[43]

The Viceroy's denouncement of the intendancy could not be ignored by the crown. Already questions in regard to its viability had been raised in America. In response to complaints the King had ordered the annulment of specific articles of the ordinance. In 1787 the crown had restored to the viceroy the authority to confirm the election of alcaldes in the capitals and to the presidents of the audiencias similar rights in their places of residence and in the surrounding territory to a distance of fifteen leagues. Intendants might continue to approve conciliar elections in small towns, provided approbation of officials was secured later from the viceroy. In 1788, the crown had rescinded Articles 6 and 28, which had required the supervision of municipal finance by the viceroy.[44] But it was highly improbable that the crown would accept de Croix's recommendation of the abolition of the office of intendant. Nevertheless, on March 16, 1790, the Council of State in a special session agreed to pass pertinent papers and documents with proposals for revision of the Ordinance of Intendants to the Council of the Indies. This body was to collect additional reports and informes concerning the utility of the institution for future study.

Although some minor changes in the operation of the intendancy were adopted in the next few years, the Council of the Indies did not seriously examine the system until 1800. The long delay may have been occasioned by the more weighty problems associated with the

42. Informe de Croix a Valdés, Lima, May 16, 1789, Expediente sobre la extinción de los Yntendencias, legajo 1118, Audiencia de Lima, A. G. I.
43. Informe de Croix a Valdés, May 16, 1789, ibid.
44. Fisher, Intendant System, p. 94.

European war, which would naturally be given priority by the government. A royal order of July 3, 1800, accompanied by informes from the Conde de Revillagigedo, the Marqués de Branciforte, both ex-viceroys of New Spain, and José Azanza, finally needled the council into action. On December 2, 1801, in an important session, with twenty-one individuals present, including Jorge Escobedo, the founder of the institution in Peru, the Marqués de Bajamar, and other notables, the council pored over reports that had been accumulating in the secretariat since 1789. In addition to de Croix's old representación and those of other officials, there was for their elucidation a recent *informe de la Contaduría* and *respuestas fiscales correspondientes al expediente de Intendencias*. Dated December 30, 1800, the informe contained among other things summaries of the views of Revillagigedo and the Bishop of Guadalajara.

With reference to municipal rights, the ecclesiastical dignitary was more explicit than the ex-viceroy of Mexico. He offered the opinion that "it would be more suitable to the treasury and to the common good to abolish the subdelegates and their agents and to transfer to the alcaldes ordinarios the responsibility for the administration of justice and the collection of the tribute, these individuals to be elected in the villas y lugares where there are ayuntamientos from the persons of greatest distinction and of proven conduct and of outstanding ability." No salary would be necessary, "since there would be no lack of vecinos who for the public service and love of His Majesty would fill these positions." In towns having no cabildos the crown should choose every year four to six deputies "who would elect one or two alcaldes to have the same powers as those chosen by the ayuntamientos. . . ."[45]

The fiscal of New Spain, in a *respuesta* of March 6, 1801, took issue with the Bishop of Guadalajara's proposal concerning the administration of justice by the local magistrates. He declared that if alcaldes mayores and corregidores were abolished and alcaldes ordinarios left as judges, "the result would be inconveniences, indeed, insuperable." Indians must not come under the jurisdiction of the local alcaldes, since the "majority of Spaniards owning haciendas, herds of cattle, and sugar mills would compel the natives to perform work for their particular interests contrary to oft-repeated laws." Exception was

45. Informe de los Srs. Contadores Gens. de 30 de Dic. de 1800, legajo 1119, Audiencia de Lima, A. G. I.

taken by the legal advisor to de Croix's accusation against the integrity of the intendants. He claimed that the charge of injustice applied to only a few, "for there is no government, however useful or essential, without weak and scandalous individuals." It would not be imperative to adduce evidence to show that "the cabildos were displeased with the intendancies, for, accustomed to an arbitrary handling of funds . . . they would little relish the creation of a junta municipal, with the public disclosure of rents and with the opportune intervention provided in the Ordinance."[46]

Supporting de Croix's position vis-à-vis the intendancies was the fiscal of Peru. In his respuesta of April 30, 1801, the attorney branded the asesores as the cause of "many disputes, rivalries, and controversies that have developed with the ayuntamientos, and with others, now over seating at the public functions and in the church, now over succession to the intendancy, now over matters of jurisdiction, ceremony, and etiquette." More natural and less likely to arouse altercation was "the system in Spain, in which the corregidor, as head of the ayuntamiento, presides over it always, and is in a better position and more qualified to give legal counsel to the intendant." While the intendancy had some merit, the older plan produced less quarreling and fewer lawsuits.[47]

In his defense of the intendancy the fiscal of the consejo sought to counter the objections raised to the conduct of the subdelegates. These officials would be less prone to extortion and malfeasance if paid fixed salaries in place of the 3 per cent accruing to them from the collection of the tribute. To forestall possible tyranny of these agents, it was proposed that municipal officials have concurrent jurisdiction with the subdelegates within the bounds of the pueblo, with the proviso that cognizance of civil and criminal cases be left as before. In towns or villages with more than thirty families the officials thus authorized should comprise the two alcaldes, the procurator, and five elected deputies.[48]

In summary, it is plain that there was manifold evidence pro and

46. Respuesta del Sor. fiscal de Nueva España, March 6, 1801, expedientes de Intendencias, *ibid*.
47. Respuesta del Sor. fiscal del Perú, April 30, 1801, Expediente de Intendencias, *ibid*.
48. Razón de los puntos qe. comprende el expediente genl. de Intendencias, *ibid*.

con as to the value of the intendancy. The *dictamen* of the council reflected the belief that no categorical conclusion could be reached. It rejected the Peruvian Viceroy's arraignment as petty and without sufficient foundation, while lauding the fairness and objectivity of Revillagigedo. Nevertheless, revisions were unavoidable. It was resolved to abolish completely the *repartimientos* and to procure more efficiency and honesty from the subdelegates, who were to be appointed thereafter from Europeans or criollos upon recommendation of a special tribunal and to be assigned to three classifications with salary corresponding to the grade. The term of office was six years. If the residence proved satisfactory, the official might anticipate promotion to a higher rank as a reward for hard work and good conduct. As to local government, the alcaldes might do business with the Indians and assume some responsibility for the abolition of the repartimientos.[49] Because of his role in introducing the system into Peru and of his first-hand knowledge of the problems involved, Escobedo was permitted to record a separate opinion. It favored the retention of the system but with certain modifications.[50]

The Council of the Indies devoted a number of sessions to the knotty question of revision of the ordinance. Meetings of February 23, February 28, and March 4, 1802, dealt with the drafting of a single code to apply uniformly throughout the colonies. Undoubtedly, the recommendations of Escobedo and Revillagigedo carried weight with other members of the council. In the discussion of a number of points that were raised the former Peruvian Visitador actively participated. Since the general sentiment prevailed that the advantages exceeded the demerits, there was little thought of scrapping the system

49. Dictamen del Consejo de Indias, Dec. 2, 1801, Expediente de Yntendencias, *ibid.*

50. Paradoxically, he remarked that "to declare yourself against the Intendancies is to be in favor of them," for they represented an effort to correct evils in administration. To strengthen the power of the intendant was imperative. "The right of confirmation of the alcalde, which was conceded even to the corregidor at one time, should be returned to the intendant, who must be allowed knowledge of the ramos of propios, arbitrios, caxas de comunidad and censos, since these are all by nature associated with their duties. . . ." Colonial intendants and corregidores could not function simultaneously as in Spain because of mutual rivalries, "nor is it practicable that there be asesores of the intendants, corregidores, or alcaldes letrados in the capitals, where there are not so many lawsuits as in Spain; and in general are inseparable from the departments of the Treasury and War the questions of Justicia and Policia and those matters that are advanced in the cabildos, which for these and other reasons must not recognize any other head than the intendant." See Voto particular del Sor. Dn. Jorge Escobedo, Expediente de Yntendencias, *ibid.*

and returning to previous administrative methods. The council proposed changes that might eliminate the outstanding weaknesses.

Work on the amended code was finally completed. On August 4, 1802, the junta of ministers, commissioned by the King on March 27 for this purpose at the recommendation of the council, announced the termination of its onerous task.[51] Whether or not great hopes were entertained among royal advisors for the success of the new Ordinance of Intendants is uncertain. Having 226 articles, with different phrasing and arrangement of material, it amounted to an essentially new code. It is needless to describe in detail the changes in general administrative procedure and in the powers set forth. Suffice it to say that the status of the subdelegates received greater attention; they were placed in specific grades with proportionate salaries and the possibility of promotion. Some modification in the authority wielded by the alcalde ordinario in the handling of municipal funds was also to be noted.[52] These were belated efforts to rectify obvious mistakes and to improve government at the primary stratum.

For good or bad, the Ordinance of 1803 never became effective. As a result of the objection of the Ministry of War at the inclusion of certain articles affecting military defenses, an order of January 11, 1804, proclaimed by the Council of the Indies two days later, invalidated the new code. Hence, with some amendments and revisions, the Ordinance of 1782 had legal force in Peru until the disruption of the region by revolution.[53]

A definitive appraisal of the operation of the intendancy in all sectors of administration throughout the empire awaits future scholarship. Meanwhile, it may be safely conjectured that the effects of the system varied from region to region. In the Viceroyalty of La Plata the intendants performed work of lasting quality.[54] In certain other areas they accomplished little of note. It was a mistake to overload them with a multiplicity of duties, the perennial curse of colonial administration. Their accomplishments would have been greater had they been more youthful and consequently more capable of the physical exertions associated with their diverse responsibilities and had there

51. Informe of the Junta to Miguel Cayetano Soler, Aug. 4, 1802, legajo 1713, Indiferente general, A. G. I.
52. Fisher, *Intendant System*, pp. 94, 95.
53. Real Orden, Jan. 11, 1804, legajo 1119, Audiencia de Lima, A. G. I.
54. Lynch, *Spanish Colonial Administration, 1782-1810*, p. 284.

not been debate in high places over the very existence of the institution. Time was also a factor. In the comparatively brief life of the intendancy "it did not appear to be integrated to the old system," but to say that "it interfered with it" is perhaps questionable.[55]

In the area of municipal development an apparent causal relationship can be established. At the end of the pre-revolutionary epoch the Peruvian cities and towns manifested greater activity, independence in outlook, and awareness of grievances than they had at the beginning. Nonetheless, a survey of the municipalities in 1792 revealed many vacancies in civic offices.[56] Was this advance not in part because of the supervisory authority invoked by the intendants and their subordinates? Admittedly, other tangible and intangible forces conducive to better administration existed. Despite the heavy hand of this newcomer to the bureaucracy, cities in the Audiencia of Lima gained concessions. Through donations to the royal treasury and the display of an uncommon aggressiveness, Lima surpassed other municipalities and secured privileges that enabled her to rank with Mexico City. But the most important feature, that of local autonomy, which might have forged a bond between the colonies and the metropolis, was not a gift of the decendants of the great reformer Charles III.

55. Viellard-Baron, "L'Etablissement des Intendants aux Indes par Charles III," p. 533.
The view that the functioning of the system was handicapped by incompetent ministers is offered by Luis Navarro García, *Intendencias en Indias*, p. 120: "The great ill-luck of Gálvez' work was that it was not continued by men of the mentality of its creator. Had this not been so, the history of the intendancies would have been otherwise."
56. Hipólito Unánue, *Guía política del Perú*, pp. 87, 99, 148.

CHAPTER XI

The Impact of
Spanish Liberalism

Like Joshua's biblical blasts before the wall of Jericho, Napoleon's trumpets in the cobbled streets of Madrid sounded the death knell of the Spanish Empire. By the terms of the Treaty of Fontainebleau, of October 24, 1807, Manuel Godoy, the Prince of Peace, permitted French troops to traverse the Pyrenees for the invasion of recalcitrant Portugal. The continued presence of foreign soldiers in the Peninsula after the speedy overrunning of the maritime state aroused apprehension among Spaniards as to the future designs of the French dictator, and on March 19, 1808, in response to the public outcry, Charles IV, who was blamed for peril to the nation, agreed to abdicate. His successor was his son Ferdinand VII, hailed by the populace as El Deseado. Like Louis XV's sobriquet of "Well-Beloved" the term became ironical at the end of his reign. Protesting that the act of abdication was consumated under duress, Charles appealed to Napoleon. In consequence both father and son were invited to Bayonne by the crafty Emperor, ostensibly for a family reconciliation, but in reality for the fulfilment of a well-concealed plan for the occupation of Spain and her colonies. Once on French soil, Ferdinand, under pressure, returned the throne to his father, who in the almost interminable game of passing the sceptre, yielded Spain to Napoleon. The latter designated his brother Joseph Bonaparte as the new ruler. Until the dissipation of the imperial dream the royal family remained as restive prisoners in an isolated French chateau.

To Napoleon's deep chagrin, the Spanish people refused to concur in the high-handed scheme. All classes of the population joined in a patriotic movement of resistance against the French. The spirit of nationalism was invoked against its creator. Appropriately enough, the call to arms came on May 2, 1808, from a municipal official, an alcalde. "Madrid falls victim to French perfidy! Spaniards, hasten to save her!" was his manifesto.[1] Beginning in the heart of the country, the uprising spread from province to province and continued, with English aid, until the eventual expulsion of the invaders. To fill the political vacuum that had existed since the imprisonment of Ferdinand VII, a Suprema Junta Central, composed of thirty-six deputies named by the provinces, formally came into being on September 25, 1808, at Aranjuez.[2] This body, governing in the name of the King, endured until January 29, 1810, when it was dissolved and replaced by a five-man Supremo Concejo de Regencia.

Meanwhile, intelligence of the abdication of the throne by Charles IV in favor of his son reached Peru. The Viceroy, audiencia, and the cabildo of Lima joined in preparations to celebrate the event in a manner befitting its importance. On August 27, 1808, the Viceroy Fernando Abascal, who had assumed his high post in Lima on July 26, 1806, informed the local council of what had transpired in Spain and directed that festivities be inaugurated. On September 9, the cabildo named commissioners to supervise the ceremonies scheduled to take place on October 1. Before this date the unhappy tale of Bonaparte's sordid treachery and deceit came in a convoy from Chile. Undaunted by the disaster, the Viceroy and the council agreed that the proclamation and the customary oath of allegiance should, notwithstanding, take place, but on the thirteenth instead of the first as originally planned. Although enthusiasm was dampened, the illumination of the public buildings and streets and the pealing of church bells continued for three days. In the cathedral a special prayer was said for the monarch's safety. On the fifteenth the cabildo issued a proclamation, expressing its abiding loyalty to the King.[3]

On the last day of the celebration the important ecclesiastical and secular bodies of the city assembled in the cathedral. From this station they made their way around the Plaza de Armas and by a side

1. Alemparte, *El cabildo en Chile colonial*, p. 388.
2. García Venero, *Historia del parlamentarismo español*, pp. 60-63.
3. Representación del cabildo de Lima al Presidente de Junta Suprema de Gobierno de España e Indias, legajo 58, Estado, Archivo histórico nacional, Madrid.

street to the Dominican monastery to honor the Virgin of Rosario. In Cuzco and other cities and towns there were similar demonstrations of affection for the deposed monarch.[4]

Mindful of the gravity of the crisis in Spain, the ayuntamiento of Lima resolved on October 25 to strengthen the Suprema Junta by recognition of its authority. Accordingly, it addressed a letter, dated October 26, to Francisco de Saavedra, president of the Suprema Junta, proclaiming its allegiance and giving an account of the following acts of loyalty by the municipality, with certifications attached:

> The capital of Peru, represented by the cabildo, has always given proof of its faithfulness to the Catholic Ruler and has enjoyed privileges from his royal liberality, honors and distinctions that it retains and that perpetuate his gratitude. In consequence, it offers its haciendas and lives in the service and defense of the sovereign, to whom it is bound by oath, and it bows to the authority of the one [body] who represents him. It recognizes the Suprema Junta de Sevilla as destined by Divine Providence, and hastens to obey its honored decisions. If distance separating it from the Peninsula—never more incommodious and intolerable—has delayed the expression of its allegiance, it is satisfied to use the opportunity presented with no little feeling of not having been the first in an obesiance due the authority of Your Excellency. . . .[5]

Toward the end of the communication a note of opportunism was struck. Aware of the greater financial dependence of the junta on the colonies, the ayuntamiento requested the rescinding of the *Real Ynstrucción de la Amortisación,* according to which many citizens' funds had been allegedly misappropriated.[6]

While it strove to hamper the advance of the French army, the newly organized Suprema Junta initiated moves to bind itself more closely with the colonies. In June, 1808, it ordered José Manuel de Goyeneche, a native of Arequipa, to sail to Montevideo and Buenos Aires and to preserve connections with this region. His mission was

4. *Ibid.*
5. Enclosed in the packet of documents, papers, etc. from Lima was an oficio of Aug. 28, 1808, from the cabildo of Buenos Aires, denouncing the tyrannical action of Napoleon in Madrid and expressing the hope that everything would be done "to incite the enthusiasm and loyalty of the citizenry for the defense of the mother country." The reply, dated Oct. 26, and likewise included, reiterates the devotion and the fidelity of the limeños to the cause of liberation.
6. Apparently the protest was ineffective.

momentarily successful.[7] Simultaneously, Napoleon dispatched emissaries to America to appeal for colonial allegiance, but with no success.[8]

The Suprema Junta's next proposal was revolutionary. No more dramatic bid for colonial adhesion to the cause could have been devised than to invite representation from the empire in the governing body of Spain. A memoria of September 30, 1808, underlined the doubts and forebodings in the colonies over their future. On October 27, the junta notified the Council of the Indies of its resolve to have deputies present in the deliberations from each of the four viceroyalties and inquired as to the best procedure for holding elections.[9] It was not until a month later that the council, unconvinced but reluctantly obedient, made its reply, and then only after a peremptory order from Saavedra. The members of this body, while unable to agree on specific conditions, were united in their concern over the wisdom of such a step.[10] With the advice of the council at hand, the Suprema Junta on January 22, 1809, issued from the Alcázar in Seville an order to the viceroys and captains-general to supervise the selection in their respective regions of one individual to share in the government of the realm. The method of choice stipulated that the ayuntamiento of each important town in a district would assemble for the election of three individuals, from whom one name was to be taken by lot. From the list presented by the cabildos the viceroy would choose three. The casting of lots would determine the final name.[11]

In these perilous times it was not unnatural for the Suprema Junta to receive suggestions and recommendations from many quarters over the ever-present issue of colonial reform. Government officials and colonists alike diagnosed the ills of the patient and offered speedy cures. It is not unlikely that some of these proposals had an influence in the formation of later policies and decrees. A lengthy memorandum, authored by an anonymous Peruvian, warrants examination because of its unusual insight into regional grievances and because of the provocative nature of the remedies.

7. Rodríguez and Calderón, *Memoria de Abascal,* vol. I, lxxxvi-lxxxix.
8. *Ibid.,* lxxxix-xciii.
9. Oficio of the Junta to the Gobernador del Consejo de Indias, Oct. 27, 1808, legajo 54D, Estado, Archivo histórico nacional, Madrid.
10. Consulta of the Gobernador del Consejo to Francisco Saavedra, Nov. 28, 1808, *ibid.*
11. Royal Order, Jan. 22, 1809, legajo 58, Estado, *ibid.*; see also García Venero, *Historia del parlamentarismo español,* p. 66.

The picture of injustice, suffering of the natives, and economic decline is not unfamiliar. The memorialist recounts the multifold wrongs endured by the "unhappy inhabitants of these immense zones" of the empire: the oppression of the Indians by the intendants and the subdelegates; the dishonesty of treasury officials; the decline of mining at Potosí and other sites; and the endless litigation, resulting in appeals to higher tribunals, more burdensome "owing to distances and increasing costs."

For the reformation of local government extraordinary measures were urged. The cabildos were composed for the most part of those "of limited vision, who to become so [members] purchase varas for which many times they do not pay and who from a mean and ridiculous interest sacrifice those of the Patria to those of the governors and prelates." To revitalize the municipal councils, the author proffered this advice:

> Order it so that there should be only two perpetual positions in the cabildo, those of alférez real and alguacil mayor, and that all the rest, including those of the justices, be elected annually to the satisfaction of the pueblos, maintaining rigorously the principle that half be Europeans and half Americans. Clothe again these cabildos, or let them be called juntas, with an authority greater than that of the governors, prelates, and tribunals, not in order that they may command and govern by themselves, but that they may watch over the conduct of all the chiefs and magistrates, and bring about the exact execution of all laws and statutes; that they may end discord among the citizenry and terminate lawsuits so that ruin may be avoided; that they may administer honestly the revenues of the state and the municipality; that they may direct the administration of the towns and the maintenance of highways; and finally, that good order may reign and disorders and public scandals be eliminated.

An even more drastic governmental change was advocated. General assemblies, comparable to those of the provinces of Alava, Guipúzcoa, and Biscay and composed of the alcaldes ordinarios of the Spanish towns, were to meet once a year or once every two years "to devise policies which are absolutely lacking now." It was suggested that the crown establish a political system "equal in all the dominions," and thus assure "an indissoluble union, without the necessity of employing a soldier in its preservation or at most only militia to aid the justices."

The anonymous proposal calls, also, for an alteration of immigration regulations: Free and unhindered passage from Spain to the Americas and vice versa ought to be permitted. The right of entry might be conferred on foreigners of Catholic faith, "provided they be laborers or artists," who could organize agricultural colonies in Chile, Buenos Aires, and Tucumán, "where land is worth little and herds are abundant." The vastness of the territory to be opened up would mean sparse settlements, with little threat from the colonists to the sovereignty of the crown.

The communication closes with a fervent exhortation and a dire warning: "I implore you by everything that is sacred in Heaven and on earth that you change or reform this fatal and tyrannical form of government. Unless this is done there will be an explosion more terrible and dangerous than that of the year '80."[12] This and similar cartas must have exerted a liberalizing impact on the Suprema Junta's outlook.

In the course of time the resistance regime extended its authority to Peru. On March 18, 1809, the cabildo of Lima at the behest of the Viceroy took an oath of loyalty to the governing committee in a *pleno y extraordinario* session, a procedure followed soon by other ayuntamientos of the audiencia.[13] The steadfastness of the capital in this critical hour was partly because of Abascal's unusual popularity with many sections of the population, including of course the privileged upper stratum.[14]

Upon receipt of the Suprema Junta's directive calling for the election of a deputy from the Viceroyalty of Peru, Abascal dispatched

12. Carta de 'un ciudadano que reside en los angullos mas remotos de nuestra monarquia a Serenismo Presidente, Ilustres Vocales de la Suprema Soberana 'Junta Central,' . . . Perú, 1809, legajo 58 F, Estado, Archivo histórico nacional, Madrid.

13. Minutes of March 18, 1809, Libros de cabildos de Lima, vol. XLI, Biblioteca municipal, Lima.

14. As Lorente points out, the Viceroy had the support of influential classes: the lawyers, because of his reorganization of their constitution and bylaws; the physicians for whom he had founded a school of medicine; the literati, who admired the establishment of a public library; and finally, the general public, who were indebted to him for the opening of a general cemetery. See Sebastián Lorente, *Historia del Perú bajo los Borbones, 1700-1821* (Lima, 1871), p. 302.

Diego Barros Arana, Compendio de *historia de América* (Santiago, 1865), II, 514, emphasizes the outlook of the aristocracy: "Lima, like Mexico, was subdued . . . not so much by the forces that guarded it, as by the influence and prestige of the high functionaries and of those titled señores who resided in it. The luxury and wealth of those two cities created in them a kind of court, which exercised a strange fascination over its inhabitants."

a circular to the cabildos in the capitals of the districts to inform them of the order and to urge immediate compliance. The idea of representation won speedy approval from the creoles. The villa of Tarma was the first to act, followed by Huancavelica and the seat of the viceroyalty. By August 31, all of the remaining cities and towns, with the exception of Arica, had conducted elections and had forwarded the names of the nominees to Lima.[15]

The elections held in the winter of 1809 belied past experience. In contrast to ordinary conciliar assemblies good order prevailed and attendance was far better than usual. With a promise of a share in the government of the realm interest was running high.

Electoral procedure lacked complete uniformity. The intendant or subdelegate presided over the election, held in the sala capitular or, if no municipal hall was standing, in the residence of the chief officer. Voting was mainly oral. The royal decree of January 22 did not stipulate this condition, but rather permitted the method of selection to be in accordance with the custom of the particular council or the preference of the presiding official. In the case of Yca the proposal of the use of the secret ballot by the subdelegate provoked a serious dispute with the capitulars, who declared that it was contrary to "immemorial custom." The cabildo overrode his suggestion and the Viceroy accepted the results despite written allegations by the presiding officer of other irregularities and favoritism.[16] From the three individuals elected by the cabildo one was selected by lot.

By the nineteenth of September Abascal had before him the nominees of the various cabildos. On the basis of conciliar preferences and the qualifications of the candidates, the Viceroy chose three indi-

15. The alcalde, who constituted the government of Arica, apologized for the lack of a formal cabildo on the grounds that the city "has lost population," but he noted that bids for the office of regidor had been made so that in time there would be a municipal corporation. See legajo 58F, Estado, Archivo histórico nacional, Madrid.
16. In the *testimonio* dispatched by the subdelegate to the Viceroy there is an expression of ultra-regalian theory: "The ayuntamientos or cabildos of this city since their inception or establishment were only to offer pareceres to those holding royal authority without the power to command or determine or execute their pareceres, and resolutions, and if they act to the contrary the justicias must not consent to it because harm and prejudice result, since they [cabildos] lack mero y mixto ymperio, having bestowed it on the prince and his ministers. Since Ferdinand and Isabella resolved to send to these places ordinary judges with fullest jurisdiction the ayuntamientos were deprived of the power to name them and so there is no one to authorize them to act to the contrary nor to remove the presiding officer and name another in his place." See *ibid*.

viduals. The casting of lots determined the final selection.[17] It was José de Silva y Olave, a man in his early sixties and a doctor in law from the University of San Marcos. He was neither the ablest nor the most experienced of the nominees in the conduct of such business. He had, however, two points in his favor. He was generally popular in the city and was attached to the cause of local rights. His dexterity as a conciliar delegate was never put to the test, for he succeeded in getting only as far as New Spain when he learned of the dissolution of the Suprema Junta and returned to Lima.[18]

For this abortive trial in representative government, the cabildo was a ready vehicle at the disposal of the Suprema Junta. But there was no opportunity for the appearance of a genuine democracy, the municipal councils at this epoch being filled with men who had purchased offices or been appointed to them. Notwithstanding, the resolution of the junta symbolized a salient break with the past, a reversal of a three-century trend. With the ascendency of absolutism, it could have come only in a time of national emergency when hostile forces threatened the very existence of Spain and her empire. However, the Peruvian delegate took no part in the deliberations of the junta, as it was dissolved on January 29, 1810. It was succeeded by the Supremo Consejo de Regencia, with five councilors, one of whom was a Spanish representative for America, Esteban Fernández de León of the Council of Spain and the Indies, later replaced by a Mexican, Miguel de Lardizábal y Uribe.[19]

This gesture toward liberalism was dwarfed by a grant of representation to the colonies in the Cortes. Only a calamity of tremendous dimensions such as that of 1808 could have resuscitated the moribund national parliament. There was some truth in the current saying that "it was in its death-throes under the House of Austria and had expired under the Bourbons."[20] In a moment of desperation and solicitude for the future, Ferdinand VII at Bayonne had decreed the convoking of this body to aid the cause of popular resistance. Earnest progressives and reformers hailed it as the culmination of two forces

17. *Ibid.*

18. Rubén Vargas Ugarte, *Historia del Perú, emancipación, 1809-1825* (Buenos Aires, 1958), pp. 111, 112.

19. Rodríguez and Calderón, *Memoria de Abascal*, vol. I, cxix-cxxxii.

20. Luis Alayza and Paz Soldán, *La constitución de Cádiz. El egregio limeño Morales y Duarez* (Lima, 1946), p. 17.

at work, the democratic tradition of Spain of the Middle Ages and the current of philosophical thought of the eighteenth century, "the medieval fueros and the new ideas."[21]

Despite the opposition of the conservatively inclined Regency Council, which delayed for a time the issuance of a summons, the Cortes opened its sessions on September 24, 1810, on the Isle of Leon, at Cadiz.[22] On hand were the representatives of the Iberian provinces, occupied and free, and of the American colonies. Time being a vital factor, the deputies for the overseas viceroyalties were chosen by creoles who chanced to be in the port at the moment. They were to serve ad interim and *como suplentes*.

The selection of colonial representatives for the Cortes from Peru by more proper methods had been initiated many months earlier. A decree of February 14, 1810, by the Regency Council authorized elections by the important cabildos of the region. Ten municipalities were to choose one deputy each.

While the concept of participation in the national government struck a responsive chord among the creoles, there was as usual uncertainty about the adoption of correct electoral usage. The experience of Trujillo is typical. Trujillo sought to select a deputy and to draw up instructions for his guidance. On August 18, 1810, the ayuntamiento received a message from the cabildo of Lima, with a viceregal oficio of August 7 instructing the body to proceed to the choice of a deputy without delay.[23] September 18 was fixed as the day for the election. On the appointed date the ayuntamiento nominated three individuals by a plurality of secret votes, from whom one was chosen by lot.[24] Because of technical points raised by the procurator-general, the cabildo declared the selection invalid until clarification of instructions had been obtained from the Viceroy. On December 24, the council went through the motions of a second election, using the same procedure but with viceregal approbation.

After numerous sessions, marked by animated debate, the Trujillo council drafted directions for the guidance of its deputy. They called for the extension of freedom from port dues to all the cities of the province, for recognition of the need to publicize the opportunities

21. Alemparte, *El cabildo en Chile colonial*, p. 415.
22. García Venero, *Historia del parlamentarismo español*, p. 93.
23. Minutes of Aug. 18, 1810, Libros de cabildos de Trujillo, vol. XVIII.
24. Minutes of Sept. 18, 1810, *ibid.*, vol. XVIII.

for exploitation of the mineral resources of the region, and for the concession of the distinction of the appellation of *muy noble y siempre leal* similar to that for Tlascala in New Spain.[25] In the main, they reflected the economic wishes of the citizenry.

The choices of the Peruvian municipalities when finally completed were as follows: Francisco Salazar (Lima), Manuel Galeano (Cuzco), Antonio Andueza (Chachapoyas), Pedro García Coronel (Trujillo), José Lorenzo Bermúdez (Tarma), José Antonio Navarrete (Piura), Mariano Rivero (Arequipa), Tadeo Gárate (Puno), Martin José Mujica (Guamanga), and Domingo Alcaraz (Huánuco). Seven of them managed to reach Spain safely and to take part in the discussions of the Cortes in 1811.[26]

Creoles in Peru might well have been proud of their delegation. It outshone those of the other viceroyalties in the intellectual endowment of the individual members and in the outstanding nature of their accomplishments. In the struggle between the liberals and the conservatives in the Cortes, the Americans constituted politically a third group, "which although progressive and inclined to reform worked solely and exclusively pro domo sua."[27] Equality of status with Spaniards and freedom of speech and of the press having been guaranteed, they strove boldly and persistently to secure other favorable concessions. Head and shoulders above any of the viceregal delegates whether ad interim or elected by the cabildos, was the Peruvian attorney Vicente Morales y Duarez.[28] When the Cortes was officially organized in September, 1810, his extraordinary gifts as a political thinker and a forceful speaker led to his election as vice-president of the body, a high honor for the criollos, hitherto regarded as inferior mentally to the people from the Peninsula. He presided over an important session of the national body in December and was one of the thirteen men responsible for the drafting of the celebrated constitution. On March 24, 1812, the Cortes elevated him to the presidency, an office that ironically gave to the Peruvian greater power than that formerly enjoyed by the imprisoned Bourbon. His untimely death one week later removed from the scene one of the most vigorous and

25. Minutes of Dec. 24, 1810, *ibid.*, vol. XVIII.
26. If Guayaquil is included, there are eleven deputies. See Vargas Ugarte, *Historia del Perú, emancipación*, p. 113.
27. Quoted in Alayza and Soldán, *Constitución de Cádiz*, p. 27.
28. *Ibid.*

idealistic protagonists of liberalism.[29] Three other personalities of more than average perceptiveness and knowledge of governmental affairs served along with Morales in the initial sessions: Blas Ostolaza, canon of the cathedral of Trujillo; Dionisio Inca Yupanqui, who, as his name might indicate, was from Cuzco and of Inca blood; and Ramón Feliú, of Ceuta.[30] In time, they were joined by the seven regularly elected Peruvian delegates.

To plead the creole cause in the national assembly required the exercise of diplomacy and tact by the colonial deputies. Spaniards of both liberal and conservative faiths shared the same antipathy and condescension toward those born in America. It is said that "Spanish liberalism had limits: the frontiers of Spain."[31] Shackled by tradition and illusion of imperial greatness, the patriots from the Peninsula could not understand the desire of the colonists for equality of rights, freedom of commerce, and abolition of restrictions on competing agricultural pursuits and manufacturing. For them America was yet a region of unexploited wealth, ultimately to enrich the metropolis. Moreover, tension was heightened by news reaching Cadiz of revolutionary movements underway in certain parts of the empire.

It was incumbent upon the Peruvian deputies to keep the cabildos of the viceroyalty informed of the debates and the resolutions of the Cortes and of the course of the war against the invaders. Be-

29. The cause of his death is unknown. After attending a banquet given in his honor by the Marquis of Wellesley, he returned to his room in an inn and was found dead some hours later by a Peruvian compatriot. See *ibid.*, pp. 34-36.
He was eulogized by one of his contemporaries in superlative terms: "There was no one in the Cortes of Cádiz who surpassed him in learning, serenity, equanimity, reasonableness, and the ability to speak precisely, clearly, and attractively." But, unlike most of the liberals of his day, he advocated the return of the Jesuits. See *ibid.*, p. 34; for the "Relación de los méritos y servicios del doctor D. Vicente Morales Duarez de la Quadra," see Valcárcel, "Perú borbónico y emancipación," pp. 434-438. His conservatism on the proposal of extension of political rights to free men of color is exposed by James F. King in an article entitled "The Colored Castes and American Representation in the Cortes of Cadiz," *Hispanic American Historical Review*, XXXIII (Feb., 1953), 39, 41, 44. See also García Venero, *Historia del parlamentarismo español*, p. 125.
30. While forthright in his denunciation of those who belittled Americans, Ostolaza was, strangely enough, such a fervent believer in divine right that he later joined a cabal to overthrow Ferdinand VII in favor of the *infante* Charles V. See Alayza and Soldán, *Constitución de Cádiz*, pp. 28-30; for more about Blas Ostolaza, consult Rubén Vargas Ugarte, "D. Blas Ostolaza, rector del seminario de Trujillo, diputado a Cortes, capellán de Ferdinando VII, víctima del liberalismo," *Revista de historia de América*, no. 49 (June, 1960), pp. 121-145.
31. Alayza and Soldán, *Constitución de Cádiz*, p. 27.

cause the city of Lima enjoyed a political primacy in the region its ayuntamiento had assumed after 1808 a leadership among the municipal bodies in relaying intelligence from Europe, in the formulating of instructions to the delegates, and in the organizing of public opinion. Municipal solidarity, later to germinate into national unity, was a task for the capitulars of the capital.

The first important communication from the delegation, dated December 26, 1810, and signed by Morales and Feliú, arrived in Lima on April 26, 1811. Addressed to the Excelentísimo Ayuntamiento of the capital, it affirmed the zealous devotion of the group to the prosecution of colonial interests.[32] Appended to this was a copy of the demands presented to the Cortes by the American and Asiatic deputies on December 16, 1810:

> I. In consequence of the decree of next October 15 it is declared that the national representation of the provinces, cities, towns, and villages of the mainland of America, its islands, and the Philippines with respect to the natives of both hemispheres, thus Spaniards as Indians and their sons, must be the same and will be the same in order and form [although respective in number] that today have and will have in the future the provinces, cities, and localities of the Peninsula and the islands of European Spain among its lawful citizens.
>
> II. The natives and inhabitants of America shall be able to sow and cultivate whatever nature and skill make possible in those climes; and in the same way may develop industry, manufacturing, and the crafts in every field.
>
> III. The Americas shall enjoy the widest permission to export their products, both natural and manufactured, to the Peninsula and to allied and neutral nations; and the importation of whatever is necessary will be permitted, whether in national or foreign ships; and in effect, all ports of America will be open for trade.
>
> IV. Free and reciprocal trade will exist between the Americas and the Asiatic possessions, with the abolition of any exclusive privilege that denies such freedom.
>
> V. Liberty of trade shall be established for the ports of America and the Philippines with the rest of Asia, any restriction to the contrary being withdrawn.

32. Dionisio Inca Yupanqui, however, addressed cartas to the cabildo of Arequipa relating the circumstances of the election of the ad interim deputies and his hopes for the relief of colonial oppression. There are three of these to be found in the Municipal Library in Lima, the first dated Sept. 22, 1810, the second, March 14, 1811, and the third undated. They were apparently separate communications and not intended for general distribution as was the case of the letter from Morales and Feliú.

IMPACT OF SPANISH LIBERALISM 209

VI. Every monopoly in the Americas shall be suppressed, but with compensation to the public treasury of the cash that is collected from the various sources, according to the taxes that are due each one.

VII. The exploitation of the quicksilver mines shall be free and open to every individual, but the administration of the output will remain the charge and responsibility of the Tribunal of Mines, with no intervention by viceroys, intendants, governors, and courts of the Real Hacienda.

VIII. Americans of Spanish blood as well as Indians and the sons of both classes shall have equal right to office with European Spaniards for every type of work and career, as well in the Cortes as in any position in the kingdom, whether they be of ecclesiastical, political, or military nature.

IX. With consideration to the natural protection of each Kingdom, it shall be stipulated that one half of the positions must go to individuals born within that territory.

X. For the most certain attainment of the above there shall be in the capitals of the viceroyalties and captaincies-general of America an advisory Junta for the designation of Americans to vacant positions in turn, in which arrangement all of the authority due the appointee will be assigned. The said Junta shall be composed of the following individuals: the senior member of the audiencia, the senior regidor, the conciliar procurator, the rector of the University, the dean of the College of Lawyers, the ranking military officer, and the most distinguished official of the Real Hacienda.

XI. In recognition of its great importance for the spread of learning and for the extension of the missions which introduce and propagate faith among the infidel Indians, the Jesuit Order shall be restored by the Cortes to the kingdoms of America.[33]

Two days after the receipt of the foregoing letter and document the ayuntamiento of Lima distributed copies to the other cabildos. In an accompanying note it declared that the communication from the Peninsula "will reveal to you the vigilance and the activity of those worthy sons in the advocating of the establishment of a true and permanent foundation for the prosperity of the Americas. . . ." Cuzco acknowledged the arrival of the dispatches on May 7 and ordered the posting of the communications from Spain in public places.[34] Similar steps were taken in other municipalities to inform the citizens of the work of the deputies.

33. Expediente sobre las propuestas remitidas por el Excmo. Cabildo de Lima a este dirigidas a él por los señores diputados desde la real isla de León, Cuzco, May 7, 1811, Ms. D331, Biblioteca nacional, Lima.
34. Ibid.

Another communication dated March 23, 1811, was received by the cabildo of Lima from the representatives in the Cortes, with the request that copies be forwarded as speedily as possible to the other ayuntamientos of Peru. It dealt primarily with the reception of the eleven proposals by the national assembly:

> The first proposition, as you will understand has two parts; one treats the law; the other the fact. The former is sanctioned: that is to say it has been resolved that national representation should be respectively equal to that of Spain and this should be one of the bases of the Constitution. The second that we sought, which even for the Cortes should be fulfilled according to that principle of the representation of Americans, convoking those who have the same qualifications as Europeans, has appeared to His Majesty's government full of so many impediments that there is no decision on accepting it.
>
> The second proposal has been conceded and by virtue thereof agriculture, industry, and the arts in America are already free of the prohibitions and trammels that up to now have prevented not only their growth but even their existence. And when the fields of Peru are overflowing with the produce that nature so bountifully offers; when everywhere are observed factories and shops that circumstances invite, the excellence of its raw materials and the skill of the natives; and when as a result of this condition, everything takes on a new aspect in Peru, we shall boast of having known how to take advantage of the situation in which providence has placed us, in order to lay the cornerstone of this building as grandiose as new and unexpected.
>
> As concerns the following propositions, it has been decreed that they be turned over to a commission for its examination. Since our determination has not been to force resolution in matters so difficult and of so high an order, and as on the other hand we are persuaded of the fact that the rights of America will be better known and respected the more they are examined, there is left to us no other thought but that of being able as soon as possible to communicate to you the favorable answer to our importunity in this area that will revive the preceding [rights].
>
> It was found convenient to postpone consideration of the sixth proposal until the general organization of the treasury is agreed upon.
>
> The seventh proposal has been approved with greater breadth than it contains. It has been ordered that the exploitation of the quicksilver mines, as well as the trade therein, be absolutely free and without restriction.
>
> As the eighth proposal contains an eternal truth it was necessary that it be approved also, and it has been approved.

But the two following in which we endeavored to make real and effective the meaning of the preceding have been deferred because they deal with the Constitution of the State on which work goes continually and which will shortly be concluded.

Finally, the eleventh proposal was rejected.

Furthermore, we inform you with special satisfaction that the government has consented to exempt the Indians from the tribute that they used to pay and afflicts them so much, not because of the amount but because of the extortions from which they suffered. The Indians, the wretched Indians will breathe, and will see for the first time at the end of three centuries that there is someone who pleads in their behalf so that they will be free forever of this annoying charge. Meanwhile, we shall consider the adoption of taxes with which to supply that section of the tribute that it yielded in benefit of those same tributaries, such as the synods of the curates; and when His Majesty's Government makes a decision on this interesting point, we shall advise you at the first opportunity. . . .[35]

A summary of the decrees issued by the Cortes up to the end of March, 1811, indicates the generous scope of concessions made to the colonials. Cognizant of unrest overseas and dominated by a coalition of liberals from the Peninsula and America, it inaugurated a series of sweeping reforms. Among them were the dismissal of unpopular viceroys and oidores, appointment of creoles to positions in the bureaucracy of the Peninsula, abolition of the Indian tribute and the repartimiento, permission to develop colonial industries formerly in competition with those of the homeland, and introduction of the right of habeas corpus. Freedom of the press, a reality in Spain since the beginning of the war with Napoleon, was voted overwhelmingly by the members of the national parliament. It was "simultaneously effect and cause of the great transformation of thought occurring in the first years of the nineteenth century, because the press succeeded in spreading new doctrines and inciting the combative instinct of the dissenters and the innovators."[36] A broad road to the realization of many goals stretched before the creoles.[37]

35. Alayza and Soldán, *La Constitución de Cádiz*, pp. 52, 53 note 1.

Julio V. González, *Filiación histórica del gobierno representativo Argentino* (Buenos Aires, 1937), p. 79, has a good summary of the role of the American representatives in the Cortes.

36. Alayza and Soldán, *Constitución de Cádiz*, p. 61.

37. Not only did the enraptured liberals dream of reforms in America, but they also contemplated transformation of the social and economic structure of the Peninsula in harmony with the philosophy of the French Revolution, thus doing away with

A scrutiny of these measures leads to the conclusion that they were generally favorable to the Peruvians. Economic discrimination still prevailed against the people of the La Plata basin and some other areas. In consequence, in these regions there was greater provocation to resentment and to acts of rebellion. To a greater degree than in most of the empire revolutionary sentiment in Peru arose from burgeoning nationalism and the spread of radical political dogma from Europe.

Privileges to Americans and Spaniards were to be guaranteed in a constitution. Approved by the Cortes in Cadiz on January 23, 1812, this remarkable document was declared in force in Spain on March 18, 1812. Its pervasive spirit of liberty and freedom is reflected in the words of the Archbishop of Mallorca, one of the drafters: "Our slavery is now ended. . . . My compatriots, inhabitants of four corners of the world: we have regained our dignity and our rights. . . . We are Spaniards! . . . We are free!"[38]

A description of all the progressive features of this extraordinary document would be extraneous. It is sufficient to say that the basic assumptions of the framers were democratic. At the outset they audaciously proclaimed the revolutionary doctrine of popular sovereignty. Articles 14 and 15 placed the law-making power, however, in the ruler and an elective body having representation from the colonies on the basis of one delegate for each 60,000 persons. The Consejo de Estado, the executive committee, was likewise to have imperial participation.

Local government, intimately related to the exercise of democracy, occupied a place in the constitution. Of 384 articles, 14 dealt solely with the election, organization, and powers of the ayuntamientos.[39]

---

privileges "denominated exclusive, prohibitory, and privative, inherent in señorios, such as hunting, fishing . . ." and depriving nobles of the title of "señor of vassals" and of having judicial rights. See *ibid.*, p. 62.

But in some matters the Cortes took the middle road. While it abolished the Inquisition, it declared a new patron for Spain in Santa Teresa de Jesús. De Tocqueville's observation that the leaders of the French Revolution did not change things as much as they believed they had may apply to this era of liberalism. See Alemparte, *El cabildo en Chile colonial*, pp. 424, 425.

38. Quoted in Alayza and Soldán, *Constitución de Cádiz*, p. 63.

39. Arts. 309-323 of the *Constitución política de la monarquía española, promulgada en Cádiz a 19 de marzo de 1812* (Cádiz, 1812).

Other sections having some bearing on local regimes are título III, capítulo III, De las juntas electorales de parroquia, arts. 35, 37-39, 41, 42, 45-48, 51-53; capítulo IV, De las juntas electorales de partido, arts. 59, 61, 63, 67-75; capítulo V, de las juntas

Cities and towns were to have councils, composed of elective alcaldes, procurators, and regidores, the number of these officials to be determined by the size of the citizen body. Presiding over this body would be the royal official, or in his absence, an alcalde.[40] The principle of vendibility having been abolished for all of these offices, the franchise was to be implemented by the citizens every December in the various municipalities for the choice of electors, who in turn would select by absolute plurality of votes all of the above-named functionaries.[41] The election of alcaldes, along with half the membership of the aldermanic body was to be annual, and an interval of two years had to elapse before re-election to any of the three offices.[42] To stand for office an individual had to be twenty-five years old with a minimum of five years' residence and citizenship in the pueblo.[43] No royal official was eligible for municipal employment.[44]

To the cabildo the constitution assigned these prerogatives:

1. To look after the health and sanitation of the population.

2. To aid the alcalde in everything that pertains to the security of persons and property of the citizens and the preservation of public order.

3. To administer and disburse funds from the propios and the arbitrios in conformity with the laws and ordinances, with power to name depositarios responsible to those naming them.

4. To make the allotment and collection of the taxes and remit them to the respective treasuries.

5. To oversee the primary schools and other educational institutions supported by public funds.

6. To take care of hospitals, houses of charity, and orphanages, under the rules prescribed for their operation.

7. To look after the construction and maintenance of roads, gravel-walks, bridges, jails, communal properties in the hills, and of all public works of need, utility, and ornamentation.

8. To draw up municipal ordinances and present them to the Cortes for its approval through the agency of a Provincial Deputation, which will prepare an informe concerning them.

9. To promote agriculture, industry, and trade, according to the

electorales de provincia, arts. 80-97; título V, capítulo II, de la administración de justicia en lo civil, arts. 282-284; capítulo III, de la administración de justicia en lo criminal, art. 286.

40. Arts. 309-312.   41. Arts. 312-314.
42. Arts. 315-316.   43. Art. 317.
44. Art. 318.

location and needs of the pueblo, in any way that will be beneficial and useful.[45]

There were limitations on the exercise of these powers. In theory a Provincial Deputation, composed of a president, an intendant, and seven individuals chosen by the electors of the district and meeting ninety days in each year, was to have general oversight of the functioning of the local councils. Article 323 specified control by this body of the disposition and use of municipal funds. At the end of the year the ayuntamiento had to file a statement of income and expenditure with the provincial committee; and, if supplementary taxes were required, approval had to be secured from it and eventually from the Cortes. Authorization to set up municipal councils in localities requiring them was also lodged in the hands of the provincial group. It was thus the intent of the crown to continue in part its traditional tutelage of local institutions.[46]

Despite these restrictions the colonial cabildos enjoyed a greater measure of liberty in the handling of their affairs than they had hitherto exercised under the Ordinance of Intendants. The constitutional innovations were an attempt to reverse previous trends and to arouse greater interest in local administration. A distinct gain was the abolition of the vendible office. Nevertheless, there was no provision for full-fledged democracy, the majority of the people being ineligible for citizenship and therefore for voting. The type of government thus instituted signified a further advance toward political control by the creoles.

For the selection of representatives to the Cortes the framers of the constitution devised a more complicated system of indirect election. Citizens assembling in a junta of the parish, with a population of not more than 200, would choose by secret ballot eleven individuals who in turn designated the parish elector. Voting would normally take place in the casa de cabildo under the direction of the crown officer or the senior alcalde. The parish electors met in the chief town of the partido, or district, to name electors to the capital, where the final act in the selection of deputies to Spain occurred.[47]

45. Art. 321.
46. While its chief authority lay in the areas of finance and public works, some overlapping and duplication of functions are noted in the promotion of trade, industry, agriculture, and education.
47. Arts. 35-46, 59-91.

Proclamation of the Constitution of 1812 by the Cortes generated a favorable response among the municipalities of Peru. Although some local officeholders believed that its provisions encroached upon their proprietary rights, a majority of the creoles regarded it as consonant with their aspirations.

Quite the contrary was the reaction of the highest official of the colonial bureaucracy. The Viceroy Abascal, a stubborn authoritarian and devoted servant of the old regime, secretly abhorred the political tenets of the French Revolution. In his memoria, written after his resignation, he condemned the constitution in unequivocal terms:

> This novelty [the Constitution] could not but leave in my mind the most vivid and saddest impression, because I saw the person of the king reduced to the simple representation of a special magistrate, his sovereignty usurped, abusing the name of the Nation with other illegal proceedings, like the alteration and transformation of its fundamental laws, in order to introduce the revolutionary principles of Democracy, of impiety and of irreligion....[48]

Nevertheless, under orders from the Regency Council, Abascal made open preparations for the execution of the articles of the constitution. On October 1 the cabildo of Lima in an extraordinary session took an oath of loyalty to the new regime and designated four days as a period of rejoicing and celebration.[49] In due course other cities followed the example of the capital. On December 3, Trujillo, having received a viceregal oficio dated November 21, together with a copy of the constitution, ordered observance of the ceremony of allegiance. Festivities in honor thereof were marked by the erection of decorative scaffolds by the guilds on street corners and in the public squares. The guilds lacking sufficient funds for this purpose, the cabildo authorized payments from the public treasury, contingent upon approval by the municipal junta.[50] Ere long the constitution had been formally accepted by all the municipalities in the firm belief that it was to become the basis for a vastly different and improved colonial policy.

No less profound was the Viceroy's antipathy toward the emancipation of the colonial press. That it would have serious repercussions

48. Rodríguez and Calderón, *Memoria de Abascal,* vol. I, p. 440.
49. Minutes of Oct. 1, 1812, Libros de cabildos de Lima, vol. XLII, Biblioteca municipal, Lima.
50. Minutes of Dec. 3, 1812, Libros de cabildos de Trujillo, vol. XVIII.

in the long run on Spanish sovereignty he had no doubt.[51] The decree authorizing this right and drawn up by the Cortes on October 10, 1810, reached the capital on April 18, 1811, and was proclaimed at once. The cabildo expressed its satisfaction at this new evidence of liberalism.[52] But as Abascal feared, it became the signal for an outburst of violent criticism of the regime. Newspapers, and broadsides, with articles denunciatory of government policies written by leading literary figures of Lima, such as Unánue, Pezet, and Larrea y Loredo appeared almost overnight and were eagerly read by the public. The most important of these publications were *El Investigador, El Peruano, El Verdadero Peruano,* and *El Satélite del Peruano.* Gaspar Rico and Manuel Villalta, editors of the last-named sheet, delivered an audacious, frontal assault on what they considered to be the inherently illiberal attitude of the Spanish officials: "We must remove from our bosom and not regard as brothers those who desire to preserve the old colonial regime and the iron sceptre that has governed for three past centuries Spain as well as the Indies."[53] This was more than conservative flesh and blood could endure. On his own initiative the Viceroy ordered the suppression of *El Satélite.*

Undeniably, the temporary abolition of censorship of the press furthered the cause of eventual freedom. It stimulated the publication of books up to that moment proscribed by the government, and it encouraged the formation among the creoles of literary clubs for the discussion of new ideas from Europe and inevitably of the dangerous subject of politics. The mushrooming of conspiracies and plots against the crown can be traced to the new concession.

Of significance also for the rise of a revolutionary feeling were the rehabilitation of the ayuntamientos and the establishment of open elections for deputies to the Cortes and to the general council in Lima. It was the aim of the regime to restore the popularly elected bodies of early Castilian history, a move "of transcendental importance."[54] Reception to these proposals by the creoles was enthusiastic. Indubitably, a majority of the vecinos of Lima and of other colonial cities

51. Abascal, normally imperturbable, was vehement in his disapprobation of this concession. See Rodríguez and Calderón, *Memoria de Abascal,* vol. I, p. cvi.

52. Minutes of April 26, 1811, Libros de cabildos de Lima, vol. XLII, Biblioteca municipal, Lima.

53. Quoted in Alayza and Soldán, *La Constitución de Cádiz,* pp. 76, 77.

54. *Ibid.,* p. 79.

highly approved, for their application heralded the development of a type of representative government that in fullness might eventually surpass what had been enjoyed in the sixteenth century.

But opposition by an influential minority was not long in coming. Lurking in the background was the element of vested interests, personified by the holders of purchaseable offices who aspired to preserve their property rights intact or to secure adequate indemnification.

When the regidores of Lima got wind in May of the effect of the provisions of the new constitution on their status, they resolved to instruct their deputy in Spain to counsel the Cortes to act cautiously and with consideration of their rights. If the system of elective regimientos were adopted for the region, they asserted, "it appears just that some means be devised for consultation of the councils, leaving intact what belongs to the cabildo of the capital. . . ."[55] Upon receipt of an oficio from the deputy in Cadiz pointing out the full intent of Article 310 for the abolition of salable offices, the indignant council determined unanimously to appeal to the National Congress for full indemnifications and for the preservation of the "honors, distinctions, benches, uniforms, etc., which make in some way more bearable the blow to some illustrious families, to the chief citizens, and to the rest of the Kingdom."[56] The attitude of the alcaldes, however, moderated their opposition. Being more in tune with popular sentiment and having no investment at stake, the magistrates refused to sign the necessary recursos. On August 18 a majority of the regidores, though still hopeful of some compensation, voted to accept the constitution and to refrain from the dispatch of memorials.[57] The selfish stand of the aldermen in Lima was seemingly echoed in the provincial cabildos. There was in actuality less justification for the recalcitrance of the ayuntamientos, for the valuation of the offices had nearly everywhere undergone major depreciation since the 1780's. Nevertheless, pride and tradition combined with economics provoked a resistance that

55. Minutes of May 12, 1812, Libros de cabildos de Lima, vol. XLII, Biblioteca municipal, Lima.
56. Minutes of July 30, 1812, ibid.
57. Minutes of Aug. 18, 1812, ibid.
The plea of the proprietary regidores was not entirely disregarded in Spain, for the cabildo of Trujillo received a royal order allowing the members of the old ayuntamiento to preserve "all the honors, prerogatives, and the use of uniforms." See minutes of Dec. 17, 1813, Libros de cabildos de Trujillo, vol. XX.

was only surmounted by a realization of the sympathy of the majority of the vecinos with the change.

With the proclamation of the new constitution in Lima during the first week of October, 1812, preparations got underway for the elections decreed by the Cortes. Preliminary to the parochial assemblies was the taking of a census of the population. The object of this was to compile an electoral roll of the citizens, whether lay or ecclesiastical, but with exclusion of members of the orders having a domicile in the parish. In November, 1812, the intendant issued a general order for the guidance and direction of the subdelegates.[58]

There is a good illustration of the act of census-taking for the city of Huancavelica. By a decree of November 22, 1812, the Viceroy authorized the chief royal officials of the city to hold elections for the choice of parochial electors. When the order was received on December 23, the intendant summoned the cabildo to meet with the curates of the town to carry out the command. On December 27 the council resolved to have a complete census of the municipal district, putting in charge the priests, "aided by men of intelligence and probity, to be named by the government." It supplied the curates with a form containing the following questions to be asked of adult males and females in every household:

Name
Race—if he or she is Spanish, Indian, mestizo, pardo, or Negro; free or slave
Status—married, bachelor, ecclesiastic or secular
Position—employment; if they work for themselves or if they are workers on the haciendas of others
Age—(even though it be conjectural)[59]

With the compilation of the lists of qualified voters the dates for the parochial elections could be set. According to the instructions of the Regency Council of May 23, 1812, those individuals chosen in the parishes selected electors to a general junta for the partido, which in turn designated the deputies for the Cortes and for the advisory council of the viceroyalty. On the basis of one deputy for each 60,000 persons the representation for the Kingdom of Peru was distributed

---

58. Expediente sobre la creación de una junta de cabildo y disposiciones cerca de la elección de diputados a Cortes, realizada en la intendencia de Huancavelica, Dec. 23, 1812, Ms. D9361, Biblioteca nacional, Lima.
59. *Ibid.*

as follows: Lima, two deputies and eight electors; Cuzco, three deputies and eight electors; Trujillo, with the bishopric of Mainas, four deputies and twelve electors; Huancavelica, one deputy and five electors; Tarma, three deputies and nine electors; Puno, three deputies and nine electors; Guayaquil, one deputy and the number of electors to be fixed by the government; Chiloe, Valdivia, and Osorno, one deputy and the number of electors to be fixed by the crown.[60]

Contrary to the Viceroy's apprehensions few signs of disorder and tumult manifested themselves during the elections. In spite of the tedious nature of census-taking, relatively little time elapsed before the meeting of the primary assemblies. There was an evident eagerness to get on with the elections. For the most part few of the delegates reached Spain to participate in the Cortes because of the brief existence of the constitution.[61]

Elections for municipal offices aroused great excitement among the liberal groups of the citizenry. The announcement by the crown of December 9 as the date for the local elections in Lima induced the patriot Unánue to rhapsodize: "My pen burning in my hands wishes to detach itself and soar to great heights to commemorate the happy dawn of the 9th day of December. . . . The rights of the citizens are reborn in Peru on this memorable day."[62] Liberals in other cities showed similar elation over the prospect of popular control of the cabildos.

The tendency to controversy and dissension—an inherent trait of municipal assemblies—soon appeared. Difficulties arose in the determination of the proper conditions for the holding of the elections. Doubts were expressed by some expiring cabildos over the interpretation of the new regulations respecting the abolition of vendible offices and the qualifications for suffrage. For example, the ayuntamiento of Lima in a session of November 13, 1812, pointed out that the constitution neither fixed the age of enfranchised citizens nor stated unequivocally that the offices of secretary, alcalde de la hermandad, and alguacil mayor were extinguished. To avoid protracted argument it decided to turn these matters over to the Viceroy for judgment.[63]

60. Vargas Ugarte, *Historia del Perú, emancipación,* p. 114.
61. *Ibid.,* pp. 114, 115.
62. Quoted in Alayza and Soldán, *La Constitución de Cádiz,* p. 79.
63. Minutes of Nov. 13, 1812, Libros de cabildos de Lima, vol. XLII, Biblioteca municipal, Lima.

For the most part elections occurred without extended delay in the cities and towns of Peru in December, 1812, and January, 1813.[64] "Public tranquility was generally not disturbed."[65] The resort to altercation and intimidation, though markedly less, was more notice-able in the interior provinces where the intendants and subdelegates lacked the firm hand of the Viceroy. Some incidents could be traced to the constant antipathy and jealousy existing among creoles and Peninsulares, which increased rather than diminished with the passage of time.[66]

How much actual authority was exercised by the local councils thus created through popular suffrage? Can one point to positive benefits resulting from their deliberations and enactments? Lamen-tably, the abbreviated life span of the Constitution of 1812 makes ade-quate answers to these questions difficult.

To assess the reality of local power in this era it is essential to bear in mind two facts or conditions. The articles of the constitution granted exceptional rights to the colonial municipal bodies, partly restoring them to the position that they had once occupied in govern-ment. In the realm of general welfare and finance they regained much that had been lost. Obviously, it was the purpose of the framers of the document to re-establish the ayuntamientos as viable administrative units representing a majority of the citizens.

But the implementation of these prerogatives hinged on a cir-cumstance that was well understood by the creoles—the wide dis-cretionary power held by the appointive officials. The decrees of a new regime, which was anathema to the colonial bureaucracy, could not overnight materially alter three hundred years of conservative theory and practice. In short, the hiatus between the law and its enforcement still persisted. The Viceroy Abascal confessed to a tortu-ous policy, "whose threads—difficult to follow—could reconcile the extremes of obeying the crown, preserving the authority of the magis-trates, suppressing the populace, rewarding the merited, maintaining armies, and giving succour to the Kingdoms of Quito, Santa Fe, Mexico, and Chile, Buenos Aires and even to the same Peninsula. . . ."[67]

64. The system of indirect election in Lima resulted in the choice of twenty-four electors, who on Dec. 19 in a session presided over by the Viceroy selected the cabildo.
65. Vargas Ugarte, *Historia del Perú, emancipación*, pp. 115, 116.
66. Rodríguez and Calderón, *Memoria de Abascal*, vol. I, p. 441.
67. *Ibid.*, p. 446.

Annoyance and vexation were his lot "owing to the repeated consultas [from the cabildo] for enlightenment in regard to its powers, offices, and ordinances."[68] It was his claim that the direction of the royal treasury, at first a function of the deputies of the province, became his duty and that in the end "the ayuntamientos were reduced to being aids of the Viceroy for the control of the food supply, the policía, the preservation of good order and public health."[69] In his mind the concept of popular rights was subversive illusion.

Other evidence does not altogether support Abascal's dour allegations. The frequency with which the Lima cabildo met during these years, eighty-one times in 1813 and ninety-two times in 1814, discloses a mounting interest by the capitulars in local issues and a growing importance of matters discussed. Greater efficiency may have ensued from a reduction in the size of the municipal corporation. Lima's elective body, the largest in the audiencia, consisted of two alcaldes ordinarios, eight regidores, and one procurador síndico, or attorney-general.[70] A vigorous remonstrance by the cabildo of Huánuco against a subdelegate confirmed the desire of a local body to maintain its constitutional privileges. On March 6, 1813, the council gave power of attorney to the municipal procurator and a regidor to appear before the asesor-general in Lima to plead its case. In turn these agents authorized a procurator of the audiencia to represent the municipality in the final argument.[71]

Yet it is doubtful if many worthwhile acts could be claimed by the constitutional cabildos. Because of the oppugnancy of the crown officials, the inexperience of many councilors, and the strong traditional loyalty that pervaded Peru, the ayuntamientos did not assert their prerogatives fully.

Notwithstanding, the five-year interval from 1808-1813, featured

68. *Ibid.*, p. 119.   69. *Ibid.*, p. 118.

70. Municipal offices held by regidores or other individuals in Trujillo as of Jan. 21, 1813, included these: alguacil mayor (regidor), alcaide de la Rl., *fiel ejecutor* (regidor), alcalde provincial (with the same powers exercised in the past), juez de agua (regidor), *defensor de menores*, juez de tierra (regidor), juez de policía (regidor), inspectors of the hospital (two regidores), junta municipal (alcalde of the 1st vote, two regidores, and the procurator), mayor de propios, maestro mayor of the guilds. See minutes of Jan. 21, 1813, Libros de cabildos de Trujillo, vol. XIX.

71. Expediente sobre los poderes que se han dado al regidor Juan Sánchez y al síndico procurador D. Guillermo Zevallos, para que en nombre del Ayuntamiento de Huánuco declaren las facultades y autoridad otorgadas a este organismo por las Cortes Españolas, Ms. D250, Biblioteca nacional, Lima.

successively by the dominance in Spain of the Suprema Junta, the Regency Council, and finally by the Cortes, was highly significant for the future. Since the formative era of the sixteenth century no time had held forth greater promise.

While positive achievements did not measure up to the rose-tinted expectations of the creoles, results were by no means negligible. The Peruvian delegation to the Cortes, headed by Morales, contributed more to the work of the assembly than any other group representing an American viceroyalty. They participated strenuously in the public debates and in the committee discussions in spite of the handicap imposed by inadequate appropriation for personal expenses stemming from limited municipal propios and from the clandestinely obstructionist tactics of the Viceroy.[72] In the multifarious aspects of municipal administration the cabildos had a larger share of freedom than in the immediate past. Greater inter-municipal correspondence bespoke a need for solidarity and mutual assistance.[73] The apparent satisfaction of many creoles with the Constitution of 1812 might have permitted a survival of imperial rule in this part of South America for some years.[74] But in 1814 allied victory over Napoleon restored to the throne in Madrid the despotic Ferdinand VII, whose first important act was to declare the fundamental document invalid. It was, however, impossible to restore the old system in every respect. Nor could the creoles forget that they had briefly enjoyed representation in the Spanish parliament and in the colonial municipal bodies. The image of what might have been could not be obliterated.

72. In vain, the cabildo of Trujillo petitioned Abascal on more than one occasion for permission to levy a tax to raise money for the expenses of the deputies in the Península. See minutes of Dec. 17, 1813, Libros de cabildos de Trujillo, vol. XIX.

73. In this period Lima was the recipient of communications from the cabildos of Panamá, Santiago de Chile, Buenos Aires, and Montevideo.

74. Alayza and Soldán, *La Constitución de Cádiz*, p. 90.

CHAPTER XII

Denouement

Ten years elapsed before the curtain dropped on the final scene in the drama of Peruvian emancipation. The triumph of autocracy, personified by Ferdinand VII, portended in 1814 the severance of ties binding creoles to the mother country. On re-ascending the throne after six years of captivity in the somber chateau of Valencay, the monarch issued a series of decrees that left little doubt of his aversion to liberalism at home and in the colonies. Well thought of at the beginning of his reign, a symbol of resistance to the invaders, he was the most hated of the Bourbons at the end. With some exaggeration, the Spanish historian Pérez Galdós has depicted his duplicity and hypocrisy: "That king who had deceived his parents, his schoolmasters, his friends, his ministers. . . , his four wives, his brother, his towns, his allies, everybody [in short], played the game even in death, for he believed that he was making us happy, delivering us from the devil."[1] Such were the worst traits in the personality of *El Deseado*.

On May 4, 1814, the King drew up in secret the decree that restored absolutism in the Peninsula and in America. Because of the lack of enough reliable troops in Madrid to quell possible demonstrations in favor of the Cortes, the order was not made public until May 11. It revoked the Constitution of 1812 and all other legislation of the Cortes, "as if such acts had never been passed."[2]

Several months went by before a copy of the decree was put in the hands of the Viceroy Abascal. The staunch defender of the old regime could hardly contain his joy. His memoria reflects his intense dislike for the constitution: "In writing and by word of mouth I have mani-

1. Quoted from Pérez Galdós, *Episodios nacionales* in Alemparte, *El cabildo en Chile colonial*, pp. 425, 426; see also Ballesteros, *Historia de España*, VII, 135-147.
2. *Ibid.*, p. 146.

fested the aversion with which I have regarded always the monstrous deformity of its establishment, with the risks and perils to which the monarchy was exposed. . . ."[3]

Other decrees from Spain abolished the reforms in local government. Royal orders of June 15 and of July 30 restored the old ayuntamientos with the political and economic prerogatives that had prevailed in 1808. They were enforced without delay and in the Viceroy's words "those bodies occupy again the place of appreciation, utility, and confidence that they have always merited from the Sovereign."[4] Although reluctant to witness its own demise the constitutional cabildo of Lima complied with Abascal's oficio. To his request for ceremonies of public rejoicing at the "happy restoration of Our August Monarch," the council rejoined indifferently that a shortage of municipal funds would limit festivities.[5] Likewise, the populace evinced no jubilation. Lima's response was characteristic of other constitutional ayuntamientos throughout the audiencia. On December 31 the regidores propietarios were duly installed and two alcaldes were elected according to the pre-Cortes method. Through the revival of the principle of vendibility the crown counted mistakenly on demonstrations of gratitude and loyalty from the upper stratum of creole society to which the regidores for the most part belonged.

The reactionary policies of 1814 furnished additional stimulus to conspiracies and plots against Spanish authorities. As early as 1809 an unsuccessful cabal, inspired by events in La Paz and Quito, had been organized in Lima. Uprisings in Tacna in 1811 and 1813 coincided with the invasion of Upper Peru by Argentine forces under Castelli and Belgrano. In 1812 Huánuco was the scene of an insurrection of more importance than the ephemeral plot in the capital. Beginning as a protest by the Indians against the excesses of a subdelegate, it developed into a movement of all classes for the expulsion of Spaniards.[6] Although without previous military experience, the alcaldes placed themselves at the head of the militia. Capably led Spanish units, directed from Lima, soon quelled the uprising and a similar

3. Rodríguez and Calderón, *Memoria de Abascal*, vol. I, p. 447.
4. *Ibid.*, p. 120.
5. Minutes of Oct. 12, 1814, Libros de cabildos de Lima, vol. XLIII, Biblioteca municipal, Lima.
6. Vargas Ugarte, *Historia del Perú, emancipación*, pp. 32, 33.

one in Guamanga.[7] In November, 1812, Cuzco was thrown into a turmoil by a dispute over the election of deputies to the Cortes. One of the factions, espousing the cause of separation, organized an armed body and occupied the city for a short time. In 1813, Guamanga, seemingly in the path of the revolutionists, summoned a cabildo abierto with the initial thought of coming to terms with the rebels, but abandoned the plan. The municipal councils of Arequipa and Arica, though toying with ideas of freedom, rallied to the Viceroy's camp. Finally, Cuzco, the center of disaffection, threw off the grip of the extremists and asserted its adherence to Ferdinand VII.[8] The general failure of these isolated, sporadic incidents may be explained by the "roots that fealty had grown among us and on the other hand by the strength of the forces available to Spain."[9] The Viceroy Abascal, in full command of all the resources of the loyalists, was, moreover, "a man of energy, perspicacity, and decision."[10]

It may be noted that most of the acts of rebellion and resistance to the crown were identified with the cabildos. The organization and promotion of conspiracies occurred generally in the sessions of the ayuntamientos under the leadership of the alcaldes. In order to enlist the backing of the vecinos the conspirators resorted to the cabildo abierto. Thus in suppressing the burgeoning revolutionary stirrings Abascal had to contend with local governmental units.

Is it possible to label the cabildo the authentic instrument of the people in the fulfilment of the doctrine of popular sovereignty of the Jesuit thinker Francisco Suarez?[11] As the chief contemporary exponent of this theory in relation to Spanish-American independence avers, it is difficult "to identify the specific juridical means of creating the democratic state" in the colonies.[12] But to strict legalists of this

7. *Ibid.*, pp. 38-40.   8. *Ibid.*, pp. 63, 64.
9. *Ibid.*, p. 69; see also Javier Prado, *Estado social del Perú durante la dominación española* (Lima, 1941), I, 193.
10. Vargas Ugarte, *Historia del Perú, emancipación*, p. 69.
11. Although all men in this concept are free and equal by nature, the social quality of man implies a regulatory, legislative power to be exercised by one or many in the interests of all. Ultimate authority is vested in the whole community rather than in a single individual. The community may by an act of will delegate the power to some one or to a group. Thus is created a contract binding upon the people and the sovereign as long as there is abstention from tyranny or injustice. See William A. Dunning, *A History of Political Theories: From Luther to Montesquieu* (New York, 1927), pp. 142-144.
12. Manuel Giménez Fernández, "Las doctrinas populistas en la independencia de Hispano-América," *Anuario de estudios Americanos*, III (1946), p. 590.

school the establishment and maintenance of law and order depend on institutional prestige based on group consent rather than on the assumption of dictatorial powers by a single individual. No other comparable agency existed in America to express in whole or in part the will of the people. Logically, the claim of the cabildo to occupy this position is not without foundation. During the era of the abolition of vendibility and the adoption of elective procedures its status as the depositary of the *poder civil* is legally more valid. Even closer to the democratic reality of Suarez is the original assembly of the citizenry, the cabildo abierto, the most natural and appropriate political organism to affirm the will of the municipality. But the cabildo or any juridical variant, being local in character, had to be succeeded ultimately by a larger body, or cortes, to represent the broader and necessarily more significant interests of the region.[13]

Linked with the question of the identification of the depositary of popular rights is the interpretation of another aspect of Suarez' concept. Did the return of Ferdinand VII automatically reinstate the agreement between the king and the people? There is little doubt but that the act of abdication created a vacuum permitting a claim to the exercise of power by the colonials in defiance of the Regency Council and the Cortes.[14] Whether or not the former contractual relationship could be restored by a declaration from Madrid is a moot point. Evidently many creoles regarded the breach in continuity as permanent.[15]

The Suarez thesis of popular control has found growing support. "In the seventeenth and eighteenth centuries," says Guillermo Furlong, "it was the European philosopher Suarez who most influenced Tucumán, Cuyo, and Paraguay in the Rio de la Plata, as much before as after 1767, and the same may be said of Upper Peru and of all Hispanic America." See *Causas y caracteres de la independencia hispanoamericana*, p. 211.

13. In the case of Buenos Aires the fiscal Villota had recourse to a cabildo abierto "pending the convocation of a 'Cortes of the Realm' to constitute the legitimate authority." See Giménez Fernández, "Las doctrinas populistas," p. 589.

14. Nevertheless, the creole José Goyeneche, inspired by Floridablanca, arrived in Buenos Aires with the hope of finding a solution in the dynastic succession of the Infanta Carlota Joaquina, daughter of Charles IV. But unable to arouse any enthusiasm among the creoles, he abandoned his design and accepted the authority of the Regency Council. See *ibid.*, pp. 580, 581.

15. It is likely that these notions were current in the colonial universities and Jesuit colleges in the eighteenth century. According to the opinion of the main advocate of this approach to the genesis of the independence movement, the expulsion of the Jesuits by Charles III was not due, as many would have it, to the fomenting of the Madrid riot, but rather to the teaching of the doctrine of popular sovereignty. See *ibid.*, pp. 546-549, 575.

To entertain such ideas or even to speculate about them was anathema to the ultra-conservative Abascal. Satisfied that Peru would go no farther along the road to revolution, the Viceroy requested permission from Ferdinand VII to resign. By a royal order of October 14, 1815, the monarch granted the petition, bestowing upon him the seemingly appropriate title of "Marquis of Concordia" in recognition of his masterful work as conciliator.[16] Teniente General Joaquín de la Pezuela, commander of the royalist army in Upper Peru, was named as his successor.

In reviewing his association with the people of Lima, Abascal recalled with pride his contributions to the improvement of municipal services. Upon entry into the capital he had ordered the paving of many streets and a general cleaning up of the city.[17] Public walks and the exits from the city to Callao, "entirely useless" in 1805, were in better condition. To lessen the incidence of nocturnal robbery he had augmented the number of watchmen making the rounds in the barrios and had seen to the collection of the tax levied upon householders for this type of protection. Citizens were encouraged to form special patrols under the command of the alcaldes to pursue thieves and keep watch over the gaming houses where disorders habitually originated. To reduce the risk of assaults upon travelers by highwaymen, he had dispatched squadrons of dragoons, aided by companies of infantry and patrols of citizens under the alcaldes, into the suburbs and into the countryside.[18] Unfortunately, many of the ills had reappeared, he declared, after 1809 during the regrettable era of conspiracies and disturbances.

Relations of church and state were affected by the problem of the Jesuits. Although Abascal had received support in his conservative policies from the ecclesiastical hierarchy, he was not an advocate of the return of the society. The cabildos, at times jealous of or hostile to the wealth of the church, nevertheless, agitated for the re-establishment of the order. Because of a strong anti-clericalism among the Spanish liberals, the Cortes in 1811 had rejected a motion of the Peruvian delegates looking to the return of the Jesuits.[19] When Ferdinand VII in 1814 restored the order and compelled restitution of all

16. Vargas Ugarte, *Historia del Perú, emancipación*, p. 124.
17. Rodríguez and Calderón, *Memoria de Abascal*, vol. I, pp. 124, 125.
18. *Ibid.*, pp. 125-127.
19. Rubén Vargas Ugarte, *Los Jesuitas del Perú, 1568-1767* (Lima, 1941), p. 207.

property hitherto unalienated, the cabildos in the important towns warmly applauded the policy. In a session of October 6, 1815, the ayuntamiento of Trujillo discussed the propriety of drawing up a memorial to hasten the return of the Jesuits "because from the moment of their exile their absence has been greatly felt on the spiritual side, in the instruction of reading and writing to the youth, and in the gifts of bread and meat they made to the poor."[20] A resolution to this effect was drafted at the next meeting.[21] No less sincere was a petition of the cabildo of Lima, of October 15, 1816, seeking the identical end. The reason given was that the Jesuits were "necessary and their absence greatly missed . . . they having been the ones to advocate public welfare and good customs with special dedication and constant zeal, observing the most rational, wise, and religious precepts. . . ."[22] Other civic voices were raised in favor of the order.[23] Despite the pleas of these bodies no Jesuits set foot in Peru until 1851. Problems of reorganization, expenses of transportation, and more importantly the development of the revolutionary movement militated against the immediate re-establishment of the order.

In addition to the desirability of the presence of the society, the improvement in justice was a matter of concern to the cabildos. For example, Trujillo memorialized the crown in 1815 for the founding of an audiencia, citing the trouble and expense involved in journeys to Lima.[24] When no answer was received from the Viceroy, the council on November 19, 1816, reiterated the appeal.[25] It is apparent that in time of crisis the crown had little thought of modifying the judiciary.[26]

Despite the temporary silencing of plots in the district of the audiencia the future course of Peru was problematical at the moment of General Pezuela's assumption of the viceregal post. San Martín had yet to accomplish the Hannibalic feat of crossing the towering snow-covered ranges of the Andes. The invasion of the central plateau

20. Minutes of Oct. 6, 1815, Libros de cabildos de Trujillo, vol. XX.
21. Minutes of Oct. 10, 1815, *ibid.*
22. Vargas Ugarte, *Jesuitas del Perú*, pp. 208, 209.
23. Municipal bodies in Cuzco, Cajamarca, and Huancavelica vigorously seconded the memorials from Lima and Trujillo. See *ibid.*, pp. 209-211.
24. Minutes of Aug. 18, 25, and Oct. 6, 1815, Libros de cabildos de Trujillo, vol. XX.
25. Minutes of Nov. 19, 1816, *ibid.*
26. There is no mention of this memorial in the memorias of Abascal and Pezuela (Vicente Rodríguez Casado and Guillermo Lohmann Villena, *Memoria de gobierno de Joaquín de la Pezuela, Virrey del Perú, 1816-1821* [Sevilla, 1947]).

of Colombia by a liberating force via the flooded lowlands of the Orinoco and the passage of the northern Andes was a chimera. Although the partisans of separation in the viceroyalty were increasing, the personality of the new administrator was a not insignificant factor in the final outcome. A native of Aragon, he had been trained in the Colegio de Artilleria, had participated in the siege of Gibraltar in 1782, and in 1804 had been sent to Peru. Abascal had given him command of the army of Upper Peru, where he had won some successes. There were excellent qualities in his make-up: bravery, generosity, intelligence, and loyalty; but his one failing was serious—a lack of "confidence in himself."[27] At this hour the choice of an irresolute man was a blunder of the first magnitude.

To allay the apprehensions of the creoles the incoming Viceroy made several modifications in the ceremony of the recibimiento. On July 7, 1816, at the hacienda Maravilla, a short distance from the city, he received the bastón, described as a "rod lined with tortoise-shell and having a head of gold with a small watch inside," from the senior general who was substituting for the momentarily indisposed Abascal.[28] The public entry, required by law, occurred almost six weeks later. In deference to the pride of the regidores there was no resort to the palio, a cause of acrimonious disputes in the past.[29] Lengthy popular festivities usually accompanying this ceremony were cut short by wartime shortages and the need to economize.[30]

Pezuela's preoccupation with military affairs left little room for a meticulous scrutiny of civic administration. By vocation a soldier, he gave priority to the enlisting and drilling of recruits for the army and to the strengthening of the fortifications along the coast. Nevertheless, some consideration of municipal matters was unavoidable. In July, 1816, he compiled a razón of salaries and taxes of the major bodies or corporations of the city, including those of the cabildo. For salaries the ayuntamiento expended the amount of 20,490 pesos 4 reales, the special *impuesto*, "tax," bringing in 1,306 pesos.[31] In January, 1817, the income from the propios, decreased by donations, taxes,

27. *Ibid.*, p. xxiv; see also Sebastián Lorente, *Historia del Perú bajo los Borbones*, p. 320.
28. Rodríguez and Lohmann, *Memoria de la Pezuela*, p. 17.
29. *Ibid.*, pp. 86, 87.   30. *Ibid.*, pp. 104, 105.
31. *Ibid.*, pp. 61-64.

and interest on debt, had to be supplemented at the Viceroy's orders for the purpose of clothing and feeding the prisoners in the jail.[32]

Royalist reverses in engagements with the insurgents absorbed Pezuela's attention in 1817. The brilliant victory of San Martín at Chacabuco would mean ultimately the loss of all of Chile. It aroused new hopes in the breasts of Peruvian patriots, leading in 1818 to the organization in Lima of another abortive conspiracy.[33] The Viceroy's efforts to increase the size of the loyalist forces in Lima, Arica, Arequipa, and Trujillo foundered on his inability to raise funds for the pay and maintenance of the soldiers. In June, 1818, he complained bitterly of the unco-operative attitude of the ayuntamiento in the face of the peril looming from the south: "The secular cabildo is so petty in a matter of such importance, to which it should contribute ... but although it is a fact that it cannot aid with its propios, it was to be hoped that with its intelligence, its taxes, and counsel it might help to a minor degree. . . ."[34]

How important the attitude of the creoles was in the struggle is shown in the efforts of the Council of the Indies to ingratiate itself with the local councils. Lima and Cuzco were singled out for special favors. Acting on a remonstrance from the ayuntamiento of Lima against the audiencia, this body instructed the Viceroy to enforce without delay the real cédula of February 21, 1808. Among other things this decree enjoined the restoration of judicial prerogatives to the cabildo of the capital, the curbing of the audiencia in the indiscriminate issuance of orders, and the application to the regidores of the titles of "Excellency" and "Señoría."[35] For its "extraordinary merit and important services," in particular the aid furnished the crown in the suppression of the uprising in La Paz, the city of Cuzco was granted the appellation of "Most Faithful."[36] It is obvious that these measures could only briefly contain the rising tides of nationalism and discontent that would eventually engulf this part of the colonial empire.

The greatest threat to the viceroyalty now presented itself from

32. *Ibid.*, p. 103.
33. Vargas Ugarte, *Historia del Perú, emancipación*, pp. 165-169.
34. Rodríguez and Lohmann, *Memoria de la Pezuela*, pp. 279, 280.
35. Real cédula, Oct. 26, 1818, Madrid, Audiencia de Lima, legajo 804, A. G. I.; for further reference to the cedula of Feb. 21, 1808, see chap. x, note 38.
36. Real cédula, Oct. 11, 1818, Audiencia de Cuzco, legajo 13, A. G. I.

Chile. San Martín, assisted by the English sympathizer and soldier of fortune Lord Cochrane, was launching an expedition for a sea and land attack on the Peruvian coast. Only the prompt dispatch of a powerful naval squadron from the Peninsula via the Straits of Magellan could have destroyed the patriots' plans—a measure no Spanish government could well execute after Trafalgar. On September 7, 1820, the liberating force landed near Pisco, where it was hailed by the inhabitants.

Meanwhile, the Viceroy's hold over Peru was loosened by the liberal revolt in Spain. The army chieftains, who espoused the cause of the Cortes, forcibly persuaded Ferdinand VII to proclaim the Constitution of 1812. To end the war in America, the new regime directed the colonial officials and the Spanish generals to propose an armistice with the revolutionary leaders looking to the granting of limited sovereignty. From dispatches brought by an American packet out of Rio de Janeiro, the Viceroy learned on July 12 of the uprising at home, but as the royal order of April 11, embodying the altered policy, was not received until September 11, no steps were taken for a number of months to insure the allegiance of the people of Lima. In compliance with orders, he formally proclaimed on September 15, 16, and 17 the liberal constitution and accepted oaths of loyalty from the populace. He commented on the absence of popular elation on the first day of the proclamation: "Not even a single 'viva' was heard, nor the least demonstration of jubilation until the oidor Osma in the plaza de San Ana threw a handful of silver coins to the crowd of Negroes and zambos who followed him and this enlivened them and they shouted several 'vivas' to see if there would be more money, but neither this group nor the chief citizens nor those of other classes showed rejoicing or aversion."[37] If the indifferent response of the populace could be interpreted as a genuine disillusion over the adoption of any policy beneficial to Peru, it might contrarily be regarded as symptomatic of a continuing sense of loyalty of the creole aristocracy toward the illiberal monarch. Whatever was the real feeling of the limeños at this time, there is no doubt that the proclamation stimulated the patriot cause by revealing to all the internal disunity and factionalism in the Peninsula.

Pezuela's orders stipulated likewise the immediate election of

37. Rodríguez and Lohmann, *Memoria de la Pezuela*, p. 763.

constitutional cabildos according to past procedure. But alert to the fact that this might create a favorable opportunity for the separatists, he put off a meeting of the ayuntamiento of Lima until October 20. In defiance of the Viceroy, the cabildo assembled on October 6 "in order that the people should not lack a constitutional cabildo, which it so much desires."[38] The body that had been dissolved in 1814 was temporarily restored. There was apparently little opposition by the proprietary regidores in contrast to their position in 1812, a sign of the growing unpopularity of the loyalist cause. Such was Pezuela's abhorrence of the idea of elections that he refused to preside over the gathering and take the oath of office from the new members. His unfriendly stand widened the gap between the administration and the creoles and encouraged the selection for key positions of men more inclined to independence.[39] On December 3 the parochial elections took place, resulting in the naming of an electoral college of twenty-four. With the Marqués de Montemira, the military governor of Lima, as the presiding officer, this group assembled on December 7 and chose by secret vote two alcaldes, sixteen regidores, and two procurators.[40] Similar electoral procedures were followed throughout the district controlled by the Viceroy.

The course before the *ayuntamiento constitucional* was difficult. Would this body avoid an immediate showdown by ostensibly accepting orders from Pezuela, though convertly working to protect the interests of a majority of citizens who seemingly favored the abolition of Spanish rule? Or would it openly break with Spain and declare for independence? Wisdom dictated patience and the first policy was adopted. By forestalling martial law, the inevitable consequence of such a pronouncement, the cabildo remained in existence and served as a buffer between the Viceroy and the citizenry.[41]

The first important act of the ayuntamiento of Lima was to forward to the Viceroy on December 16 a petition from seventy-two citizens seeking a resumption of negotiations with San Martín.[42]

38. Gamio, *La municipalidad de Lima y la emancipación, 1821*, p. 13. ·
39. *Ibid.*, pp. 14, 15.
40. Acta de elección del Exmo. Ayunt. Constitucional, año 1820, Lima, Dec. 7, 1820, Ms. D1055, Biblioteca nacional, Lima. For a similar proceeding see Acta del establecimiento del ayuntamiento constitucional del pueblo de San Pedro de Callamarca (province of Huancavelica), March 11, 1821, Ms. D10336, Biblioteca nacional, Lima.
41. Gamio, *La municipalidad de Lima*, pp. 21, 22.
42. *Ibid.*, p. 38, note 12.

This was a matter that had already engaged the attention of Pezuela. It was a number of months before both sides agreed to send agents to a conference for the discussion of terms of peace. In reality, San Martín did not believe an accord possible, as his demand for unconditional independence would be unacceptable. But he regarded the postponement of fighting as a boon to the cause as it permitted further propagation of the ideas of freedom and liberation throughout the countryside.[43] The conference opened at Miraflores on September 25 with a cessation of fighting for eight days. The deputies for the Argentine General asserted that the Constitution of 1812 did not provide sufficient guarantees for self-government and protection of individual rights. Other points of controversy developed, making it clear that no firm basis for an understanding could be reached. On October 1, the Peruvian delegates left the scene of the conference and three days later fighting broke out anew. Because Lima was strongly defended by thick walls and a large garrison to man them and by its proximity to the well-nigh impregnable fortress of Real Felipe at Callao, San Martín bypassed the city and began the conquest of the north. On November 1, his force disembarked at Ancón. The advantages of this port were its facilities for provisioning the army and its location as a center for the dissemination of revolutionary tracts and broadsides among the people of northern Peru. From these provinces and from Lima by escape at night recruits swelled the size of the liberating array.

The movement for emancipation grew apace. The presence of San Martín, the budding nationalism, and the deepened distrust of the Spaniards inspired declarations of independence by a number of municipalities. It was fitting that the ayuntamiento take these decisive steps, for no other corporate body or association of citizens could with more legal authority and more solemnity terminate the bonds between colonists and the mother country. To the pueblo of Supe belongs the distinction of making the first declaration, in April, 1819, of full separation from Spain within the territorial limits of present-day Peru. The procedure was generally typical of that followed by other towns throughout the colonies. The proclamation was delivered in a cabildo abierto, summoned by the town fathers.[44]

43. Vargas Ugarte, *Historia del Perú, emancipación*, p. 186. See also Ballesteros, *Historia de España*, VII, 414.
44. Rodríguez and Lohmann, *Memoria de la Pezuela*, p. 447.

It was not until a year later that the cabildos of Yca, Tarma, and Lambayeque were emboldened to break away by like action. On December 29, 1820, the important provincial city of Trujillo, led by the intendant the Marqués de Torre Tagle, seceded by what was to all intents and purposes a cabildo abierto. In the sala de ayuntamiento surrounded by regidores and citizens of note, the Marqués explained the purpose of the meeting, read aloud a letter from San Martín, and then proposed a declaration of independence. The announcement was greeted with shouts of approval from the hall, and when the Marqués stepped out on the balcony to repeat the proclamation there was vociferous approval from the crowd in the plaza.[45]

The propitious outcome of events in Trujillo and Lambayeque had its effect. In Piura, the oldest city of the viceroyalty, the obstacles in the way of liberation were greater than elsewhere, the Viceroy having converted it into a royalist base to counter invasion by sea. But the arrival on January 3 of an invitation from Torre Tagle to cast off Spanish domination tempted the alcalde to take action. The next day a cabildo abierto, meeting in the Franciscan monastery, resolved to join hands with the patriot groups in Trujillo. The presence at the doors of the monastery of a sizable body of townspeople, whose huzzas and cheers were felt by the participants in the solemn conclave within, gave a semblance of democracy to the proceedings.[46] The overwhelming show of sentiment in the municipality induced the Spanish garrison, despite the resistance of the commandant, to lay down its arms and unite with the patriots. Cajamarca, Chachapoyas, Jaén, and Mainas imitated the example of Piura, the leaders in the movement in all these towns being the alcaldes. By the end of May, all of the northern part of Peru had declared for independence, and, in consequence, men and money were soon reaching the Argentine General from this region.[47]

Among the high-ranking Spanish officers there was dissension and dismay over the loss of Chile and the advance of the patriot forces into Peru. Censure of Pezuela's conduct of the war, at first occasional, became more vocal. Had he reinforced the royalist army in Chile instead of the units in Upper Peru, it is possible that San

45. Vargas Ugarte, *Historia del Perú, emancipación*, pp. 240, 241.
46. *Ibid.*, pp. 242, 243 note 12, 260, 261.
47. *Ibid.*, p. 244.

Martín could have been driven back over the Andes and the war in this theater prolonged many years.[48] Excessive cautiousness and indecision at critical moments had permitted a build-up of the revolutionary forces with an imminent threat to the capital itself. Mounting opposition to his strategy culminated in his forcible removal on January 29, 1821, by a coterie of officers who demanded as head of the loyalists the general in command of the army in Upper Peru, José de La Serna.[49] To their chagrin La Serna proved to be "no genius" and his unlawful assumption of authority, albeit confirmed in Madrid, further weakened Spanish influence in the colony.[50]

An additional complication for the crown in America was the appearance of special commissioners from Spain. The Cortes had sent them to win over the revolutionists with fresh proposals of peace. The emissary to Chile, later to Peru, Manuel Abreu, a *capitán de fragata*, reached Lima the first week in April, 1822, to confer with La Serna. Compelled to adopt a more conciliatory position by the presence of the commissioner, the Viceroy requested a conference in May with San Martín. The meeting, taking place first at Punchauca, later at Miraflores, held forth some promise of success initially, in view of the Protector's leaning toward monarchism. Eventually negotiations were dissolved as they had been in the past over Spain's unwillingness to accept Peruvian independence, and hostilities were resumed. Abreu's contribution had been slight and had added to the confusion in royalist deliberations.[51]

In Lima the constitutional ayuntamiento had no choice but to submit, perforce begrudgingly, to the Viceroy's commands. Any other course would have meant quick disaster for that body and rule solely by the military. Demands for money and supplies were met, however, by evasive tactics. On February 10, at the instigation of the Viceroy, the cabildo appointed two regidores to requisition cattle from the hacendados, but made it clear to him that both the army and the populace would suffer hunger and even starvation if the assessment were not conducted with circumspection and if the mountain passes by which all types of food were brought to the city were not cleared of

48. Rodríguez and Lohmann, *Memoria de la Pezuela,* pp. xxxii, xxxiii.
49. Vargas Ugarte, *Historia del Perú, emancipación,* pp. 221, 222.
50. Rodríguez and Lohmann, *Memoria de la Pezuela,* p. xxxiv.
51. Vargas Ugarte, *Historia del Perú, emancipación,* pp. 275-282.

guerillas.[52] Again, the council demurred at the imposition of an extraordinary war tax: "The capital is not in a position to bear an unusual levy for the prosecution of the war." Holding out as long as possible, the cabildo finally yielded on condition that the tax should be applied equitably.[53] In its relations with the Viceroy the council apparently acted in the best interests of the city, which were those of Peru.[54]

The worsening of the military situation along the coast made paramount for the royalists a consideration in June of the evacuation of the capital. The plight of the Spanish forces prompted the surreptitious dispatch of an anonymous letter to the alcalde the Conde de San Isidro, appealing to the cabildo to approach the Viceroy to urge negotiations with San Martín. The ayuntamiento accepted the suggestion in the belief that it was indicative of public opinion. On June 7, though fearful of reprisal, it daringly forwarded a petition to La Serna.[55] Its recommendation was lost upon the Viceroy, then deeply engaged in stringent measures of defense for the fortress of Real Felipe at Callao. In the first week of July, La Serna sallied from the city for the sierras, followed by General Canterac on July 27.[56] The Marqués de Montemira, a person not unwilling to negotiate with San Martín, remained in the city as military and political governor.

The Viceroy's departure presaged the fall of the capital. Apprehension as to possible revenge by the army upon the populace for its acceptance of royalist rule was silenced by a message from San Martín to the cabildo on July 6, in which full protection for all the inhabitants of the city was assured. The council replied the following day, attesting to the loyalty of the citizenry to his cause.[57] On July 8, by secret vote, it chose Manuel Pérez de Tudela to serve as its representative in company with others selected by the Spanish governor to confer with San Martín.[58] The next day elements of the patriot army

52. Gamio, *La municipalidad de Lima*, p. 26.
53. *Ibid.*, pp. 26-28.
54. Vargas Ugarte, *Historia del Perú, emancipación*, p. 283.
55. "The happiness of the capital and of all the kingdom depends solely on peace; and this on a 'yes' from Your Excellency. The cabildo hopes to secure it and offers Your Excellency in the name of the generous people that it represents a constant and everlasting gratitude." Quoted in Gamio, *La municipalidad de Lima*, p. 31.
56. Vargas Ugarte, *Historia del Perú, emancipación*, pp. 287-288.
57. Minutes of July 7, 1821, Libros de cabildos de Lima, vol. XLV, Biblioteca municipal, Lima.
58. Minutes of July 8, 1821, *ibid.*, vol. XLV.

joyfully paraded into the city and on the thirteenth the Protector entered incognito to plan with the Marqués de Montemira for the occupation of the city. To rally full support to the cause of liberation San Martín, in an oficio of July 14, urged the cabildo to call a general junta of "reputable citizens, who representing a majority of the people would ascertain if the general view is in favor of independence."[59] The ayuntamiento agreed at once to summon a cabildo abierto for this purpose. In determining the names of those to be invited to the assembly, the council had recourse to the latest rolls of citizens drawn up when the Spanish authorities were collecting the special war contribution. From this source, aided by the advice of commissioners from the cuarteles, who knew many of the citizens, it prepared a representative list of people to whom invitations were carried that very evening. The news spread rapidly throughout the city, causing much excitement in private homes and coffee shops, where "independence" was the toast of the hour.

On July 15 the most famous cabildo abierto in the history of Peru was observed. Among those attending the meeting at 11:00 A.M. in the sala capitular were the Archbishop of Lima, the heads of the monasteries, delegates from the legal and cultural bodies, and members of the aristocracy. The presiding officer was the Conde de San Isidro.[60] After the message from San Martín was read, Dr. José de Arríz, former fiscal of the audiencia, delivered an impassioned harangue in favor of liberty and freedom for Peru. He concluded with a ringing exhortation to the assembly for action: "This city is the first in this [part of] America. For three hundred years it has been the center of government, the example and regulator of everything. Cuzco, Arequipa, Guamanga, all the villas and towns have at this moment their eyes fixed on her. They await her heroic decision."[61] Prolonged applause greeted his peroration. When the alcalde called for an expression of opinion, a spontaneous ovation broke out, indicating that the vote for emancipation had already been cast. Upon the completion of the acuerdo, members of the convocation filed past the secretary's

59. Quoted in Gamio, *La municipalidad de Lima*, pp. 45, 46.
60. The Conde was alcalde in 1817 and again in 1821. Trained as a naval officer, he had taken part in 1803 in a scientific expedition to Coromandel, Manila, and the Malacca Straits, after which he had returned to Lima. See Mendiburu, *Diccionario histórico-biografico del Perú*, X, 35.
61. Gamio, *La municipalidad de Lima*, p. 55.

table to sign the document of independence from Spain. Since only a
limited number of individuals participated in the cabildo abierto, it
was decided to allow all citizens of the municipality to visit the sala
during the next four days to add their signatures to those of the
members of the assembly.

Through still another cabildo abierto the capitulars sought to
identify themselves with the sentiment of the community. A convocation of prominent citizens was held on the nineteenth to select "the
most esteemed of His Country and the most worthy through his
services to her" to unfurl the new national banner.[62] The choice fell
upon the Conde de la Vega del Ren, a regidor long known as a
liberal thinker and as a valiant champion of the cause.[63]

It was a happy function of the ayuntamiento to organize the fiestas
in honor of independence. At the Protector's suggestion three days
were set aside for this purpose. Curiously enough, in form and se-
quence the ceremonials adhered in good measure to those employed
on the occasion of the accession of Philip V in 1701 and of Ferdinand
VII in 1808, save that the standard bearer bore aloft through the
streets the flag of the new nation.

Civic celebrations began at seven o'clock in the evening of July 27,
with the pealing of church bells and the illumination of the streets
and public buildings. As darkness fell, the officers of the gremios
set off fireworks in the principal squares to the lively satisfaction
of the crowds that thronged the avenues and byways. The plaza de
armas, scene of many a royal act of homage, was the focus for the
ceremonies opening another chapter in the history of the region. The
following day witnessed the official proclamation of independence.
Shortly before ten o'clock in the morning the ayuntamiento in full
regalia and accompanied by guests reached the portals of the casa de
cabildo, situated on the plaza and facing the cathedral. Assembling
in the sala, the capitulars saw the alcalde pin a red band across the
chest of the Conde de la Vega and hand to the standard bearer the
flag of the new nation. From the town hall the civic officials and

62. The selection of an individual for this purpose was proposed by San Martín,
though not necessarily by a cabildo abierto. See *ibid*., pp. 70, 71.

63. Born in Lima, the Conde de la Vega had been closely associated with its
municipal government for a number of years, serving as alcalde ordinario in 1791,
1792, and 1810, and as regidor of the constitutional cabildo in 1813 and 1820. See
Mendiburu, *Diccionario histórico-biográfico del Perú*, XI, 224.

the leading citizens proceeded across the plaza to the former viceregal palace to greet the Protector and the governor of the city, the Marqués de Montemira. Here in a brief act the Governor received the national flag. Leaving the viceregal residence, San Martín, followed by the Governor and the municipal representatives, marched to a platform, "hung with tapestry and having railings with balusters," which had been erected on the plaza. The Protector hastily mounted the steps, seized the flag borne by the Marqués de Montemira, waved it to the crowd, and in a vibrant voice proclaimed the independence of Peru. When the cries of "Viva la Patria, viva la libertad, and viva la independencia," had subsided, he descended and made his way to three squares in other parts of the city, where platforms had been raised. Here the same ceremony was repeated. The procession finally returned, exhausted, to the palace, and the flag now carried by the standard bearer was given back to the alcalde to be put in a conspicuous place for all to see. The festivities concluded that evening with a stately reception and a gala ball honoring the Argentine General. On the last day all of the actors in the drama gathered in the spacious cathedral to witness the sacrificial Mass performed by the Archbishop. With the termination of the religious service the regidores entered the hall of the ayuntamiento to take individual oaths of loyalty to the new government.[64] The cabildo prescribed that all citizens must acknowledge the sovereignty of the present regime by presenting themselves at the residence of the district commissioner or of the alcalde de barrio to swear allegiance in a similar fashion.[65]

There was another, not insignificant, role played by the cabildo of the capital in the formation of modern Peru. It was an instrument of political transition in the development of local and governing institutions for the republic. Because of its collaboration in the last stage of emancipation San Martín, by a decree of August 6, 1821, confirmed the continuance in office of the members of the cabildo. Thus the colonial body became the first town council of the national state.[66] During the following months it accomplished much important work: the choice of a junta for the preservation of the liberty of the press; the establishment of a commission, comprising two aldermen

64. A moving description of these patriotic scenes is to be found in Gamio, *La municipalidad de Lima*, pp. 83-115.
65. *Ibid.*, pp. 116-124.   66. *Ibid.*, p. 134.

and two vecinos, to be supplemented by representatives of the hacendados selected by the cabildo at a later time, for the purpose of setting up a national bank; and finally the designation of a body to draw up with the approval of the President of the Department the ordinances regulating future conciliar elections.[67] Even though Lima subsequently passed under royal control for two separate periods, from June 18 to July 16, 1823, and from February 27 off and on to December 7, 1824, the framework for the organization of civic government remained. After the realization of the national phase the municipal council of the capital served as underpinning to a central structure whose form was constantly being altered by a bewildering succession of dictators. Further prosecution of the conflict with Spain and the formulation of urgent domestic policies were, however, relegated by San Martín to a congress, with the members being chosen through indirect election from districts into which the country was divided rather than from the municipalities. Thereafter organs of the national government predominated and in part superseded the local units.

Even though Lima had been liberated, the fate of the remaining municipalities in the audiencia had yet to be decided. The Spanish authorities, their position more precarious, adopted harsher methods to reinforce their cause. They compelled local councils under their control to render assistance through forced enlistment of troops, requisitioning of supplies for man and beast, and donation of sums of money. While harboring sentiments of resentment and of hope for eventual independence, the magistrates had no other course but to urge acceptance of royal commands.

Guamanga's experience is probably typical of the way in which municipal councils were exploited by the Spanish army in the last stage of the revolution. Elections for the positions of alcalde and regidor continued to be held in accord with the provisions of the Constitution of 1812. With the consent of the *jefe militar*, they selected the police officials and minor functionaries.[68] Because of the virtual impossibility of getting aid from the Peninsula, the Spanish authorities sought money and provisions from the colonists. On August 10, 1823, the

67. *Ibid.*, pp. 145-147.
68. Minutes of Jan. 2, 1823, Libros de cabildos de la ciudad de Guamanga, desde octubre 29 de 1822 hasta junio de 1825, Biblioteca nacional, Lima.

intendant ordered the cabildo to appoint two regidores from the hacendados to see to the prompt collection of taxes, necessary for the government.[69] Again on June 19, 1824, the council was requested to furnish beef for the troops quartered in the area.[70] Expropriation of supplies entailed hardships for the inhabitants.

In 1822 the resumption of the highly successful campaign to free the remainder of Peru hinged on San Martín's decisions. With the termination of the Guayaquil Conference in July of that year, the Argentine General retraced his steps to Lima, tendered his resignation as Protector to the junta, and in a short while withdrew to Chile, Buenos Aires, and finally to Europe as an exile. There was no dangerous rival to challenge the inordinate aspirations of the Liberator of the North for martial glory and political dominance. In August, 1823, General William Miller, acting under orders from Bolívar's brilliant protégé Sucre, freed Arequipa, the cabildo being permitted "to continue in the exercise of its respective functions."[71] Nevertheless, while pledging support to the patriot cause, the ayuntamiento refused to fulfil a request from Sucre for 100,000 pesos—regarded as excessive, though to be guaranteed by the confiscation of royalist estates—until the General appeared in person before that body.[72] After the victory on August 6, 1824, at Junín, Bolívar's forces drove royal garrisons from Tarma, Jauja, and Huancayo. By the end of October, Huancavelica, Huanta, and Guamanga were also in the hands of the revolutionists. Sucre's spectacular triumph over La Serna at Ayacucho on December 9 prompted the capitulation of a royalist pocket at Cuzco, the last significant municipality to be liberated. The expulsion of the Spanish from Peru was well-nigh total. Only the fortress of San Felipe at Callao held out for another year.

In the course of the revolution the Peruvian cabildos had not followed a direct, undeviating path to the realization of independence. Creoles were divided in loyalties at the outset and often based their stand opportunely on the advance or retreat of the opposing armies. Through the ayuntamientos, headed by the alcaldes, they made their wishes felt in the civil struggle. As the seat of a viceroyalty for nearly three hundred years, the City of the Kings, like the capital of New

69. Minutes of Aug. 10, 1823, *ibid.*   70. Minutes of Jan. 19, 1824, *ibid.*
71. Vargas Ugarte, *Historia del Perú, emancipación*, p. 406.
72. *Ibid.*, pp. 407, 408.

Spain, had a redoubtable number of loyalists among its proud, affluent aristocracy. Surely, the presence of a huge Indian population, resentful of exploitation, was a deterrent to the adoption of a hasty policy that might lead to racial strife with unforeseeable consequences. With the successive Spanish defeats the allegiance of many to the crown waned. Nationalism took greater hold and claimed more adherents. Through the cabildo abierto the sovereignty of the Bourbons over the territory was formally ended. Upon the achievement of independence the local units became an integral part of the governmental machinery and were recognized as such in the new constitution of the republic.

In conclusion, one might speculate as to whether the crown's grant of full self-government would have preserved the integrity of the empire. Perhaps it would have postponed the break between sovereign and colonist. But in the light of past events it could hardly have forestalled the development of a nationalism that was fortified by the historical accident of Napoleonic ambition and subsequently by the blind, uninformed policy of Ferdinand VII. If one assumes the inevitability of separation, the policies of the newly formed state might have been directed to the benefit of its citizens to a greater degree by individuals trained and experienced in the art of colonial administration.

EPILOGUE

The story of the Peruvian cabildo from founding to absorption into the national state has been told in this and an earlier volume. Judged by the canons of nineteenth-century liberalism and democracy, the cabildo was woefully lacking. Indeed, an approximation of true representation occurred only in two epochs. During the sixteenth century the struggle of the settlers against the aborigines created a milieu marked by lessened class consciousness which was suitable for the growth of a kind of self-government. But like a vine, the local institution drooped under the strong rays of Hapsburg and Bourbon autocracy and was revived only by the more propitious climate of the late eighteenth century. The distinct and distant environment of the New World, the spread of the ideas of the Enlightenment, and the examples of the French and American revolutions nurtured concepts of nationalism and popular rights. Jesuit doctrines, kept alive in the lecture halls of the colonial universities, furnished philosophical justification for independence. Both in Peru and in the Peninsula, the municipal council became the legal instrument for the implementation of popular sovereignty. In the words of Victor Belaúnde: "The cabildo was the bridge between Spain and America . . . if Spain planted cabildos she had to reap the harvest of nations."[1] In the transition from colony to republic the council assumed a vital role of directing collective action against a reactionary ruler.

Today the average citizen takes for granted the many requisite services performed by the modern municipality. To the creole of the colonial era, functions that we regard as routine and ordinary were more highly prized because they were not as routine nor as easily come by. Moreover, in times of sudden stress and emergency the municipal council was the primary organ of security for the community. That it was at times corrupt, inefficient, and neglectful of the interests of the people cannot be gainsaid. Nevertheless, it represented a partial survival of the independent spirit of the medieval

1. *Causas y caracteres de la independencia hispanoamericana,* p. 141.

Castilian ciudad and simultaneously a practical, covert concession of Bourbon authoritarianism to a basic aspiration for autonomy. Legally, the powers of the cabildo were limited. Yet, in a region where law enforcement was dilatory and where viceroys and intendants understood plainly the need to curry favor with the landed aristocracy and merchants, its influence was greater than has hitherto been recognized by the generality of historians.[2]

2. Charles C. Griffin in his essay entitled "Unidad y variedad en la historia americana" (*Ensayos sobre la historia del Nuevo Mundo* [Mexico City, 1951]), p. 110, shares this view: "We must not deny that the Spanish system of government had as its base the omnipotence of the crown; but this power was exercised by means of juridical and political institutions to which the kings themselves submitted. There was moreover an enormous difference between theory and practice. Some high officials of the Spanish regime in America sympathized with the people that they governed and represented, clearly in an imperfect fashion, the interests of the creole class. The power exercised by the crown over governors in America was not always effective. There are cases of governors in remote regions—Paraguay, New Mexico— who functioned contrary to royal orders and supported themselves with the weight of public opinion. Likewise, the American cabildo, although imperfect and oligarchical, did not cease enjoying in a limited mode an autonomous government."

APPENDIX I

RETURNS FROM THE SALE OR LEASING OF ROYAL AND MUNICIPAL OFFICES FOR THE AUDIENCIA OF LIMA FOR PARTICULAR YEARS

A. OFICIOS 1710

Oficios Reales

(Sales under diverse conditions, crown usually getting one-third of value, plus a small charge for confirmation)

	pesos	reales
Receptor of Real Audiencia (value: 1,000 pesos)	300	
Escribano de Juzgado de Censos de Indios (value: 3,500)	1,666	5
Fiador de escribano de Provincia	14	7½
Receptor de Real Audiencia	100	
Ensayador de Lima	7,000	
Capitán de Sala de Armas (value: 4,000)	1,000	
Contador ordenador (value: 3,500)	1,500	
Escribano público del Rey (value: 2,500) (confirmation?)	133	3
Procurador número (value: 2,400) (part payment?)	500	
Factor of Caja de Potosí (value: 11,000)	3,000	
Alguacil maior del Gral de Puertas desta Rno. (value: 40,000 but renounced in his favor)	20,000	
	35,214	7½

Oficios Municipales

Alguacil maior of Lima (value: 30,000)	10,000	
Escribano de cabildo de Yca (confirmation)	50	
Escribano público y cabildo de Villa de Chancay (yalue: 1,500)	500	
Regidor de Lima (value: 11,000)	3,666	5½
Escribano público de Lima (value: 3,500) (leasing?)	500	
Alférez real de Chachapoyas (confirmation)	30	
	14,746	5½

Oficios Reales y Municipales

Arequipa	2,303	1
La Paz	5,858	2
Oruro	3,093	4
	11,254	7

MEDIA ANATA 1710

Media Anata: normally one-half of salary of office for first year and one-third of all other emoluments of the recipient of a public office, favor, concession, whether permanent or temporary, with exemption as a general rule for salaries of offices filled annually by election, such as alcalde ordinario, procurator, etc.

Media anata for royal offices
(the length of the list precludes enumeration of specific fees, etc.)

Media anata for municipal offices	*pesos*	*reales*
Regidor of La Paz	16	6
Alcalde provincial of La Paz	12	
Sargento of Santa Hermandad—Arequipa	6	7
Regidor of Lima	376	6
Regidor of Cochabamba	73	3
Escribano publico	16	2
Sargento-Santa Hermandad Arequipa	7	7
Alférez real of Chachapoyas	24	
Alcalde provincial of Saña	78	6
Escribano público y cabildo of Latacunga	8	2

Regidor of Saña	10	
Alférez real of Saña	12	
Regidor of Guamanga	26	6
Escribano público del numero (Lima)	124	7
Alcalde de Leon de Huánuco	27	4
Escribano público y cabildo (Chancay)	58	2
Depositario (Arequipa)	100	
Regidor (Guamanga)	35	7
Alguacil maior Lima	1,000	
License to build a grist mill	15	
License to construct a bridge	20	
Maestro mayor de examinar de labrar paños (Riobamba)	10	
Maestro mayor de fábricas Guayaquil	20	
Alguacil—Huaylas	50	
	2,131	1

B. Oficios 1725

Oficios reales	*pesos*	*reales*
Real casa	286	3
Fiador de escribano de cárceles	96	2½
Procurador número (Audiencia)	50	
Contador (Audiencia)	1,000	
Procurador	146	5½
Receptor	100	
	1,679	3

Oficios municipales		
Alférez real Yca (value: 2,050)	683	3
Escribano público (value: 6,100)	2,500	
Depositario general Lima (value: 12,500)	3,000	
Alcalde provincial Chancay (value: 2,000) (confirmation?)	266	6
Escribano público	400	
	6,850	1

Oficios reales y municipales		
Trujillo	1,286	3
Oruro	1,125	

La Paz	3,737	4¾
Potosí	12,766	2
	18,915	1¾

MEDIA ANATA 1725

Oficios reales	*pesos*	*reales*
(as above)		
Total	302	½

Oficios municipales

Alcalde de Leon de Huánuco	27	4
Alférez real Yca	68	3
Fiel ejecutor of Saña	50	
	145	7

Oficios reales y municipales

Trujillo	59	
Saña	57	
Arequipa	1,223	1½
La Paz	160	4
Potosí	15,957	6½
Oruro	3,293	
	20,750	4

c. OFICIOS 1755

Oficios reales	*pesos*	*reales*
Alguacil maior (Audiencia)	13,333	2½
5 Procuradores del numero (leasing at 50 pesos each)	250	
11 Receptores (leasing at 50 pesos each)	600	
Escribano de cámara	4,500	
Procurador	283	5
Escribano de bienes de difuntos	327	6½
Receptor (leasing, 2 yrs.)	100	
Chanciller (Audiencia)	916	5½
	20,261	3½

Oficios municipales

    Alguacil maior (Lima, part payment,
        value in 1751: 24,000)   1,500
    Escribano de cabildo (leasing)   750
    Alcalde provincial (leasing)   250
    Alcalde provincial (resignation of office)   4,000
                                6,500

Oficios reales y municipales

    Pasco   73
    Trujillo   1,200
    Arequipa   300
    Cuzco   4,272
    Oruro   1,743   3½
    La Paz   3,766   6
                              11,355   1½

Media anata and sisa*

    Saña, Pasco, Jauja, Trujillo
    Caylloma, Arequipa, Arica,
    Piura, Cuzco, Oruro   1,755   2½

*The tax was lumped on this occasion with the excise on foodstuffs, or the sisa. If the media anata was collected for this year in the district of Lima, it was not so reported.

SOURCE. Cuentas de Real Hacienda y Caxa de Lima, legajos 1762, 1766, 1772, Contaduría General, A. G. I.

APPENDIX II

SELECTED LISTS OF PURCHASE PRICES FOR MUNICIPAL OFFICES IN THE AUDIENCIA OF LIMA (in pesos)

A. REGIDOR

Lima		Arequipa		Yca	
1700	11,000	1710	2,300	1718	200
1710	11,000	1718	1,500	1768	400
1719	11,000	1735	1,600	1769	700*
1734	11,000	1743	1,000		
1760	6,000				
1764	4,500				
1769	4,500				
1771	6,000				
1777	4,000				

Guamanga		Cuzco		Piura	
1719	800	1696	3,000	1697	450
1731	920	1706	4,000	1750	425
		1713	4,000	1751	2,000*
		1752	1,500		

Trujillo		Huancavelica	
1704	600	1714	4,500*
1729	1,600*	1731	4,500*
1738	500		
1743	1,675*		
1756	500		

B. ESCRIBANO DE CABILDO

Lima		Yca		Piura	
(escribano mayor)					
1713	45,000	1718	800	1699	5,120
1737	45,000	1767	1,300		
1760	18,000**				

(*escribano*)

1707   3,000

Cuzco		Trujillo		Arequipa	
1702	4,050	1704	4,000	1709	4,000
1737	3,550	1751	4,000	1754	4,000

Huancavelica

(*escribano mayor*)

1740   9,500

*And the office of the fiel ejecutor.
**Probably due to unfavorable court judgment.

C. DEPOSITARIO GENERAL

Lima		Cuzco		Piura	
1723	25,000	1710	12,700	1750	2,000
		1734	12,100		
		1743	12,100		

Arequipa		Moquegua	
1710	3,000	1735	1,600
1713	3,000		

D. ALCALDE PROVINCIAL (DE HERMANDAD)

Lima		Cuzco		Piura	
1738	25,000	1700	18,000	1713	2,800
		1734	6,000	1725	2,500
		1745	18,000	1756	2,500
				1770	4,000

Arequipa		Guamanga		Trujillo	
1708	8,000	1717	6,000	1716	6,000

Huancavelica		Yca		Huánuco	
1733	8,000	1734	3,525	1696	4,800
		1772	3,525		

E. ALFÉREZ REAL

Lima		Cuzco		Piura	
1747	20,000	1702	8,000	1697	450
1774	12,500	1752	3,000	1731	800

Arequipa		Guamanga		Trujillo	
1705	4,000	1701	3,000	1701	1,300
1734	1,500	1724	3,000		
		1743	3,000		

Yca		Huánuco	
1755	1,600	1718	1,200
		1780	525

F. ALGUACIL MAYOR

Lima		Piura		Tarma	
1730	30,000	1742	1,100	1707	2,000
1748	24,000			1738	2,600
1755	26,050				

Arequipa		Trujillo		Guamanga	
1708	6,400	1710	4,000	1733	2,375
1756	7,000	1733	3,600		

Yca		Huánuco		Cajamarca	
1721	3,525	1714	3,000	1701	5,000

SOURCES. In the compilation of these figures the following sources were consulted: Expedientes, oficios, legajos 422, 457; Confirmaciones de oficios, legajos 449, 450-452, 454, 455, 457-462; Cuentas de Real Hacienda, legajos 1137-1141, 1143, 1146, Audiencia de Lima, A. G. I.

BIBLIOGRAPHY

I. Special Guides, Bibliographies, Encyclopedias, and Dictionaries

Alcedo, Antonio de. *Diccionario geográfico-histórico de las Indias occidentales, o America: es a saber de los reynos del Perú, Nueva España, Tierra Firme, Chile y Nuevo Reyno de Granada.* . . . 5 tomos. Madrid, 1786-1789.
Catálogo de la sección colonial del archivo histórico, ministerio de hacienda y comercio, República del Perú. Lima, 1944.
Diccionario de historia de España desde sus orígenes hasta el fin del reinado de Alfonso XIII. 2 tomos. Madrid, 1952.
Domínguez Bordona, Jesús. *Catálogo de la biblioteca de palacio, manuscritos de América.* Tomo IX. Madrid, 1935.
Gayangos y Arce Pascual de. *Catalogue of the Manuscripts in the Spanish Language in the British Museum.* 4 vols. London, 1875-1893.
Handbook of Latin-American Studies. 24 vols. Vols. 1-13, Cambridge, Mass., 1936-1951; Vols. 14-26, Gainesville, Fla., 1951-1964.
Humphreys, R. A. *Latin American History: A Guide to the Literature in English.* Oxford, 1958.
Jones, Cecil K. *A Bibliography of Latin-American Bibliographies* (2nd. ed.). Washington, 1942.
Mendiburu, Manuel de. *Diccionario histórico-biográfico del Perú* (2nd. ed.). 11 tomos, Lima, 1931-1934; appendices, 4 tomos, Lima, 1935-1938.
Paz, Julián. *Catálogo de manuscritos de América existentes en la Biblioteca Nacional.* Madrid, 1933.
Porras Barrenechea, Raúl. *Fuentes históricas peruanas.* Lima, 1954.
Reales cédulas, reales órdenes, decretos, autos y bandos que se guardan en el archivo histórico, ministerio de hacienda y comercio, República del Perú. Lima, 1947.
Smith, Robert S. *Indice del archivo del Tribunal del Consulado de Lima, con un estudio histórico de esta institución.* Lima, 1948.
Vargas Ugarte, Rubén. *Biblioteca peruana, manuscritos peruanos* (1) *en las bibliotecas del extranjero,* Lima, 1935, (2) *en el archivo de Indias,* Lima, 1938, (3) *en la biblioteca nacional de Lima,* Lima, 1940, (4) *en las bibliotecas de América,* Lima, 1945, (5) *en las bibliotecas y archivos*

de Europa y América (suplemento), Buenos Aires, 1947, (6) *impresos peruanos publicados en el extranjero*, Lima, 1949.
——. *Manual de estudios peruanistas*. Lima, 1952.

II. PRIMARY SOURCES

1. *Archives*

Archivo de la Universidad de Cuzco.
    Libros de actas del cabildo de Cuzco, 1712-1824, vols. 20-30.
Archivo general de Indias, Sevilla.
    Audiencia de Cuzco, legajo 13.
    Audiencia de Lima, legajos 410-412, 414, 416, 417, 420-423, 428, 449-
        452, 454, 455, 456, 457-462, 593, 640, 642, 643, 646, 787, 792, 793,
        801, 802, 804, 805, 819, 1117-1119, 1137-1141, 1143, 1146, 1151,
        1156, 1161, 1223.
    Audiencia de Quito, legajo 139.
    Contaduría general, legajos 1760-1767, 1770, 1771, 1772.
    Indiferente general, legajos 652, 1713.
    Papeles de Cuba, legajos 180, 1802.
Archivo histórico de hacienda y comercío, Lima, legajo 14.
Archivo histórico nacional, Madrid.
    Consejo de Indias, legajos 20292, 21293.
    Estado, legajos 58, 54D.
Archivo nacional, Lima.
    Cabildos, legajos 1, 3, 4, 8, 10, residencias, legajo 24.
Biblioteca de Academia de Historia, Madrid.
    Ms. 9-9-7n-1999.
Biblioteca municipal, Arequipa.
    Libros de acuerdos de cabildo, 1697-1833, vols. 23-51.
Biblioteca municipal, Lima.
    Libros de cabildos, 1700-1821, vols. XXXIII-XLV.
    Libros de cédulas y provisiones, 1609-1821, vols. XVIII-XXXI.
Biblioteca municipal, Trujillo.
    Libros de cabildos, 1701-1838, vols. 12-24.
Biblioteca nacional, Lima.
    Libros de cabildos de la ciudad Guamanga, desde octubre 29 de
        1822 hasta junio de 1825.
    Mss. D250, D331, D1055, D9361, D10336.
Biblioteca nacional, Madrid.
    Ms. 11026.

2. Printed documents and contemporary works

Barriaga, Víctor A. (ed). *Memorias para la historia de Arequipa, 1786-1796.* 3 tomos. Arequipa, 1941-1948.

Bustamante Carlos Inca, Calixto, alias Concolorcorvo. *El Lazarillo de ciegos caminantes desde Buenos Aires hasta Lima, 1773.* Buenos Aires, 1942.

Cangas, Gregorio de. "Descripción de la ciudad de Lima," *Revista histórica* (Perú, 1941), XIV, 325-342.

Castillo de Bobadilla, Jerónimo. *Política para corregidores, y señores de vasallos en tiempo de paz y de guerra....* 2 vols. Madrid, 1775.

Colección de documentos inéditos para la historia de España. 113 vols. Madrid, 1842-1895.

Colección de documentos inéditos relativos al descubrimiento, conquista, y organización de las antiguas posesiones españolas de América y Oceanía, sacados de los archivos del reyno y muy especialmente del de Indias. 42 vols. Madrid, 1864-1884.

Colección de documentos inéditos relativos al descubrimiento, conquista y organización de las antiguas posesiones españolas de ultramar. 25 vols. Madrid, 1885-1932.

Constitución política de la monarquía española, promulgada en Cadiz a 19 de Marzo de 1812. Cadiz, 1812.

Fernan-Núñez, Conde de. *Vida, de Carlos III, publicada con la biografía del autor, apéndices y notas por A. Morel-Fatio y A. Paz y Melia y un prólogo de D. Juan Valera.* 2 tomos. Madrid, 1898.

Fonseca, Fabián de and Carlos de Urrutia. *Historia general de Real Hacienda escrita por órden del Virey Conde de Revillagigedo.* 6 tomos. Mexico City, 1845-1853.

Humbolt, Alexander von. *Ensayo político sobre la isla de Cuba.* La Habana, 1959.

———. *Essai politique sur le royaume de la Nouvelle Espagne.* 5 vols. Paris, 1825.

Juan, Jorge y Ulloa, Antonio de. *Noticias secretas de América.* Buenos Aires, 1953.

———. *A Voyage to South America, Describing at large the Spanish cities, towns, provinces, etc. on that extensive continent...* (3rd. ed.). 2 vols. London, 1772.

Konetzke, Richard. *Colección de Documentos para la Historia de la Formación social de Hispanoamérica 1493-1810.* Vol. III, tomo I, 1691-1779. Madrid, 1962.

Larco Herrera, Alberto (ed.). *Anales de cabildo, Ciudad de Trujillo, del 8 de octubre de 1794 al 17 de setiembre de 1802.* Lima, n.d.

León Pinelo, Antonio de. *Tratado de confirmaciones de encomiendas, oficios i casos, en que se requieren para las Indias occidentales.* Madrid, 1630.

Libro del cabildo de la ciudad de San Miguel de Piura, año 1737 a 1748. Lima, 1939.

Llano Zapata, José Eusebio de. *Memorias histórico-físicas-apologéticas de la América Meridional.* Lima, 1904.

Loayza, Francisco A. (ed.). *Estado del Perú, códice escrito en 1780 y que contiene datos importantes sobre la revolución de José Gabriel Túpac Amaru por Raphael José Sahuaraura Titu Atauchi.* Lima, 1944.

Memorias de los virreyes que han gobernado el Perú durante el tiempo del coloniaje español. 6 vols. Lima, 1859.

Muro Orejón, Antonio (ed.). *Cedulario Americano del siglo XVIII, colección de disposiciones legales indianas desde 1680 a 1800, contenidas en los cedularios del Archivo General de Indias.* Vol. I (cedulas de Carlos II, 1679-1700). Sevilla, 1956.

Nuevo reglamento de policía agregado a la instrucción de alcaldes de barrios. Lima, 1786.

Recopilación de leyes de los reinos de las Indias (5th ed.). 2 vols. Madrid, 1841.

Rodríguez Casado, Vicente and Calderón Quijano, José Antonio (eds.). *Memoria de gobierno de José Fernando de Abascal y Souso,* 2 tomos. Sevilla, 1944.

Rodríguez Casado, Vicente and Lohmann Villena, Guillermo (eds.). *Memoria de gobierno de Joaquín de la Pezuela, Virrey del Perú, 1816-1821.* Sevilla, 1947.

Rodríguez Casado, Vicente and Pérez Embid, Florentino (eds.). *Memoria de gobierno de Manuel de Amat y Junient, 1761-1776.* Sevilla, 1947.

Rodríguez de Campomanes, Pedro. *Discurso sobre la educación popular de los artesanos y su fomento.* Madrid, 1775.

Santayana Bustillo, Lorenzo de. *Govierno político de los pueblos de España y el corregidor, alcalde, y juez en ellos.* Zaragoza, 1742.

Solórzano Pereira, Juan de. *Política indiana* [1647]. 5 tomos. Madrid, 1930.

Ulloa, Antonio de. *Noticias Americanas: entretenimiento físico-histórico sobre la América meridional y la septentrional oriental.* Buenos Aires, n.d.

Unánue, José Hipólito. *Guía política, eclesiástica y militar del virreinato del Perú, para el año de 1793 Compuesta por orden del Superior Gobierno* Lima, n.d.

Valcárcel, Daniel (ed.). *Cosme Bueno, Geografía del Perú virreinal, siglo XVIII.* Lima, 1951.

III. Secondary Sources

1. Articles

Aiton, Arthur S. "Spanish Colonial Reorganization Under the Family Compact," *Hispanic American Historical Review*, XII (1932), 269-280.

Artola, Miguel. "Campillo y las reformas de Carlos III," *Revista de Indias*, XII (1952) 685-714.

Basadre, Jorge. "Notas sobre la experiencia histórica peruana," *Revista histórica* (Perú, 1952), XIX, 5-40.

Bromley, Juan. "Los libros de cédulas y provisiones del archivo histórico de la municipalidad de Lima," *Revista histórica* (1952), XIX, 61-202.

————. "Recibimiento de virreyes en Lima," *Revista histórica*, XX, 5-108.

Castañeda, Carlos. "The Corregidor in Spanish Colonial Administration," *Hispanic American Historical Review*, IX (1929), 446-470.

Céspedes del Castillo, Guillermo. "Lima y Buenos Aires, Repercussiones económicas y políticas de la creación del virreinato del Plata," *Anuario de estudios Americanos*, III (1946), 669-874.

————. "Reorganización de la hacienda virreinal peruana en el siglo XVIII," *Anuario de historia del derecho español*, XXIII (1953), 329-369.

————. "La Visita como institución Indiana," *Anuario de estudios Americanos*, III (1946), 984-1025.

Christelow, Allan. "French Interest in the Spanish Empire during the Ministry of the Duc de Choiseul, 1759-1771," *Hispanic American Historical Review*, XXI (1941), 515-537.

Desdevises du Dezert, George N. "Les institutions de L'Espagne au XVIIIe siècle," *Revue Hispanique*, LXX (June, 1927), 1-556.

Dunbar Temple, Ella. "Periodismo peruano del siglo XVIII," *Mercurio peruano*, XXV, 428-461.

Durand Flores, Luis. "El juicio de residencia en el Perú republicano," *Anuario de estudios Americanos*, X (1953), 339-456.

Ezquerra Abadía, Ramón. "Unpresupuesto Americano: el del cabildo de Nueva Orleans al terminar la soberanía española," *Anuario de estudios Americanos*, V (1948), 675-701.

García y Fernández Castañon, Cesar. "Ordenanzas municipales y de pueblos," *Revista de ciencias jurídicas y sociales*, IV (1921), 243-276, 356-381, 566-583.

Gates, Eunice J. "Don José Antonio de Areche: His Own Defense," *Hispanic American Historical Review*, VIII (Feb., 1928), 14-42.

Giménez Fernández, Manuel. "Las doctrinas populistas en la independencia de Hispano-América," *Anuario de estudios Americanos*, III (1946), 519-655.

Griffin, Charles C. "Unidad y variedad en la historia americana," *Ensayos sobre la historia del Nuevo Mundo* (Mexico City), 1951, pp. 99-123.

Hanke, Lewis. "The Portuguese in Spanish America, with Special Reference to the Villa Imperial de Potosí," *Revista de historia de América* (June, 1961), pp. 1-48.

Harth-Terre, Emilio. "Un balcón para Micaela Villegas," *El Comercio* (Lima), July 13, 1959.

King, James F. "The Colored Castes and American Representation in the Cortes of Cadiz," *Hispanic American Historical Review*, XXXIII (Feb., 1953), 33-64.

Lohmann Villena, Guillermo. "El corregidor de Lima, estudio histórico-jurídico," *Revista histórica* (Peru, 1953), XX, 153-180.

Lynch, John. "Intendants and cabildos in the Viceroyalty of the Rio de la Plata, 1782-1810," *Hispanic American Historical Review*, XXXV (Aug., 1955), 337-362.

Morse, Richard M. "Some Characteristics of Latin American Urban History," *American Historical Review*, LXVII (Jan., 1962), 317-338.

Muñoz Pérez, José. "La idea de América en Campomanes," *Anuario de estudios Americanos*, X, (1953), 209-264.

Muro Orejón, Antonio. "El ayuntamiento de Sevilla modelo de los municipios Americanos," *Anales de la Universidad Hispalense*, XX (1960), 69-85.

Pérez Búa, Manuel. "Las reformas de Carlos III en el régimen local de España," *Revista de ciencias jurídicas y sociales*, no. 2 (1919), pp. 219-247.

Pierson, William W. "Some Reflections on the Cabildo as an Institution," *Hispanic American Historical Review*, V (1922), 573-596.

Romero, Carlos A. "Los orígenes del periodismo en el Perú. De la relación al diario, 1594-1790," *Revista histórica* (Peru, 1939), XII, 246-312.

Sanz, Luis Santiago. "El proyecto de extinción del régimen de las intendencias de América y la Ordenanza General de 1803," *Revista del instituto de historia del derecho* (Buenos Aires), no. 5 (1953), pp. 123-185.

Valcárcel, Carlos Daniel. "Morales Duárez, prócer peruano," *Revista de Indias*, XXI, nos. 85-86, pp. 505-509.

———. "Perú borbónico y emancipación," *Revista de historia de América*, no. 50 (Dec., 1960), pp. 315-438.

Vargas Ugarte, Rubén. "D. Blas Ostolaza, rector del seminario de Trujillo, diputado a Cortes, capellán de Fernando VII, víctima del liberalismo," *Revista de historia de América*, no. 49 (June, 1960), pp. 121-145.

Vázquez de Acuña, Isidoro. "El ministro de Indias, Don José de Gálvez, Marqués de Sonora," *Revista de Indias*, XIX (July-Dec., 1959), 449-473.

Viellard-Baron, Alain. "L'Etablissement des Intendants aux Indes par Charles III," *Revista de Indias*, XII (1952), 521-546.

———. "L'Intendant Americain el l'intendant français," *Revista de Indias,* XI (1951), 237-250.

2. Books

Alayza, Luis and Soldán, Paz. *La constitución de Cádiz: El egregio limeño Morales y Duárez.* Lima, 1946.

Alemparte, Julio. *El cabildo en Chile colonial.* Santiago, Chile, 1940.

Altamira, Rafael, *et al. Contribuciones a la historia municipal de América.* Mexico City, 1951.

———. *Historia de España y de la civilización española.* 4 tomos. Barcelona, 1900-1911.

———. *A History of Spain from the Beginnings to the Present Day* (1st ed.). Translated by Muna Lee. Toronto, New York, and London, 1949.

Antequera, José María. *Historia de la legislación española desde los tiempos más remotos hasta nuestros días.* Madrid, 1874.

Ayala, F. Javier de. *Ideas políticas de Juan de Solórzano.* Sevilla, 1946.

Ayarragaray, Lucas. *La iglesia en América y la dominación española* (2nd. ed.). Buenos Aires, 1935.

Ballesteros y Beretta, Antonio. *Historia de España y su influencia en la historia universal* (2nd. ed.). 11 vols. Barcelona, Buenos Aires, 1929-1950.

Barra, Felipe de la. *Monografía histórica del Real Felipe del Callao y guía del museo histórico-militar* (2nd. ed.). Lima, 1957.

Barros Arana, Diego. *Compendio de historia de América.* 2 vols. Santiago, 1865.

Basadre, Jorge. *Meditaciones sobre el destino histórico del Perú.* Lima, n.d.

Bayle, Constantino. *Los cabildos seculares en la América española.* Madrid, 1952.

Béthencourt Massieu, Antonio. *Patiño en la política internacional de Felipe V.* Valladolid, 1954.

Boleslao, Lewin. *La rebelión de Túpac Amaru y los orígenes de la emancipación Americana.* Buenos Aires, n.d.

Cardell, Carlos. *La casa de Borbón en España.* Madrid, 1954.

Causas y caracteres de la independencia hispano-americana (Congreso hispano-americano de historia). Madrid, 1953.

Chapman, Charles E. *A History of Spain.* New York, 1927.

Cox, William. *Memoirs of the Kings of Spain of the House of Bourbon* (2nd. ed.). London, 1815.

Danvila y Collado, Manuel. *Reinado de Carlos III.* 6 tomos. Madrid, 1893-96.

Darrío Arrús, M. *El Callao en la época del coloniaje.* Callao, 1904.

Desdevises du Dezert, George N. *L'Espagne de l'Ancien Regime: Les Institutions.* Paris, 1899.

Dunning, William A. *A History of Political Theories: From Luther to Montesquieu.* New York, 1927.

Ferrer del Río, Antonio. *Historia del reinado de Carlos III en España.* Madrid, 1856.

Fisher, Lillian E. *The Intendant System in Spanish America.* Berkeley, Calif., 1929.

——. *The Viceregal Administration in the Spanish-American Colonies.* Berkeley, Calif., 1926.

Gamio Palacio, Fernando. *La municipalidad de Lima y la emancipación, 1821.* Lima, 1944.

García, Juan Agustín. *La ciudad indiana: Buenos Aires desde 1600 hasta mediados del siglo XVIII.* Buenos Aires, 1954.

García Venero, Maximiano. *Historia del parlamentarismo español (1810-1833).* Madrid, 1946.

González, Julio. *Filiación histórica del gobierno representativo Argentino.* Buenos Aires, 1937.

Haring, Clarence H. *The Spanish Empire in America.* New York, 1947.

Herr, Richard. *The Eighteenth-Century Revolution in Spain.* Princeton, N. J., 1958.

Hume, Martin A. S. *The Spanish People: Their Origin, Growth, and Influence.* London, 1901.

Lafuente, Modesto. *Historia general de España.* 22 tomos. Madrid, 1850-1859.

Lohmann Villena, Guillermo. *El corregidor de indios en el Perú bajo los Austrias.* Madrid, 1957.

Lorente, Sebastián. *Historia del Perú bajo los Borbones, 1700-1821.* Lima, 1871.

Lynch, John. *Spanish Colonial Administration, 1782-1810: The Intendant System in the Viceroyalty of the Río de la Plata.* London, 1958.

Madariaga, Salvador de. *El auge del imperio español en América.* Buenos Aires, 1955.

——. *El ocaso del imperio español en América.* Buenos Aires, 1955.

——. *The Rise of the Spanish American Empire.* New York, 1949.

Mariluz Urquijo, José María. *Ensayo sobre los juicios de residencia indianos.* Sevilla, 1952.

Means, Philip A. *Fall of the Inca Empire and the Spanish Rule in Peru, 1530-1780.* New York, 1932.

Monografías históricas sobre la ciudad de Lima. 2 tomos. Lima, 1935.

Moore, John Preston. *The Cabildo in Peru Under the Hapsburgs: A Study in the Origins and Powers of the Town Council in the Viceroyalty of Peru, 1530-1700.* Durham, N. C., 1954.

Navarro García, Luis. *Intendencias en Indias.* Sevilla, 1959.

Ortega y Gasset, José. *Invertebrate Spain.* Translated by Mildred Adams. London, 1937.

Ots Capdequí, José María. *El estado español en Indias* (3rd. ed.). Mexico City, 1957.

———. *Instituciones de gobierno del Nuevo Reino de Granada, durante el siglo XVIII.* Bogotá, 1950.

———. *Instituciones sociales de la América española en el período colonial.* La Plata, Buenos Aires, 1934.

———. *Manual de historia del derecho español en las Indias y del derecho propiamente indiano.* Buenos Aires, 1945.

Palacio Atard, Vicente. *Areche y Guirior: Observaciones sobre el fracaso de una visita al Perú.* Sevilla, 1946.

Parry, J. H. *The Audiencia of New Galicia in the Sixteenth Century: A Study in Spanish Colonial Government.* Cambridge, 1948.

———. *The Sale of Public Office in the Spanish Indies Under the Hapsburgs.* Berkeley and Los Angeles, 1953.

Patrón, Pablo, *Lima antigua. Estudio biográfico del autor por Evaristo San Cristóval.* Lima, 1935.

Prado, Javier. *Estado social del Perú durante la dominación española (estudio histórico-sociológico). (Colección de libros y documentos referentes a la historia del Perú,* 3a. serie, *Historiadores clásicos,* Tomo I). Lima, 1941.

Priestley, Herbert I. *José de Gálvez, Visitor-General of New Spain, 1765-1771.* Berkeley, Calif., 1916.

Ramos Pérez, Demetrio. *Historia de la colonización española en América.* Madrid, 1947.

Riva-Agüero, José de la. *Historia del Perú (selección).* 2 tomos. Lima, 1953.

Rodríguez Villa, Antonio. *Patiño y Campillo: reseña histórico-biográfica de estos dos ministros de Felipe V.* Madrid, 1882.

Romero, Emilio. *Historia económica y financiera del Peru, antiguo Perú y virreynato.* Lima, 1937.

Rousseau, François. *Le Règne de Charles III d'Espagne.* 2 vols. Paris, 1907.

Ruiz Guiñazú, Enrique. *La magistratura indiana.* Buenos Aires, 1916.

Schäfer, Ernesto. *El consejo real y supremo de las Indias, su historia, organización y labor administrativa hasta la terminación de la casa de Austria.* 2 vols. Sevilla, 1935-1947.

Silva Santisteban, Fernando. *Los obrajes en el virreinato del Perú.* Lima, 1964.

Valcárcel, Daniel. *Ignacio de Castro, humanista tacneño y gran cusqueñista (1732-1792).* Lima, 1953.

Valega, José M. *El virreinato del Perú, historia crítica de la época colonial en todos sus aspectos.* Lima, 1939.

Vargas Ugarte, Rubén. *Historia del Perú, virreinato (siglo XVIII), 1700-1790.* Lima, 1956.

———. *Historia del Perú (siglo XVIII).* Buenos Aires, 1957.

———. *Historia del Perú, emancipación, 1809-25*. Buenos Aires, 1958.

———. *Los Jesuitas del Perú, 1568-1767*. Lima, 1941.

Vidaurre, Pedro. *Relación cronológica de los alcaldes que han presidido el ayuntamiento de Lima desde su fundación hasta nuestros días*. Lima, 1889.

Whitaker, Arthur P. *The Huancavelica Mecury Mine, a Contribution to the History of the Bourbon Renaissance in the Spanish Empire*. Cambridge, Mass., 1941.

——— (ed.). *Latin-America and the Enlightenment* (2nd. ed.). Ithaca, N. Y., 1961.

Wiesse, Carlos. *Historia del Perú colonial* (5th ed.). Lima, 1937.

Zavala, Silvio A. *New Viewpoints on the Spanish Colonization of America*. Philadelphia, 1943.

INDEX

Abascal, José Fernando, viceroy of Peru, 154, 182 n., 222; proclaims Ferdinand VII's accession to throne, 198; instructs cabildos to elect deputies to Spain, 202, 203; executes articles of Constitution of 1812, 215, 216; sets policy toward cabildos, 220, 221; withdraws liberal decrees, 223-225; resignation of, 227
Abogados, in Castile, 12; authorized establishment of colegio of, 184; colegio created, 186
Abreu, Manuel, 235
Acordada, 157
Alava, 8, 11, 201
Alcabala, 35, 42, 43, 125, 148, 154, 191; assessed in the town, 117, 118; Escobedo affirms need for care in collection of, 148; objection by Lima to high rate of, 182; see also Taxation
Alcaide, 221 n.
Alcalde de barrio, 155, 157, 158; election of, in Spain, 22; appointed in Lima, 84; selected by the visitor-general, 151; protests by the cabildo of Lima against, 160, 161
Alcalde de corte, 75
Alcalde de crimen, 157; encroaches on jurisdiction of alcalde ordinario, 77, 78
Alcalde de la hermandad, 149, 181, 219; election of, in Castile, 12; intervention by crown in judgments of, 80, 81
Alcalde de los soldados, 53
Alcalde de los vecinos, 53
Alcalde mayor, 10, 133, 134, 192
Alcalde ordinario, 142-144, 148, 150, 157, 158, 160, 167, 169, 217, 224; selection and authority of, in Castile, 11; chosen by cabildo, 53-57; dispatched by Lima to Callao, 74, 75; cognizance of in civil and criminal law, 77, 78; appeals from, 78-80; collects tribute from Indians, 134; strife over elections of, 139; contention with tenientes letrados, 139; tribute gathered by, 140; functioning according to Ordinance of Intendants,

143-147; cabildo of Lima trys to restore powers of, 160, 161; reforms in duties of, in Arequipa, 167; restoration of annual election of, 184; treatment of, 190; confirmation by viceroy of election of, 191; criticism of, 192; proposal to extend powers of, 194; to take part in assembly, 201; election according to Constitution of 1812, 213; see also Cabildo
Alcalde provincial, 60, 154 n., 221 n.
Alcaraz, Domingo, deputy to Cortes from Huánuco, 206
Alcázar, in Sevilla, 200
Alcudia, 9
Alférez real, 154 n., 156, 201; sale of office of, 60; social prestige of, 88, 89
Alguacil mayor, 149, 201, 219, 221 n.; sale of office of, 60
Almagro, Diego, 141
Almojarifazgo, 116, 191
Alvarez y Jiménez, Antonio, intendant of Arequipa: undertakes reforms in district, 166-169; eulogized by cabildo of city, 170, 171
Amat y Juniet, Manuel de, viceroy of Peru, 73, 90, 104, 107, 113, 118, 119, 127; alludes to rivalries in conciliar elections, 58; fixes number of assessors in Lima, 76, 77; blames alcaldes provinciales for banditry, 81; sets up system of street lighting in the capital, 84; organizes a colonial militia, 85
Ancón, 233
Andalucía, 10, 11, 24
Andueza, Antonio, deputy to Cortes from Chachapoyas, 206
Anjou, Duke of; see Philip V
Apoderado; see Procurator
Aragon, 14, 17, 19, 22, 229; loss of privileges of, 9; local councils in, 11
Aranceles, drawn up by cabildo, 73
Aranda, Conde de, President of Council of Castile, 7, 19 n., 24; informs king of

Regidor, 142, 150, 154 n., 159, 162, 169, 170, 177, 178, 180 n., 183, 217, 221, 224, 232; number and rights of, in Castilian town, 10, 11; rights of, in Castile, 13, 14; conditions of sale or transfer of office of, 59, 60; involved in illegal business in Piura, 70, 71; prestige curtailed by intendant, 160; Lima cabildo complains of number of, 178; opposition to election by proprietary official, 217, 218; see also Alcalde ordinario, Cabildo
Regidor de cano proprietario, 188
Registration of titles, resumption of right of, 178
Reglamento, drawn up by intendant for each town, 144
Reglamento de policía (for Lima), 158, 159
Repartimiento, 194
Residencia: removal of by Charles IV, 17; as institution, 32; effectiveness of, 32 n., 33 n.; dropped for local officials, 183
Revenue; see Exchequer
Revillagigedo, Juan Vicente de Güemes Pacheco de Padilla, Conde de, viceroy of New Spain, 190 n., 194; supports the intendancy, 192
Rico, Gaspar, 216
Rimac, 83, 84, 94, 115
Rio de la Plata, province, 40
Riobamba, 48 n., 49 n.
Rivera y Zavala, Tadeo Bravo de, 179 n.; offers memorial to the crown, 185, 186; announces assent of crown to petition of cabildo, 187, 188
Rivero, Mariano, deputy to Cortes from Arequipa, 206
Rosario, Virgin of, 199

Saavedra, Fernando, intendant of Trujillo, praised by cabildo, 171
Saavedra, Francisco de, President of the Suprema Junta, 199, 200
Salaries, municipal officials of Lima, 111 n.
Salazar, Francisco, deputy from Lima to Cortes, 206
Sale of offices, 167; criticism of practice by Charles III, 18, 19; as a source of revenue from colonies, 34-38; of royal

posts, 38; failure of Charles III to end practice in America, 41, 42; a cause for contention, 59; complaints over excessive valuation, 61, 62; confirmation of titles, 62-64; purchase of office of alferez in Cuzco, 88 n., 89 n.; intendant to abide by regulations for, 146; a problem for Cuzco, 148; amounts recorded by treasury in Lima, 153, 154; restrictions on proprietary rights, 161, 162; abolished by Constitution of 1812, 213, 214; revival of practice, 224; see also Cabildo
Salic Law, 26
Salinas, Marqués de, 124
San Andrés, hospital, 86, 186, 187
San Isidro, Conde de, alcalde de Lima, role of, in act of independence, 236, 237
San Lázaro, 91
San Lorenzo, 161
San Luis Potosí, intendancy of, 133
San Marcos, University of, 51 n., 122 n., 179, 204
San Martín, José de, 228; conquers coastal region of Peru, 230-241; resigns his command, 241
Saña, cabildo, 115 n.
—, municipality, 149, 153 n.
Sandoval y Davalos, Andrés de, 96
Santa Ana, 86
Santa Clara, 159
Santa Cruz, district of, 40
—, procession of, 163
Santa cruzada, 102 n.
Santa Fe, audiencia of, 40
—, viceroyalty of, 39, 64, 182; see also New Granada
Santa Fe de Bogotá, 183; see also Bogotá
Santa Hermandad, 146
Santa Teresa de Jesús, 212 n.
Santayana Bustillo, Lorenzo de, 15
Santiago, Order of, 47
Santiago de Chile, cabildo, 59, 119, 172 n., 184; revenues of, 116 n.
—, city, 183
Santo Buono, Príncipe de, viceroy of Peru, 116; against right of sanctuary, 81, 82
Sargentos mayores, 147
Secret ballot, use of, 54, 55
Segovia, Juan José de, 139
Seminario crítico, 176